7⁵⁰

KNOWING
the
HEART
of
GOD

Knowing

the

Heart

of

God

A Year *of* Daily Readings
to Help You Abide *in* Him

John Eldredge

Thomas Nelson
Since 1798

NASHVILLE   DALLAS   MEXICO CITY   RIO DE JANEIRO

Published in Nashville, Tennessee, by Thomas Nelson. Thomas Nelson is a registered trademark of Thomas Nelson, Inc.

Published in association with Yates & Yates, www.yates2.com.

Thomas Nelson, Inc. titles may be purchased in bulk for educational, business, fund-raising, or sales promotional use. For information, please e-mail SpecialMarkets@ThomasNelson.com.

Unless otherwise noted, Scripture quotations are taken from HOLY BIBLE: NEW INTERNATIONAL VERSION®. © 1973, 1978, 1984 by International Bible Society. Used by permission of Zondervan Publishing House. All rights reserved.

Scripture quotations marked NASB are from NEW AMERICAN STANDARD BIBLE®. © The Lockman Foundation 1960, 1962, 1963, 1968, 1971, 1972, 1973, 1975, 1977. Used by permission.

Scripture quotations marked MSG are from The Message by Eugene H. Peterson. © 1993, 1994, 1995, 1996, 2000. Used by permission of NavPress Publishing Group. All rights reserved.

Library of Congress Cataloging-in-Publication Data Available

ISBN 978-1-4002-0252-2

Printed in the United States of America
13 14 15 QG 7 6 5 4 3

Intimacy with God. This is the heartbeat of the Christian life, our deepest need, our most important aim. Some people will tell you it is obedience. Others will say right doctrine or, perhaps, evangelism. Though these are good things, essential even, in the Christian life, they are not the point. First comes intimacy with God.

There is no greater treasure on this earth, nothing more worthy of your most earnest searching, than to know the heart of God.

We often forget this and chase other things, much to our frustration and dismay. We may even think that we cannot find the heart of God. We may harbor doubts about what we will find if we do discover his heart; but we must take the risk. We must fight through every enemy to get to this great treasure. For when we find the true heart of God, we find a surprise that is greater than we dreamed. His heart is better than we thought. He is our deepest joy.

You can know the heart of God. You can connect with him in deep and satisfying ways. This devotional will help you. In these pages, day by day, you will find new insights and refreshing reminders—of your own heart and how it reflects the heart of God, of the battle and how to gain victory, and of the intimacy and life available to us in God. My prayer is that *Knowing the Heart of God* will encourage you daily, teach you to abide in the Father, and help you find the life he offers.

KNOWING

the

HEART

of

GOD

Stand at the crossroads and look;
ask for the ancient paths,
ask where the good way is, and walk in it,
and you will find rest for your souls.
—JEREMIAH 6:16

One of the most haunting experiences I have ever had took place on an early summer day in Alaska. After a twenty minute walk through a spruce forest, we were led into a broad, open meadow about four hundred yards across. "They're sleeping now, but they'll be back tonight," our guide said. "C'mere—I want to show you something." We followed him to a trail of massive footprints, with a stride of about two feet between them, pressed down into the bog and making a path through it. "It's a marked trail," he said. A path created by the footprints of the bears. "This one is probably centuries old. For as long as the bears have been on this island, they've taken this path. The cubs follow their elders, putting their feet exactly where the older bears walk. That's how they learn to cross this place." I began to walk in the marked trail, stepping into the firm, deep-worn places where bears had walked for centuries.

I'm not sure how to describe the experience, but for some reason the word *holy* comes to mind. An ancient and fearful path through a wild and untamed place. A proven way. I was haunted by it, could have followed that path for a long, long time. It awakened some deep, ancient yearning in me. There is a path laid down for centuries by men who have gone before us. A marked trail. And there *is* a Father ready to show us that path and help us follow it.

❧ FATHERED BY GOD, IX

> *If you, then, though you are evil, know how to give good gifts to your children, how much more will your Father in heaven give good gifts to those who ask him!*
>
> — MATTHEW 7:11

George MacDonald was so right when he said, "The hardest, gladdest thing in the world is to cry *Father!* from a full heart . . . the refusal to look up to God as our father is the one central wrong in the whole human affair; the inability, the one central misery." The one central misery. That's worth thinking about. I didn't used to believe it, really. You see, this fatherlessness has become so normal — *our* normal — we don't even think about it much.

That is why Jesus kept coming back to this central issue, over and over, driving at it in his teachings, his parables, his penetrating questions. If you look again, through the lens that most of us feel fundamentally fatherless, I think you'll find it very close indeed to the center of Jesus' mission. "Which of you, if his son asks for bread, will give him a stone? Or if he asks for a fish, will give him a snake?" (Matt. 7:9–10). Well? We rush ahead to the rest of the passage, but I think Jesus is asking us a real question and he wants a real answer. I expect he paused here, his penetrating, compassionate eyes scanning the listeners before him. Well? I hesitate. I guess you're right. I wouldn't, and apart from the exceptionally wicked man, I can't think of any decent father — even if he is self-absorbed — who would do such a thing. Jesus continues, "If you, then, though you are evil, know how to give good gifts to your children, how much more will your Father in heaven give good gifts to those who ask him!" (v. 11).

❖ *FATHERED BY GOD, 29–30*

Look at the birds of the air. . . Consider the lilies in the field.
Are you not much more valuable to your true Father than they?
—MATTHEW 6:26, 28

L ook at the birds of the air. Consider the lilies in the field. Are
you not much more valuable to your true Father than they?
(Matt. 6:26, 28). Hmmm. I'm not sure how to answer. I mean, of
course, there's the "right" answer. And then there is the wound in
our hearts toward fatherhood, and there is also the way our lives
have gone. "What do you think? If a man owns a hundred sheep,
and one of them wanders away, will he not leave the ninety-nine on
the hills and go to look for the one that wandered off?" (Matt.18:12).
Yet another question, pressing into the submerged fears in our
hearts, another question wanting another answer. Well? Wouldn't
he? "And if he finds it, I tell you the truth, he is happier about that
one sheep than about the ninety-nine that did not wander off. In
the same way your Father in heaven is not willing that any of these
little ones should be lost" (vv. 13–14).

Wherever you are in your ability to believe it at this moment
in your life, at least you can see what Jesus is driving at. You have
a good Father. He is better than you thought. He cares. He really
does. He's kind and generous. He's out for your best. This is absolutely central to the teaching of Jesus.

❧ *FATHERED BY GOD, 31–32*

*Then they said, "Come, let us build ourselves a city, with a tower that
reaches to the heavens, so that we may make a name for ourselves and
not be scattered over the face of the whole earth."*

—GENESIS 11:4

I've spent too many years trying to figure out life on my own.
Reading books, attending classes, always keeping an eye out for
folks who seemed to be getting the hang of things. I'd notice that
the neighbors' kids seemed to be doing well, and I'd think to
myself, *What do they do that I'm not doing?* I'd walk away from a
conversation with someone who seemed to be on top of the world,
and afterward I'd think, *She seems so well read. I should read more.*
I'd hear that a colleague was doing well financially, and quickly I'd
jump to, *He spends time managing his money. I ought to do that.*
We do this all the time, all of us, this monitoring and assessing and
observing and adjusting, trying to find the keys to make life work.

We end up with quite a list. But the only lasting fruit it seems
to bear is that it ties us up in knots. Am I supposed to be reading
now or exercising or monitoring my fat intake or creating a teach-
able moment with my son?

The good news is you can't figure out life like that. You can't
possibly master enough principles and disciplines to ensure that
your life works out. You weren't meant to, and God won't let you.
For he knows that if we succeed without him, we will be infinitely
farther from him. That whole approach to life smacks more of the
infamous folks who raised the tower of Babel than it does of those
who walked with God in the garden in the cool of the day.

In the end, I'd much rather have God.

❖ *WALKING WITH GOD, IX–X*

I spoke to the prophets,
gave them many visions
and told parables through them.
—HOSEA 12:10

Life, you'll notice, is a story. Life doesn't come to us like a math problem. It comes to us the way that a story does, scene by scene. You wake up. What will happen next? You don't get to know—you have to enter in, take the journey as it comes. The sun might be shining. There might be a tornado outside. Your friends might call and invite you to go sailing. You might lose your job.

Life unfolds like a drama. When it comes to figuring out this life you're living, you'd do well to know the rest of the story.

You come home one night to find that your car has been totaled. Now, all you know is that you loaned it for a couple of hours to your teenage daughter, and now here it is, all smashed up. Isn't the first thing out of your mouth, "What *happened*?"

In other words, "Tell me the story."

Somebody has some explaining to do, and that can be done only in hearing the tale *they* have to tell. Careful now—you might jump to the wrong conclusion. Doesn't it make a difference to know that she wasn't speeding, that in fact the other car ran a red light? It changes the way you feel about the whole thing. Thank God, she's all right.

Truth be told, you need to know the rest of the story if you want to understand just about anything in life. Love affairs, layoffs, the collapse of empires, your child's day at school—none of it makes sense without a story.

❀ EPIC, 2–4

*But Moses said to God, "Who am I, that I should go to Pharaoh
and bring the Israelites out of Egypt?"*
—EXODUS 3:11

If you want to get to know someone, you need to know *their* story.
Their life is a story. It, too, has a past and a future. It, too, unfolds
in a series of scenes over the course of time. Why is Grandfather so
silent? Why does he drink too much? Well, let me tell you. There
was a terrible battle in World War II, in the South Pacific, on an
island called Okinawa. Tens of thousands of American men died
or were wounded there; some of them were your grandfather's best
friends. He was there, too, and saw things he has never been able
to forget.

"But in order to make you understand," explained novelist
Virginia Woolf, "to give you my life, I must tell you a story."

I expect all of us, at one time or another, in an attempt to
understand our lives or to discover what we ought to do, have
gone to someone else with our stories. This is not merely the prov-
ince of psychotherapists and priests, but of any good friend. "Tell
me what happened. Tell me your story, and I'll try to help you
make some sense of it."

We humans share these lingering questions: "Who am I really?
Why am I here? Where will I find life? What does God want of
me?" The answers to these questions seem to come only when we
know the rest of the story.

If life is a story, what is the plot? What is your role to play? It
would be good to know that, wouldn't it? What is this all about?

❧ *EPIC, 6–7*

The Lord is with you when you are with him. If you seek him,
he will be found by you.
—2 CHRONICLES 15:2

Some years into our spiritual journey, after the waves of anticipation that mark the beginning of any pilgrimage have begun to ebb, after we have entered life's middle years of service and busyness, a voice speaks to us in the midst of all we are doing. *There is something missing in all of this,* it suggests. *There is something more.*

The voice often comes in the middle of the night or in the early hours of morning, when our hearts are most vulnerable and our thoughts unedited. At first, we mistake the source of this voice and assume it is just our imagination. We fluff up our pillow, roll over, and go back to sleep. Days, weeks, even months go by and the voice speaks again: *Aren't you thirsty? Listen to your heart. There is something missing.*

We listen and we are aware of . . . a sigh. And under the sigh is something dangerous, something that feels adulterous and disloyal to the religion we are serving. We sense a passion deep within; it feels reckless, wild.

We tell ourselves that this small, passionate voice is an intruder who has gained entry because we have not been diligent enough in practicing our religion. We tell ourselves that the malaise of spirit we feel even as we step up our religious activity is a sign of spiritual immaturity and we scold our heart for its lack of fervor.

Sometime later, the voice in our heart dares to speak again. *Listen to me—there is something missing in all this. You long to be in a love affair, an adventure. You were made for something more. You know it.*

❖ *THE SACRED ROMANCE, 1–2*

Speak, LORD, for your servant is listening.
—1 SAMUEL 3:9

When the young prophet Samuel heard the voice of God calling to him in the night, his priestly mentor, Eli, told him how to respond. Samuel discovered that it was God calling. Rather than ignoring the voice, or rebuking it, Samuel learned to listen.

In our modern, pragmatic world we often have no such mentor, so we do not understand it is God speaking to us in our heart. Having so long been out of touch with our deepest longing, we fail to recognize the voice and the One who is calling to us through it. Frustrated by our heart's continuing sabotage of a dutiful Christian life, some of us silence the voice by locking our heart away in the attic, feeding it only the bread and water of duty and obligation until it is almost dead, the voice now small and weak. We make sure to maintain enough distance between ourselves and others, and even between ourselves and our own heart, to keep hidden the practical agnosticism we are living now that our inner life has been divorced from our outer life. Having thus appeased our heart, we nonetheless are forced to give up our spiritual journey because our heart will no longer come with us. But sometimes in the night, when our defenses are down, we still hear it call to us, oh so faintly—a distant whisper. Come morning, the new day's activities scream for our attention, the sound of the cry is gone, and we congratulate ourselves on finally overcoming the flesh.

❂   *THE SACRED ROMANCE, 2–3*

He redeems your life from the pit
and crowns you with love and compassion,
who satisfies your desires with good things
so that your youth is renewed like the eagle's.

—PSALM 103:4–5

For most of us, life feels like a movie we've arrived at forty-five minutes late. Something important seems to be going on . . . maybe. I mean, good things do happen, sometimes beautiful things. You meet someone, fall in love. You find work that is yours to fulfill. But tragic things happen too. You fall out of love, or the other person falls out of love with you. Work becomes punishment. Everything starts to feel like an endless routine.

If there is meaning to this life, then why do our days seem so *random*? What is this drama we've been dropped into the middle of? If there is a God, what sort of story is he telling here? At some point, we begin to wonder if Macbeth wasn't right after all: Is life a tale "told by an idiot, full of sound and fury, signifying nothing"?

No wonder we keep losing heart.

We find ourselves in the middle of a story that is sometimes wonderful, sometimes awful, often a confusing mixture of both, and we haven't a clue how to make sense of it all. It's like we're holding in our hands some pages torn out of a book. These pages are the days of our lives. Fragments of a story. They seem important, or at least we long to know they are, but what does it all mean? If only we could find the book that contains the rest of the story.

G.K. Chesterton had it right when he said, "With every step of our lives we enter into the middle of some story which we are certain to misunderstand."

❧ *Epic*, 7–9

For the eyes of the LORD range throughout the earth to strengthen those whose hearts are fully committed to him.

—2 CHRONICLES 16:9

The heart is central. That I would even need to remind you of this only shows how far we have fallen from the life we were meant to live—or how powerful the spell has been. The subject of the heart is addressed in the Bible more than any other topic—more than "works" or "serve," more than "believe" or "obey," more than money and even more than worship. Maybe God knows something we've forgotten. But of course—all those other things are matters of the heart. Consider but a few passages:

> Love the LORD your God with all your heart and with all your soul and with all your strength. (Deut. 6:5) (Jesus called this the greatest of all the commandments—and notice that the heart comes first.)
>
> Man looks at the outward appearance, but the LORD looks at the heart. (1 Sam. 16:7)
>
> Where your treasure is, there your heart will be also. (Luke 12:34)
>
> Trust in the LORD with all your heart, and lean not on your own understanding. (Prov. 3:5)
>
> Your word I have treasured in my heart, that I may not sin against You. (Ps. 119:11 NASB)
>
> These people honor me with their lips, but their hearts are far from me. (Matt 15:8)

❀ WAKING THE DEAD, 39–40

Blessed are the pure in heart, for they will see God.
—MATTHEW 5:8

There are few things more crucial to us than our own lives. And there are few things we are less clear about.

This journey we are taking is hardly down the yellow brick road. Then again, that's not a bad analogy at all. We may set out in the light, with hope and joy, but eventually, our path always seems to lead us through dark woods, shrouded with a low-lying mist. Where is this abundant life that Christ supposedly promised? Where is God when we need him most? What is to become of us?

The cumulative effect of days upon years that we do not really understand is a subtle *erosion*. We come to doubt our place, we come to question God's intentions toward us, and we lose track of the most important things in life.

We're not fully convinced that God's offer to us *is* life. We have forgotten that the heart is central. And we had no idea that we were born into a world at war.

❂ WAKING THE DEAD, *1–2*

Where your treasure is, there your heart will be also.
—LUKE 12:34

In the end, it doesn't matter how well we have performed or what we have accomplished—a life without heart is not worth living. For out of this wellspring of our soul flow all true caring and all meaningful work, all real worship and all sacrifice. Our faith, hope, and love issue from this fount as well. It is in our heart that we first hear the voice of God and it is in the heart that we come to know him and learn to live in his love.

To lose heart is to lose everything. And a "loss of heart" best describes most men and women in our day. It isn't just the addictions and affairs and depression and heartaches, though, God knows, there are enough of these to cause even the best of us to lose heart. But there is the busyness, the drivenness, the fact that most of us are living merely to survive.

Indeed, the many forces driving modern life have not only assaulted the life of our hearts, they have also dismantled the hearts' habitat—that geography of mystery and transcendence we knew so well as children.

All of us have had, at one time or another, the sense that something important, perhaps the only important thing, had been explained away or tarnished and lost to us forever. Sometimes little by little, sometimes in large chunks, life has appropriated the terrain meant to sustain and nourish the wilder life of the heart, forcing it to retreat as an endangered species into smaller, more secluded, and often darker geographies for its survival. As this happens, something is lost, something vital.

❖ *THE SACRED ROMANCE, 3–5*

In the beginning God created the heavens and the earth.
—GENESIS 1:1

A Story. An Epic.
Something hidden in the ancient past.
Something dangerous now unfolding.
Something waiting in the future for us to discover.
Some crucial role for us to play.

Christianity, in its true form, tells us that there is an Author and that he is good, the essence of all that is good and beautiful and true, for he is the source of all these things. It tells us that he has set our heart's longings within us, for he has made us to live in an Epic. It warns that the truth is always in danger of being twisted and corrupted and stolen from us because there is a Villain in the story who hates our hearts and wants to destroy us. It calls us up into a Story that is truer and deeper than any other, and assures us that there we will find the meaning of our lives.

What if?

What if all the great stories that have ever moved you, brought you joy or tears—what if they are telling you something about the *true* Story into which you were born, the Epic into which you have been cast?

We won't begin to understand our lives, or what this gospel is that Christianity speaks of, until we understand the Story in which we have found ourselves. For when you were born, you were born into an Epic that has already been under way for quite some time. It is a Story of beauty and intimacy and adventure, a Story of danger and loss and heroism and betrayal.

❖ *EPIC, 14–15*

On what were the world's footings set,
or who laid its cornerstone—
while the morning stars sang together
and all the angels shouted for joy?
—JOB 38:6–7

If you learned about Eden in Sunday school, you missed some-thing. Imagine the most beautiful scenes you have ever known on this earth—rain forests, the prairie in full bloom, storm clouds over the African savanna, the Alps under a winter snow. Then imagine it all on the day it was born. And it doesn't stop there.

Into this world God opens his hand, and the animals spring forth. Birds, in every shape and size and song take wing. All the creatures of the sea leap into it—fishes of a thousand colors and designs. Thundering across the plains race immense herds of horses, buffalo, antelope, and deer. It is more astonishing than we could possibly imagine.

We have grown dull toward this world in which we live; we have forgotten that it is not *normal* or *scientific*. It is fantastic. It is a fairy tale through and through. Really now. Elephants? Caterpillars? Snow? At what point did you lose your wonder at it all?

Even so, once in a while something will come along and shock us right out of our dullness and resignation. We come around a cor-ner, and there before us is a cricket, a peacock, a stag with horns as big as he is. Perhaps we come upon a waterfall, or the clouds have made a rainbow in a circle round the sun. And for a moment we realize that we were born into a world as astonishing as any fairy tale. A world made for romance.

❂ *EPIC, 44–45*

The LORD God took the man and put him in the Garden of Eden to work it and take care of it. And the LORD God commanded the man, "You are free to eat from any tree in the garden; but you must not eat from the tree of the knowledge of good and evil, for when you eat of it you will surely die."

—GENESIS 2:15–17

He enables us to love. He gives us the greatest treasure in all creation: a heart. For he intends that we should be his intimate allies—to borrow Dan Allender's phrase—who join in the Sacred Circle of intimacy that is the core of the universe, to share in this great Romance.

Just as we have lost our wonder at the world around us, we have forgotten what a treasure the human heart is. All of the happiness we have ever known and all of the happiness we hope to find is unreachable without a heart. You could not live or love or laugh or cry had God not given you a heart.

And with that heart comes something that just staggers me. God gives us the freedom to reject him. He gives to each of us a will of our own.

Good grief, *why*? He knows what free-willed creatures can do. He has already suffered one massive betrayal in the rebellion of the angels. He knows how we will use our freedom, what misery and suffering, what hell will be unleashed on earth because of our choices. *Why*? Is he out of his mind?

The answer is as simple and staggering as this: if you want a world where love is real, you must allow each person the freedom to choose.

❀ *EPIC, 50–51*

For it is by grace you have been saved, through faith—and this not from yourselves, it is the gift of God—not by works, so that no one can boast.
—EPHESIANS 2:8–9

It is tragic for any person to lose touch with the life of the heart but especially so for those of us who once heard the call in our hearts and recognized it as the voice of Jesus of Nazareth. We may remember him inviting us to a life of beauty, intimacy, and adventure that we thought was lost. For others of us, when he called, it felt for the first time in our lives as if our heart had finally found a home. We responded in faith, in hope, and in love and began the journey we call the Christian life. Each day seemed a new adventure as we rediscovered the world with God by our side.

But for many of us, the waves of first love ebbed away in the whirlwind of Christian service and activity, and we began to lose the Romance. Our faith began to feel more like a series of problems that needed to be solved or principles that had to be mastered before we could finally enter into the abundant life promised us by Christ. We moved our spiritual life into the outer world of activity, and internally we drifted. We sensed that something was wrong and we perhaps tried to fix it—by tinkering with our outer life. We tried the latest spiritual fad, or a new church, or simply redoubled our commitment to make faith work. Still, we found ourselves weary, jaded, or simply bored. Others of us immersed ourselves in busyness without really asking where all the activity was headed.

❧ *THE SACRED ROMANCE, 7–8*

Now the LORD God had planted a garden in the east,
in Eden; and there he put the man he had formed.
—GENESIS 2:8

It is our deepest need, as human beings, to learn to live intimately with God. It is what we were made for. Back in the beginning of our story, before the fall of humanity, before we sent the world spinning off its axis, there was a paradise called Eden. In that garden of life as it was meant to be, there lived the first man and woman. Their story is important to us because whatever they were, and whatever they had, we also were meant to be and to have. And what they enjoyed above all the other delights of that place was this— they walked with God. They talked with him, and he with them.

For this you and I were made. And this we *must* recover.

❖ WALKING WITH GOD, IX

He calls his own sheep by name and leads them out. When he has brought out all his own, he goes on ahead of them, and his sheep follow him because they know his voice.

— JOHN 10:3–4

One assumption I am making is that an intimate, conversational walk with God is available, and is meant to be normal. I assume that if you *don't* find that kind of relationship with God, your spiritual life will be stunted.

We can't find life without God, and we can't find God if we don't know how to walk intimately with him. A passage from the Gospel of John will show you what I'm getting at. Jesus is talking about his relationship with us, how he is the Good Shepherd and we are his sheep. Listen to how he describes the relationship:

"I tell you the truth, the man who does not enter the sheep pen by the gate, but climbs in by some other way, is a thief and a robber. The man who enters by the gate is the shepherd of his sheep. The watchman opens the gate for him, and the sheep listen to his voice. He calls his own sheep by name and leads them out. When he has brought out all his own, he goes on ahead of them, and his sheep follow him because they know his voice. . . . Whoever enters through me will be saved. He will come in and go out and find pasture. The thief comes only to steal and kill and destroy; I have come that they may have life and have it to the full" (John 10:1–4, 9–10).

The sheep live in dangerous country. The only way they can move securely in and out and find pasture is to follow their shepherd closely.

❖ WALKING WITH GOD, 7–8

O LORD, you know me.
—PSALM 139:1

G od certainly knows *us* intimately.

> *O LORD, you have searched me*
> *and you know me.*
> *You know when I sit and when I rise;*
> *you perceive my thoughts from afar.*
> *You discern my going out and my lying down;*
> *you are familiar with all my ways.*
> *Before a word is on my tongue*
> *you know it completely, O LORD . . .*
> *For you created my inmost being;*
> *you knit me together in my mother's womb.*
> *All the days ordained for me*
> *were written in your book*
> *before one of them came to be. (Psalm 139:1–4, 13, 16)*

Whatever else we might believe about intimacy with God at this point, the truth is that God knows us *very* intimately. He knows what time you went to bed last night. He knows what you dreamed about. He knows what you had for breakfast this morning. He knows where you left your car keys, what you think about your aunt, and why you're going to dodge your boss at 2:30 today. The Scriptures make that very clear. You are known. Intimately.

But does God seek intimacy *with* us?

❖ WALKING WITH GOD, 9–11

Your word I have treasured in my heart,
that I may not sin against You.
—PSALM 119:11 NASB

We all share the same dilemma—we long for life and we're not sure where to find it. We wonder if we ever do find it, can we make it last? The longing for life within us seems incongruent with the life we find around us. What is available seems at times close to what we want, but never quite a fit. Our days come to us as a riddle, and the answers aren't handed out with our birth certificates. We must journey to find the life we prize. And the guide we have been given is the desire set deep within, the desire we often overlook or mistake for something else or even choose to ignore.

The greatest human tragedy is simply to give up the search. There is nothing of greater importance than the life of our deep heart. To lose heart is to lose everything. And if we are to bring our heart along in our life's journey, we simply must not, we cannot, abandon this desire.

Gerald May writes in *The Awakened Heart*:

There is a desire within each of us, in the deep center of ourselves that we call our heart. We were born with it, it is never completely satisfied, and it never dies. We are often unaware of it, but it is always awake. . . . Our true identity, our reason for being, is to be found in this desire.

The clue to who we really are and why we are here comes to us through our heart's desire.

❧ *THE JOURNEY OF DESIRE, 2*

So God created man in his own image, in the image of God he created him; male and female he created them.
—GENESIS 1:27

We all—men and women—were created in the image of God. Fearfully and wonderfully made, fashioned as living icons of the bravest, wisest, most stunning Person who ever existed. That glory was shared with us; we were—to borrow Chesterton's phrase—"statues of God walking about in a Garden," endowed with a strength and beauty all our own. All that we ever wished we could be, we were—and more. We were fully alive.

When I look at the night sky and see the work of your fingers—
    the moon and the stars you have set in place—
what are mortals that you should think of us,
    mere humans that you should care for us?
For you made us only a little lower than God,
    and you crowned us with glory and honor. (Ps. 8:3–5 NLT)

I daresay we've heard a bit about original sin but not nearly enough about original glory, which comes *before* sin and is deeper in our nature. We were crowned with glory and honor. Why does a woman long to be beautiful? Why does a man hope to be found brave? Because we remember, if only faintly, that we were once more than we are now. The reason you doubt there could be a glory to your life is because that glory has been the object of a long and brutal war.

❖ WAKING THE DEAD, *13–14*

But the LORD God called to the man, "Where are you?"
—GENESIS 3:9

On the day Adam and Eve fell from grace, they ran off and hid in the bushes. And God came looking for them. He called to Adam, "Where are you?" (Gen. 3:9). Thus began the long and painful story of God's pursuit of mankind. Though we betrayed him and fell into the hands of the Evil One, God did not abandon us. Even a quick read of the Old Testament would be enough to convince you that *rescue* is God's plan. First with Noah, then with Abraham, and then with the nation Israel, you see God looking for a people who will turn to him from the heart, be his intimate allies once more.

The dramatic archetype is the exodus, where God goes to war against the Egyptian taskmasters to set his captive people free.

Four hundred years they languished in a life of despair. Suddenly—blood. Hail. Locusts. Darkness. Death. Plague after plague descends on Egypt like the blows of some unrelenting ax. Pharaoh releases his grip, but only for a moment. The fleeing slaves are pinned against the Red Sea when Egypt makes a last charge, hurtling down on them in chariots. God drowns those soldiers in the sea, every last one of them. Standing in shock and joy on the opposite shore, the Hebrews proclaim, "The LORD is a warrior" (Ex. 15:3). God is a warrior. He has come to rescue us.

❖ *EPIC*, 61–62

Love the Lord your God with all your heart . . .
—LUKE 10:27

Above all else, the Christian life is a love affair of the heart. It cannot be lived primarily as a set of principles or ethics. It cannot be managed with steps and programs. It cannot be lived exclusively as a moral code leading to righteousness. In response to a religious expert who asked him what he must do to obtain real life, Jesus asked a question in return: "What is written in the Law? . . . How do you read it?"

> The man answered: "'Love the Lord your God with all your heart and with all your soul and with all your strength and with all your mind'; and, 'Love your neighbor as yourself.'"
> "You have answered correctly," Jesus replied. "Do this and you will live." (Luke 10:26–28, emphasis added)

The truth of the gospel is intended to free us to love God and others with our whole heart. When we ignore this heart aspect of our faith and try to live out our religion solely as correct doctrine or ethics, our passion is crippled, or perverted, and the divorce of our soul from the heart "that God has given us" is deepened.

❀ *THE SACRED ROMANCE, 8*

All my longings lie open before you, O Lord;
my sighing is not hidden from you.
—PSALM 38:9

George Eliot wrote, "It seems to me we can never give up long-ing and wishing while we are alive. There are certain things we feel to be beautiful and good, and we must hunger for them."

There is a secret set within each of our hearts. It often goes unno-ticed, we rarely can put words to it, and yet it guides us throughout the days of our lives. This secret remains hidden for the most part in our deepest selves. It is simply the desire for life as it was meant to be. Isn't there a life you have been searching for all your days? You may not always be aware of your search, and there are times when you seem to have abandoned looking altogether. But again and again it returns to us, this yearning that cries out for the life we prize. It is elusive, to be sure. It seems to come and go at will. Seasons may pass until it surfaces again.

And though it seems to taunt us, and may at times cause us great pain, we know when it returns that it is priceless. For if we could recover this desire, unearth it from beneath all other distractions, and embrace it as our deepest treasure, we would discover the secret of our existence.

❖ *THE JOURNEY OF DESIRE, 1–2*

Hope deferred makes the heart sick,
but a longing fulfilled is a tree of life.
—PROVERBS 13:12

In all of our hearts lies a longing for a Sacred Romance. It will not go away in spite of our efforts over the years to anesthetize or ignore its song, or attach it to a single person or endeavor. It is a Romance couched in mystery and set deeply within us. It cannot be categorized into propositional truths or fully known any more than studying the anatomy of a corpse would help us know the person who once inhabited it.

Philosophers call this Romance: this heart-yearning set within us, the longing for transcendence; the desire to be part of something larger than ourselves, to be part of something out of the ordinary that is good. We experience transcendence in a small but powerful way when our city's football team wins the big game against tremendous odds. The deepest part of our heart longs to be bound together in some heroic purpose with others of like mind and spirit.

Indeed, if we reflect on the journey of our heart, the Romance has most often come to us in the form of two deep desires: the longing for adventure that *requires* something of us, and the desire for intimacy—to have someone truly know us for ourselves, while at the same time inviting us to *know* them. The emphasis is perhaps more on adventure for men and slightly more on intimacy for women. Yet, both desires are strong in us. And these two desires come together in us all as a longing to be in a relationship of heroic proportions.

❧ *THE SACRED ROMANCE, 19*

*Love the LORD your God with all your heart and with all your soul
and with all your strength.*

—DEUTERONOMY 6:5

The sense of being part of some bigger story—a purposeful adventure that is the Christian life—begins to drain away again after those first-love years, in spite of everything we can do to stop it. Instead of feeling like a love affair with God, your life begins to feel more like a series of repetitive behaviors, like reading the same chapter of a book or writing the same novel over and over. The orthodoxy we try to live out, defined as "Believe and Behave Accordingly," is not a sufficient story line to satisfy whatever turmoil and longing our heart is trying to tell us about. Somehow our head and heart are on separate journeys and neither feels like life.

Eventually this division of head and heart culminates in one of two directions. We can either deaden our heart or divide our life into two parts, where our outer story becomes the theater of the "should" and our inner story the theater of needs, the place where we quench the thirst of our heart with whatever water is available. Whichever path we choose—heart deadness or heart and head separation—the arrows of Satan find their mark and we lose heart.

This is the story of all our lives, in one way or another. The haunting of the Romance and the Message of the Arrows are so radically different and they seem so mutually exclusive that they split our hearts in two. In every way that the Romance is full of beauty and wonder, the Arrows are equally powerful in their ugliness and devastation.

❧ *THE SACRED ROMANCE, 30–31*

For I tell you that unless your righteousness surpasses that of the Pharisees and the teachers of the law, you will certainly not enter the kingdom of heaven.
—MATTHEW 5:20

What makes the Day of Judgment so unnerving is that all our posing and all our charades will be pulled back, all secrets will be made known, and our Lord will "expose the motives of men's *hearts*" (1 Cor. 4:5, emphasis added).

This is the point of the famous Sermon on the Mount. Jesus first says we haven't a hope of heaven unless our righteousness "surpasses that of the Pharisees" (Matt. 5:20). How can that be? They were fastidious rule keepers, pillars of the church, model citizens. Yes, Jesus says, and most of it was hypocrisy. The Pharisees prayed to impress men with their spirituality. They gave offerings to impress men with their generosity. Their actions looked good, but their motives were not. Their hearts, as the saying goes, weren't in the right place. A person's character is determined by his or her motives, and motive is always a matter of the heart. This is what Scripture means when it says that man looks at the outward appearance but God looks at the heart. God doesn't judge us by our looks or our intelligence; he judges us by our hearts.

Oh, the joy of living from right motives, from a clean heart! I doubt that those who want to dismiss the heart want to dismiss our consciences, set aside the importance of character.

❦   WAKING THE DEAD, 43–44

I will give them a heart to know me, that I am the LORD. They will be my people, and I will be their God, for they will return to me with all their heart.

—JEREMIAH 24:7

God created us in freedom to be his intimate allies, and he will not give up on us. He seeks his allies still. Not religion. Not good church people. But lovers. Allies. Friends of the deepest sort.

It is the most beautiful of all love stories.

Have you noticed that in the great stories the hero must often die to win the freedom of his beloved? William Wallace is slowly and brutally tortured for daring to oppose the wicked king. He is executed (upon a cross), and yet his death breaks the grip that darkness has held over Scotland. Neo is the Chosen One, faster and more daring than any other before him. Even so, he is killed—shot in the chest at point-blank range. His death and resurrection shatter the power of the Matrix, set the captives free. They are all pictures of an even greater sacrifice.

"The Son of Man . . . came to give his life as a ransom for many" (Matt. 20:28).

Remember, God warned us in the Garden that the price of our mistrust and disobedience would be death. Not just a physical death but a *spiritual* death—to be separated from God and life and all the beauty, intimacy, and adventure forever. Through an act of our own free will, we became the hostages of the Kingdom of Darkness and death. The only way out is ransom.

❖ *EPIC*, 66–67

*If a man owns a hundred sheep, and one of them wanders away, will
he not leave the ninety-nine on the hills and go to look for the one?*
—MATTHEW 18:12

The coming of Jesus of Nazareth was not unlike the opening
scenes of *Saving Private Ryan*. A dangerous mission, a great
invasion, a daring raid into enemy territory to save the free world,
but also to save one man.

Jesus told a story like that in order to shed light on his own coming: "If a man owns a hundred sheep, and one of them wanders
away, will he not leave the ninety-nine on the hills and go to look
for the one?" (Matt. 18:12). In the midst of the great invasion, like
the storming of the beaches at Normandy, God sets his eye on one
lost soul. On you.

Historically speaking, Jesus of Nazareth was betrayed by one of
his followers, handed over to the Romans by the Jewish religious
leaders, and crucified. But there was a larger Story unfolding in that
death. He gave his life willingly to ransom us from the Evil One, to
pay the price for our betrayal, and to prove for all time and beyond
any shadow of doubt that the heart of God is good. And that your
heart matters to him; it matters more than tongue can tell.

"He has rescued us from the dominion of darkness and
brought us into the kingdom of the Son he loves, in whom we
have redemption, the forgiveness of sins" (Col. 1:13–14).

❖ *EPIC*, 67–68

Then the man and his wife . . . hid from the LORD God among the trees
of the garden. But the LORD God called to the man, "Where are you?"
—GENESIS 3:8–9

The first man and woman, Adam and Eve, knew God and talked with him. And even after their fall, God goes looking for them. What a beautiful story. It tells us that even in our sin God still wants us and comes looking for us. The rest of the Bible continues the story of God seeking us out, calling us back to himself.

> The LORD is with you when you are with him. If you seek
>   him, he will be found by you. (2 Chronicles 15:2)
> I will give them a heart to know me, that I am the LORD.
>   They will be my people, and I will be their God, for they
>   will return to me with all their heart. (Jeremiah 24:7)
> Come near to God and he will come near to you. (James 4:8)
> Let us draw near to God. (Hebrews 10:22)

Intimacy with God is the purpose of our lives. It's why God created us. Not simply to believe in him. Not only to obey him. God created us for intimate fellowship with himself, and in doing so he established the goal of our existence—to know him, love him, and live our lives in an intimate relationship with him. Jesus says that eternal life is to know God (John 17:3). Not just "know about" like you know about the ozone layer or Ulysses S. Grant. He means "to know" as two people know each other, know as Jesus knows the Father—intimately.

❖ WALKING WITH GOD, *11–12*

*I'm no longer calling you servants because servants don't understand
what their master is thinking and planning. No, I've named you friends
because I've let you in on everything I've heard from the Father.*
—JOHN 15:15 *The Message*

He means know as two people know each other, to know as
Jesus knows the Father—intimately. But does God speak to
his people?

Can you imagine any relationship where there is no communication whatsoever? What would you think if you met two good
friends for coffee, and you knew that they'd been at the café for an
hour before you arrived, but as you sat down and asked them, "So,
what have you been talking about?" they said, "Nothing."

"Nothing?"

"Nothing. We don't talk to each other. But we're really
good friends."

Jesus calls us his friends: "I'm no longer calling you servants
because servants don't understand what their master is thinking
and planning. No, I've named you friends because I've let you in on
everything I've heard from the Father" (John 15:15 *The Message*).

Or what would you think about a father if you asked him,
"What have you been talking to your children about lately?" and
he said, "Nothing. I don't talk to them. But I love them very much."
Wouldn't you say the relationship was missing something? And
aren't you God's son or daughter? "Yet to all who received him,
to those who believed in his name, he gave the right to become
children of God" (John 1:12).

❖ WALKING WITH GOD, *12–13*

"The LORD, the God of heaven . . . spoke to me."
—GENESIS 24:7

Now, I know, I know—the prevailing belief is that God speaks to his people *only* through the Bible. And let me make this clear: he does speak to us first and foremost through the Bible. That is the basis for our relationship. The Bible is the eternal and unchanging word of God to us. It is such a gift, to have right there in black and white God's thoughts toward us. We know right off the bat that any other supposed revelation from God that contradicts the Bible is not to be trusted. So I am not minimizing in any way the authority of the Scripture or the fact that God speaks to us through the Bible. However, many Christians believe that God *only* speaks to us through the Bible. The irony of that belief is that's not what the Bible says.

First off, the Bible is filled with stories of God talking to his people. Abraham, who is called the friend of God, said, "The LORD, the God of heaven, who brought me out of my father's household and my native land and who spoke to me . . ." (Genesis 24:7). God spoke to Moses "as a man speaks with his friend" (Exodus 33:11). And David: "In the course of time, David inquired of the LORD. 'Shall I go up to one of the towns of Judah?' he asked. The LORD said, 'Go up.' David asked, 'Where shall I go?' 'To Hebron,' the LORD answered" (2 Samuel 2:1). The Lord spoke to Noah. The Lord spoke to Gideon. The Lord spoke to Samuel. The list goes on and on.

❖ *WALKING WITH GOD, 13*

In the course of time, David inquired of the LORD. "Shall I go up to one of the towns of Judah?" he asked. The LORD said, "Go up." David asked, "Where shall I go?" "To Hebron," the LORD answered.

—2 SAMUEL 2:1

The Bible is filled with stories of God talking to his people. I can hear the objections even now: "But that was different. Those were special people called to special tasks." And we are not special people called to special tasks? I refuse to believe that. And I doubt that you want to believe it either, in your heart of hearts. But for the sake of the argument, notice that God also speaks to "less important" characters in the Bible. God spoke to Hagar, the servant girl of Sarah, as she was running away. "She gave this name to the LORD who spoke to her: 'You are the God who sees me,'" (Gen. 16:13). In the New Testament, God speaks to a man named Ananias who plays a small role in seven verses in Acts 9:

The Lord called to him in a vision, "Ananias!"

"Yes, Lord," he answered.

The Lord told him, "Go to the house of Judas on Straight Street and ask for a man from Tarsus named Saul. . . ."

"Lord," Ananias answered, "I have heard many reports about this man and all the harm he has done to your saints in Jerusalem. And he has come here with authority from the chief priests to arrest all who call on your name."

But the Lord said to Ananias, "Go!" (vv. 10–11, 13–15)

Now, if God doesn't *also* speak to us, why would he have given us all these stories of his speaking to others?

❀ WALKING WITH GOD, *13–14* | 33

Be imitators of God, therefore, as dearly loved children and live a life of love, just as Christ loved us and gave himself up for us as a fragrant offering and sacrifice to God.
—EPHESIANS 5:1–2

I love watching a herd of horses grazing in an open pasture, or running free across the wide, sage-covered plateaus in Montana. I love hiking in the high country when the wildflowers are blooming—the purple lupine and the Indian paintbrush when it's turning magenta. I love thunder clouds, massive ones. My family loves to sit outside on summer nights and watch the lightning, hear the thunder as a storm rolls in across Colorado. I love water, too—the ocean, streams, lakes, rivers, waterfalls, rain. I love jumping off high rocks into lakes with my boys. I love old barns, windmills, the West. I love vineyards. I love it when Stasi is loving something, love watching her delight. I love my boys. I love God.

Everything you love is what makes a life worth living. Take a moment, set the book down, and make a list of all the things you love. Don't edit yourself; don't worry about prioritizing or anything of that sort. Simply think of all the things you love. Whether it's the people in your life or the things that bring you joy or the places that are dear to you or your God, you could not love them if you did not have a heart. Loving requires a heart alive and awake and free. A life filled with loving is a life most like the one that God lives, which is life as it was meant to be (Eph. 5:1–2).

And is it even possible to love *without* your heart?

❂ WAKING THE DEAD, 47–48

My son, do not despise the LORD's discipline
and do not resent his rebuke,
because the LORD disciplines those he loves,
as a father the son he delights in.
—PROVERBS 3:11–12

Everyone has been betrayed by someone, some more profoundly than others. Betrayal is a violation that strikes at the core of our being. To make ourselves vulnerable and to entrust our well-being to another, only to be harmed by the person upon whom our hopes were set, is among the worst pain of human experience.

Sometimes the way God treats us feels like betrayal. We find ourselves in a dangerous world, unable to find the water our thirsty souls so desperately need. Our rope won't take the bucket to the bottom of the well. We know God has the ability to draw water for us, but oftentimes he won't. We feel wronged. After all, doesn't Scripture say that if we have the power to do someone good, we should do it (Prov. 3:27)? So why doesn't God?

As I spoke with a friend about her painful life, how reckless and unpredictable God seems, she turned to me and with pleading eyes asked the question we all ask somewhere deep within: "How can I trust a lover who is so wild?" Indeed, how do we learn to trust him, and then love him in return? There's only one possible answer: You could love him if you *knew* his heart is good.

❧ *THE SACRED ROMANCE, 70*

Surely God is good to Israel,
to those who are pure in heart.
—PSALM 73:1

Does God have a good heart? When we think of God as Author, the Grand Chess Player, the Mind Behind It All, we doubt his heart. As Melville said, "The reason the mass of men fear God and at bottom dislike him is because they rather distrust his heart, and fancy him all brain, like a watch." Do you relate to the author when reading a novel or watching a film? Caught up in the action, do you even think about the author? We identify with the characters in the story precisely because they are *in* the story. They face life as we do, on the ground, and their struggles win our sympathy because they are our struggles also. We love the hero because he is one of us, and yet somehow rises above the fray to be better and wiser and more loving as we hope one day we might prove to be.

The Author stands behind, beyond. His omniscience and omnipotence may be what create the drama, but they are also what separate us from him. Power and knowledge don't qualify for heart.

We root for the hero and heroine, even come to love them, because they are living *in* the drama. They feel the heartache, they suffer loss and summon courage and shed their own blood in their struggles against evil. What if? Just what if we saw God not as Author, the cosmic mastermind behind all human experience, but as the central character *in* the larger story? What could we learn about his heart?

❂ *THE SACRED ROMANCE, 71–72*

"The goal is for all of them to become one heart and mind—
Just as you, Father, are in me and I in you,
So they might be one heart and mind with us."
—JOHN 17:22–23 *The Message*

The story that is the Sacred Romance begins not with God alone, the Author at his desk, but God in relationship, intimacy beyond our wildest imagination. Heroic intimacy. The Trinity is at the center of the universe; perfect relationship is the heart of all reality. Think of your best moments of love or friendship or creative partnership, the best times with family or friends around the dinner table, your richest conversations, the simple acts of kindness that sometimes seem like the only things that make life worth living. Like the shimmer of sunlight on a lake, these are reflections of the love that flows among the Trinity. We long for intimacy because we are made in the image of perfect intimacy.

Our story begins with the hero in love. As Buechner reminds us, "God does not need the Creation in order to have something to love because within himself love happens."

Real love creates a generous openness. Have you ever been so caught up in something that you just had to share it? When you are walking alone in the woods, something takes your breath away—a sunset, a waterfall, the simple song of a bird—and you think, *If only my beloved were here.* The best things in life were meant to be shared. That is why married lovers want to increase their joy by having children. And so it is with God.

❧ *THE SACRED ROMANCE, 73–74*

"You will find me," God says, "when you seek me with all your heart."
—JEREMIAH 29:13

The heart is the connecting point, the meeting place between any two persons. The kind of deep soul intimacy we crave with God and with others can be experienced only from the heart.

I know a man who took his daughter to dinner; she was surprised, delighted. For years she had been hoping he would pursue her. When they were seated, he pulled out his Day Timer and began to review the goals he had set for her that year. "I wanted to burst into tears and run out of the restaurant," she said. We don't want to be someone's project; we want to be the desire of their heart. Gerald May laments, "By worshiping efficiency, the human race has achieved the highest level of efficiency in history, but how much have we grown in love?"

We've done the same to our relationship with God. Christians have spent their whole lives mastering all sorts of principles, done their duty, carried on the programs of their church . . . and never known God intimately, heart to heart. The point is not an efficient life—the point is intimacy with God.

❀ WAKING THE DEAD, 48–49

Then they brought him a demon-possessed man who was blind and mute, and Jesus healed him, so that he could both talk and see.
—MATTHEW 12:22

When Jesus touched the blind, they could *see*; all the beauty of the world opened before them. When he touched the deaf, they were able to *hear*; for the first time in their lives they heard laughter and music and their children's voices. He touched the lame, and they *jumped* to their feet and began to dance. And he called the dead back to *life* and gave them to their families.

Do you see? Wherever humanity was broken, Jesus restored it. The coming of the kingdom of God *restores* the world he made.

God has been whispering this secret to us through creation itself, every year, at springtime, ever since we left the Garden. Sure, winter has its joys. The wonder of snowfall at midnight, the rush of a sled down a hill, the magic of the holidays. But if winter ever came for good and never left we would be desolate. Every tree leafless, every flower gone, the grasses on the hillsides dry and brittle. The world forever cold, silent, bleak.

After months and months of winter, I long for the return of summer. Sunshine, warmth, color, and the long days of adventure. The garden blossoms in all its beauty. The meadows soft and green. Vacation. Holiday. Isn't this what we most deeply long for?

If we listen, we will discover something of epic joy and wonder. The restoration of the world played out before us each spring and summer is *precisely* what God is promising us about our lives. Every miracle Jesus ever did was pointing to this Restoration, the day he makes all things new.

❖ *EPIC, 82–83*

Then the LORD God said to the woman, "What is this you have done?"
The woman said, "The serpent deceived me, and I ate."
—GENESIS 3:13

Can you imagine if on your honeymoon one of you sneaked off for a rendezvous with a perfect stranger? Adam and Eve kicked off the honeymoon by sleeping with the enemy. Then comes one of the most poignant verses in all Scripture. "What is this you have done?" (Gen. 3:13). You can almost hear the shock, the pain of betrayal in God's voice. The fall of Adam and Eve mustn't be pictured as a crime like theft, but as a betrayal of love. In love God creates us for love and we give him the back of our hand. Why? Satan convinces us to side with him by sowing the seed of doubt, just as he did with our first parents: "God's heart really isn't good. He's holding out on you. You've got to take things into your own hands." And then Paradise was lost.

Yet there was something about the heart of God that the angels and our first parents had not yet seen. Here, at the lowest point in our relationship, God announces his intention never to abandon us but to seek us out and to win us back. "I will come for you." *Grace* reveals a new element of God's heart. Up till this point we knew he was rich, famous, influential, even generous. Yet, behind all that can lurk a heart that is less than good. Thankfully, grace removes all doubt.

❀ *THE SACRED ROMANCE*, 78–79

The Spirit of the Sovereign LORD is upon me.
—ISAIAH 61:1

Christ did not die for an idea. He died for a person, and that person is you. But ask any number of people why Christ came, and you'll receive any number of answers, but rarely the real one. "He came to bring world peace." "He came to teach us the way of love." "He came to die so that we might go to heaven." "He came to bring economic justice." On and on it goes, much of it based on a partial truth. But wouldn't it be better to let him speak for himself?

Jesus steps into the scene. He reaches back to a four-hundred-year-old prophecy to tell us why he's come. He quotes from Isaiah 61:1, which goes like this:

> The Spirit of the Sovereign LORD is upon me,
>   because the LORD has anointed me
>   to preach good news to the poor.
> He has sent me to bind up the brokenhearted,
>   to proclaim freedom for the captives
> and release from darkness for the prisoners.

Christ could have chosen any one of a thousand other passages to explain his life purpose. But he did not. He chose this one; this is the heart of his mission. Everything else he says and does finds its place under this banner: "I am here to give you back your heart and set you free." *That's* why it is said, "the glory of God is man fully alive." It's what he said he came to do. But of course. How can it bring God glory for his very image, his own children, to remain so badly marred, broken, captive?

❖ *WAKING THE DEAD, 50–51*

*God demonstrates his own love for us in this: While we were still
sinners, Christ died for us.*
—ROMANS 5:8

Here is Kierkegaard's version of the story:

Suppose there was a king who loved a humble maiden.
The king was like no other king. Every statesman trembled
before his power. . . . And yet this mighty king was melted
by love for a humble maiden. How could he declare his
love for her? In an odd sort of way, his kingliness tied his
hands. If he brought her to the palace and crowned her
head with jewels and clothed her body in royal robes,
she would surely not resist—no one dared resist him. But
would she love him?

She would say she loved him, of course, but would she
truly? . . . How could he know? If he rode to her forest cottage in his royal carriage, with an armed escort waving
bright banners, that too would overwhelm her. He did not
want a cringing subject. He wanted a lover, an equal. . . .
For it is only in love that the unequal can be made equal.
(*Disappointment with God*)

The king clothes himself as a beggar and renounces his throne
in order to win her hand. The Incarnation, the life and the death of
Jesus, answers once and for all the question, "What is God's heart
toward me?"

❖ *THE SACRED ROMANCE, 80–81*

God so loved the world that he gave his one and only Son.
—JOHN 3:16

What is God like? Is his heart good? We know he is the initiator from first to last. As Simon Tugwell reminds, God is the one pursuing us:

> So long as we imagine that it is we who have to look for
> God, we must often lose heart. But it is the other way about;
> He is looking for us. And so we can afford to recognize that
> very often we are not looking for God; far from it, we are in
> full flight from him, in high rebellion against him. And He
> knows that and has taken it into account. He has followed
> us into our own darkness; there where we thought finally
> to escape him, we run straight into his arms. So we do not
> have to erect a false piety for ourselves, to give us the hope
> of salvation. Our hope is in his determination to save us,
> and he will not give in. (*Prayer*)

When we feel that life is finally up to us it becomes suffocating. When we are the main character, the world is so small there's barely room to move. It frees our souls to have something going on before us that involves us, had us in mind, yet doesn't depend on us or culminate in us, but invites us up into something larger.

❂ *THE SACRED ROMANCE, 81–82*

He has made everything beautiful in its time. He has also set eternity in the hearts of men; yet they cannot fathom what God has done from beginning to end.

—ECCLESIASTES 3:11

They lived happily ever after.

These may be the most beautiful and haunting words in the entire library of mankind. Why does the end of a great story leave us with a lump in our throats and an ache in our hearts? If we haven't become entirely cynical, some of the best endings can even bring us to tears.

Because God has set eternity in our hearts. Every story we tell is our attempt to put into words and images what God has written there, on our hearts. Think of the stories that you love. Remember how they end. This is written on the human heart, this longing for happily ever after.

You see, every story has an ending. Every story. Including yours. Have you ever faced this? Even if you do manage to find a little taste of Eden in this life, even if you are one of the fortunate souls who find some love and happiness in the world, you cannot hang on to it. You know this. Your health cannot hold out forever. Age will conquer you. One by one your friends and loved ones will slip from your hand. Your work will remain unfinished. Your time on this stage will come to an end. Like every other person gone before you, you will breathe your last breath.

And then what? Is that the end of the Story?

If that is the end, this Story is a tragedy. Macbeth was right. "Life is a tale told by an idiot, full of sound and fury, signifying nothing." Is there no way out? Do we have a future?

*I will give you a new heart and put a new spirit in you; I will remove
from you your heart of stone and give you a heart of flesh. And I will
put my Spirit in you and move you to follow my decrees and be careful
to keep my laws.*

—EZEKIEL 36:26–27

This we now know: the heart is central. It matters—deeply.
When we see with the eyes of the heart, which is to say, when
we see mythically, we begin to awaken, and what we discover is
that things are not what they seem. We *are* at war. We must fight
for the life God intends for us, which is to say, we must fight for
our heart, for it is the wellspring of that life within us.

Standing in the way of the path to life—the way of the heart—
is a monstrous barrier. It has stopped far too many pilgrims dead
in their tracks, for far too long. There is a widespread belief among
Christians today that the heart is desperately wicked—even after a
person comes to Christ.

It is a crippling belief.

And for the "true" believer it is untrue.

❖ *WAKING THE DEAD*, 53–54

*But the Lord replied, "You hypocrite! You work on the Sabbath
day! Don't you untie your ox or your donkey from their stalls on the
Sabbath and lead them out for water? And all the people rejoiced at the
wonderful things he did.*

—LUKE 13:10–17 NLT

Jesus saw a woman who had been crippled by an evil spirit. She
had been bent double for eighteen years and was unable to
stand up straight. When Jesus saw her, he called her over and
said, "Woman, you are healed of your sickness!" Then he touched
her, and instantly she could stand straight. How she praised and
thanked God! But the leader in charge of the synagogue was
indignant that Jesus had healed her on the Sabbath day.

Now—is Jesus more like Mother Teresa or William Wallace?
The answer is . . . it depends. If you're a leper, an outcast, a
pariah of society whom no one has *ever* touched because you are
"unclean," if all you have ever longed for is just one kind word,
then Christ is the incarnation of tender mercy. He reaches out
and touches you. On the other hand, if you're a Pharisee, one of
those self-appointed doctrine police . . . watch out. On more than
one occasion Jesus "picks a fight" with those notorious hypocrites.
Take the story of the crippled woman in Luke 13.

Does Jesus tiptoe around the issue, so as not to "rock the boat"
(the preference of so many of our leaders today)? Does he drop the
subject in order to "preserve church unity"? Nope. He walks right
into it, he baits them, he picks a fight. Christ draws the enemy
out, exposes him for what he is, and calls him into account in
front of everyone. The Lord is a *gentleman*???

❖ *WILD AT HEART,* 24–25

So they bound him with two new ropes and led him up from the rock.
As he approached Lehi, the Philistines came toward him shouting.
The Spirit of the LORD came upon him in power. The ropes on his
arms became like charred flax, and the bindings dropped from his
hands. Finding a fresh jawbone of a donkey, he grabbed it and struck
down a thousand men.

—JUDGES 15:13–15

G od has a battle to fight, and the battle is for our freedom. As
Tremper Longman says, "Virtually every book of the Bible
. . . tells us about God's warring activity." I wonder if the Egyptians
who kept Israel under the whip would describe Yahweh as a
Really Nice Guy? Plagues, pestilence, the death of every firstborn—that doesn't seem very gentlemanly now, does it?

You remember that wild man, Samson? He's got a pretty impressive masculine résumé: killed a lion with his bare hands, pummeled
and stripped thirty Philistines when they used his wife against him,
and finally, after they burned her to death, he killed a thousand
men with the jawbone of a donkey. But did you notice? All those
events happened when *"the Spirit of the Lord* came upon him"
(Judg. 15:14, emphasis added). Now, let me make one thing clear:
I am not advocating a sort of "macho man" image. I'm not suggesting we all head off to the gym and then to the beach to kick sand
in the faces of wimpy Pharisees. I am attempting to rescue us from
a very, very mistaken image we have of God—especially of Jesus—
and therefore of men as his image-bearers. Dorothy Sayers wrote
that the church has "very efficiently pared the claws of the Lion of
Judah," making him "a fitting household pet for pale curates and
pious old ladies." Is that the God you find in the Bible?

❧ *WILD AT HEART, 25–27*

> *And God said, "Let the land produce living creatures according to their kinds: livestock, creatures that move along the ground, and wild animals, each according to its kind." And it was so.*
> —GENESIS 1:24

If you have any doubts as to whether or not God loves wildness, spend a night in the woods . . . alone. Take a walk out in a thunderstorm. Go for a swim with a pod of killer whales. Get a bull moose mad at you. Whose idea was this, anyway? The Great Barrier Reef with its great white sharks, the jungles of India with their tigers, the deserts of the Southwest with all those rattlesnakes—would you describe them as "nice" places? Most of the earth is not safe; but it's good.

That thought struck me a little too late when I was hiking in to find the upper Kenai River in Alaska. My buddy Craig and I were after the salmon and giant rainbow trout that live in those icy waters. We were warned about bears but didn't really take it seriously until we were deep into the woods. Grizzly sign was everywhere—salmon strewn about the trail, their heads bitten off. Piles of droppings the size of small dogs. Huge claw marks on the trees, about headlevel. *We're dead*, I thought. *What are we doing out here?*

It then occurred to me that after God made all this, he pronounced it *good*, for heaven's sake. It's his way of letting us know he rather prefers adventure, danger, risk, the element of surprise. This whole creation is unapologetically *wild*. God loves it that way.

❖ WILD AT HEART, 29–30

The fact is that Christ has been raised from the dead. He has become the first of a great harvest of those who will be raised to life again.
—1 CORINTHIANS 15:20 NLT

The resurrection of Jesus was the first of many, the forerunner of our own. He paved the way, as the saying goes.

God knew what he was doing from the very beginning. He decided from the outset to shape the lives of those who love him along the same lines as the life of his Son. The Son stands first in the line of humanity he restored. (Rom. 8:29 *The Message*)

So we, too, shall live and never die. Creation will be restored, and *we* will be restored. And we shall share it together. "Today," Jesus said to the thief on the cross, "you will be with me in paradise" (Luke 23:43). Imagine that. Imagine being reunited with the ones you love, and with all the great and noble hearts of this Story, in paradise.

We will walk with God in the Garden in the cool of the day. We will see our Jesus face-to-face. We will hear him laugh. All that has ever stood between us will be swept away, and our hearts will be released to real loving. It begins with a great party, what the Scriptures call the "wedding feast of the Lamb" (Rev. 19:9 NLT).

Imagine the stories that you'll hear. And all the questions that shall finally have answers. And the answers won't be one-word answers but story after story, a feast of wonder and laughter and glad tears.

❧ EPIC, 87–88

*If, while we seek to be justified in Christ, it becomes evident that
we ourselves are sinners, does that mean that Christ promotes sin?
Absolutely not.*

—GALATIANS 2:17

In an attempt to uphold the sovereignty of God, theologians have overstated their case, leaving us with a chess-player God making all his moves and all ours too. But clearly, this is not so. God is not threatened by human free will. From a human perspective, he took the biggest risk of all when he gave humanity the freedom to reject him—not just once but every single day. Does God cause a person to sin? "Absolutely not!" says Paul (Gal. 2:17). Fallen angels and men use their powers to commit horrendous daily evil. Does God stop every bullet fired at an innocent victim? Does he prevent teenage liaisons from producing teenage pregnancies? There is something much "riskier" going on here than we're often willing to admit.

Most of us do everything we can to *reduce* the element of risk in our lives. We wear our seat belts, watch our cholesterol, and practice birth control. I know some couples who have decided against having children altogether; they simply aren't willing to chance the heartache children often bring. God seems to fly in the face of all caution. Even though he *knew* what would happen, what heartbreak and suffering and devastation would follow upon our disobedience, God chose to have children. And unlike some hyper-controlling parents, who take away every element of choice they can from their children, God gave us a remarkable choice. He did not *make* Adam and Eve obey him. He took a risk. A staggering risk, with staggering consequences.

❖ *WILD AT HEART*, 30–31

> *"Sir," the invalid replied, "I have no one to help me into the pool when the water is stirred. While I am trying to get in, someone else goes down ahead of me." Then Jesus said to him, "Get up! Pick up your mat and walk." At once the man was cured; he picked up his mat and walked.*

—JOHN 5:7–9

The shriveled figure lay in the sun like a pile of rags dumped there by accident. He was disabled, dropped off there every morning by someone in his family, and picked up again at the end of the day. A rumor was going around that sometimes (no one really knew when) an angel would stir the waters, and the first one in would be healed. Sort of a lottery, if you will.

It had been so long since anyone had actually *spoken* to him, he thought the question was meant for someone else. Squinting upward into the sun, the misshapen man asked the fellow to repeat himself; perhaps he had misheard. Although the voice was kind, the question felt harsh, even cruel.

"Do you want to get well?"

He sat speechless, blinking into the sun. Slowly, the words seeped into his consciousness, like a voice calling him out of a dream. *Do I want to get well?* Slowly, like a wheel long rusted, his mind began to turn over. *What kind of question is that? Why else would I be lying here? Why else would I have spent every day for the past thirty-eight seasons lying here? He is mocking me.* But now that his vision had adjusted to the glare, he could see the inquisitor's face, his eyes. The face was as kind as the voice he heard. Apparently, the man meant what he said, and he was waiting for an answer. "Do you want to get well? What is it that you want?"

❖ THE JOURNEY OF DESIRE, 33–34

This is the way to have eternal life–to know you, the only true God, and Jesus Christ, the one you sent to earth.

—JOHN 17:3 NLT

And life *is* the offer, friends. Let us not forget that.

There is no simpler or more beautiful way to say it than this: Act Four in the story God is telling is the restoration of life as it was always meant to be. It is the return of the beauty, the intimacy, and the adventure we were created to enjoy and have longed for every day of our lives. And yet, *better*, for it is immortal. We can never lose it again. It cannot be taken away. Sunrise and sunset tell the tale every day, remembering Eden's glory, foretelling Eden's return. And what adventures shall unfold when we are given the kingdom that was always meant to be ours. Listen to this:

> Then the King will say to those on his right, "Come, you who are blessed by my Father; take your inheritance, *the kingdom prepared for you since the creation of the world.*" (Matt. 25:34, emphasis added)

Adam and Eve, and all their sons and daughters after them, were created to reign over the earth—to explore and discover and create and do all those things you see people do when they are at their very best.

That is our destiny.

❖ *EPIC*, 92–94

You will not fear the terror of night,
nor the arrow that flies by day.
—PSALM 91:5

At some point we all face the same decision—what will we do with the Arrows we've known? Maybe a better way to say it is, what have they tempted us to do? However they come to us, whether through a loss we experience as abandonment or some deep violation we feel as abuse, their message is always the same: Kill your heart. Divorce it, neglect it, run from it, or indulge it with some anesthetic (our various addictions). Think of how you've handled the affliction that has pierced your own heart. How did the Arrows come to you? Where did they land? Are they still there? What have you done as a result?

To say we all face a decision when we're pierced by an Arrow is misleading. It makes the process sound so rational, as though we have the option of coolly assessing the situation and choosing a logical response. Life isn't like that—the heart cannot be managed in a detached sort of way (certainly not when we are young, when the most defining Arrows strike). It feels more like an ambush and our response is at a gut level. We may never put words to it. Our deepest convictions are formed without conscious effort, but the effect is a shift deep in our soul. Commitments form never to be in that position again, never to know that sort of pain again. The result is an approach to life that we often call our personality. If you'll listen carefully to your life, you may begin to see how it has been shaped by the unique Arrows you've known and the particular convictions you've embraced as a result.

❀ *THE SACRED ROMANCE, 27–28*

> *The water I give will be an artesian spring within, gushing fountains of endless life.*
>
> —JOHN 4:14 *The Message*

This may come as a surprise to you: Christianity is not an invitation to become a moral person. It is not a program for getting us in line or for reforming society. At its core, Christianity begins with an invitation to *desire*.

Look again at the way Jesus relates to people. There is the Samaritan woman Jesus meets at the well. She arrives alone in the heat of the day to draw water, and they both know why. By coming when the sun is high, she is less likely to run into anyone. You see, her sexual lifestyle has earned her a "reputation." Back in those days, having one partner after another wasn't looked so highly upon. She's on her sixth lover, and so she'd rather bear the scorching rays of the sun than face the searing words of the "decent" women of the town who come at evening to draw water. She succeeds in avoiding the women but runs into God instead.

What does he choose to talk to her about—her immorality? No, he speaks to her about her *thirst*: "If you knew the generosity of God and who I am, you would be asking *me* for a drink, and I would give you fresh, living water" (John 4:10 *The Message*). Remarkable. He doesn't give a little sermon about purity; he doesn't even mention it, except to say that he knows what her life has been like: "You've had five husbands, and the man you're living with now isn't even your husband" (John 4:18 *The Message*). In other words, now that we both know it, let's talk about your heart's real thirst, since the life you've chosen obviously isn't working.

❖ THE JOURNEY OF DESIRE, 35–36

But while he was still a long way off, his father saw him and was filled with compassion for him; he ran to his son, threw his arms around him and kissed him.

—LUKE 15:20

Jesus told the prodigal son story to try to get it into our hearts how he feels about us. Yes, he ran off to Vegas with the family fortune, blew it all on cheap whores and high-stakes poker. Yes, we have done the same, more or less. But that is not the point of the story. It is about the father's heart. "But while he was still a long way off, his father saw him and was filled with compassion for him; he ran to his son, threw his arms around him and kissed him" (Luke 15:20).

This is the kind of Father you have. This is how he feels about you. *This* is the purpose for which Christ came.

> But when the time had fully come, God sent his Son, born of a woman, born under law, to redeem those under law, that we might receive the full rights of sons. Because you are sons, God sent the Spirit of his Son into our hearts, the Spirit who calls out, "*Abba*, Father." So you are no longer a slave, but a son; and since you are a son, God has made you also an heir. (Gal. 4:4–7)

When a man gives his life to Jesus Christ, when he turns as the prodigal son turned for home and is reconciled to the Father, many remarkable things take place. At the core of them is a true sonship.

❀ *FATHERED BY GOD, 33*

Every good and perfect gift is from above, coming down from the
Father of the heavenly lights.
—JAMES 1:16–17

A few of us were talking about our fathers the other night and sharing some of the good memories we have of them. Morgan told us of his father, who had a ritual of a poker game each week. The kids would be sent to bed long before their father got home, but the next morning they'd wake to find his winnings on the kitchen table, divided into piles for each of his children to take as their own. Treasure. Booty. For no other reason than "you are my beloved sons and daughters."

My grandfather had long quit smoking by the time I knew him, and he had taken up a love for butterscotch LifeSavers as a sort of substitute. He always carried a roll of them in the glove box of his pickup, and we'd be rolling down the road and he'd flip open the box and ask me, "Cigarette?" I loved it, love butterscotch LifeSavers to this day.

There was an old caretaker who lived on the ranch, a crusty old cowboy named Bill who lived in a trailer out by the horses. One summer afternoon Bill—who'd taken a liking to me—called me over to his trailer and said, "I've got something for you." He reached in his pocket and pulled out an old pocketknife, his own, worn from years of ranch work, and handed it to me.

What a treasure that was, for a boy with his very own pocketknife is a boy with endless possibilities before him. That small gift made my summer.

You are noticed. Your heart matters. Your father adores you.

❀ FATHERED BY GOD, 48–49

Keep me as the apple of your eye.
—PSALM 17:8

A boy yearns to know that he is prized.
This is more than just being loved in a generic sort of way. "Of course I love you—you're my son." A boy can see right through anything false in that. He yearns to know he is *adored. Uniquely.* That he holds a special place in his father's heart, a place no one and nothing else can rival.

Without this certainty in the core of his being, the boy will misinterpret the stages and lessons that are to come, for as a young man he will soon be tested, and he will face battles and challenges as a warrior, and those tests and challenges often feel to men like a form of rejection or coldheartedness on the part of God, because he does not first know in his heart of hearts that he *is* the beloved son. "The son of my right hand," as Benjamin was called; or "the son of my delight," as surely Joseph knew; or "my beloved son in whom I am so pleased," as the Father said of Jesus. Without this bedrock of affirmation, a man will move unsteadily through his life, trying to prove his worth and earn belovedness through performance or achievement, through sex, or in a thousand other ways.

Quite often he doesn't know this is his search. He simply finds himself uncertain in some core place inside, ruled by fears and the opinions of others, yearning for someone to notice him. He longs for comfort, and it makes him uneasy because at thirty-seven or fifty-one shouldn't he be beyond that now? A young place in his heart is yearning for something never received.

❖ *FATHERED BY GOD, 50*

Because you are sons, God sent the Spirit of his Son into our hearts,
the Spirit who calls out, "Abba, Father." So you are no longer a slave,
but a son; and since you are a son, God has also made you also an heir.
—GALATIANS 4:6–7

Come back for a moment to Jesus' probing questions regarding our feelings about God as Father. He almost seems puzzled. "Are you not much more valuable than they? Will he not leave the ninety-nine on the hills and go off to look for the one that wandered off? How much more will your Father in heaven give good gifts to those who ask him!" In other words, don't you know how your Father feels about you? Jesus did. He walked through the world knowing he was the beloved Son, the favored One. It's what enabled him to live as he did. As Jan Bovenmars wrote:

> Jesus had the Heart of a Son . . . *knew* himself to be the Son, felt very much like a Beloved Son, looked on God as "Abba," his dear Father, lived in a Father-Son relationship. The divine relationship Son-Father filled his human heart; it was his secret, his joy; a constant awareness; a basic attitude that determined his behavior. (*A Biblical Spirituality of the Heart*)

This relationship was meant to be our secret, our joy also. We were meant to *know* this too. First through our earthly fathers and then, by the extension of fatherhood, to our Father in the heavens. But few there are who came through their boyhood with such knowledge intact, without a trace of doubt.

❁ FATHERED BY GOD, 51–52

> *When he came near the den, he called to Daniel in an anguished voice,*
> *"Daniel, servant of the living God, has your God, whom you serve*
> *continually, been able to rescue you from the lions?"*
> —DANIEL 6:20

This is the world God has made. This is the world that is still going on. And he doesn't walk away from the mess we've made of it. Now he lives, almost cheerfully, certainly heroically, in a dynamic relationship with us and with our world.

"Then the Lord intervened" is perhaps the single most common phrase about him in Scripture, in one form or another. Look at the stories he writes. There's the one where the children of Israel are pinned against the Red Sea, no way out, with Pharaoh and his army barreling down on them in murderous fury. Then God shows up.

There's Shadrach, Meshach, and Abednego, who get rescued only *after* they're thrown into the fiery furnace. Then God shows up.

He lets the mob kill Jesus, bury him . . . then he shows up.

Do you know why God loves writing such incredible stories? Because *he loves to come through*. He loves to show us that he has what it takes.

❖   WILD AT HEART, 31–32

Joshua told the people, "Consecrate yourselves, for tomorrow the LORD will do amazing things among you."
—JOSHUA 3:5

God's relationship with us and with our world is just that: a *relationship*. As with every relationship, there's a certain amount of unpredictability, and the ever-present likelihood that you'll get hurt. The ultimate risk anyone ever takes is to love, for as C. S. Lewis writes, "Love anything and your heart will be wrung and possibly broken. If you want to make sure of keeping it intact you must give it to no one, not even an animal." But God does give it, again and again and again, until he is literally bleeding from it all. God's willingness to risk is just astounding—far beyond what any of us would do were we in his position.

Trying to reconcile God's sovereignty and man's free will has stumped the church for ages. We must humbly acknowledge that there's a great deal of mystery involved, but for those aware of the discussion, I am not advocating open theism. Nevertheless, there is definitely something wild in the heart of God.

❧ *WILD AT HEART, 32*

David, wearing a linen ephod, danced before the LORD with all his might.
—2 SAMUEL 6:14

D are we forget King David? Yes, his passions got him in a heap of trouble—and gave us our book of *worship*, the Psalms. Sure, Peter was a hotheaded disciple always quick with a reply. Remember in the Garden of Gethsemane—he's the one who lopped off the ear of the high priest's servant. But he was also the first to acknowledge that Jesus was the Messiah, and despite his Good Friday betrayals, he became a key apostle, contributed important pieces to the Scripture, and followed Jesus all the way to his own crucifixion, asking to be nailed to the cross upside down because he was not worthy to die in the manner of his Lord. Surely we remember that Paul was once Saul, the fiery young Pharisee "advancing in Judaism beyond many Jews of my own age and . . . extremely zealous for the traditions of my fathers" (Gal 1:14). His zeal made him the foremost persecutor of the church. When Christ knocked him off his donkey on the Damascus road, Paul was hunting down the church, "uttering threats with every breath" (Acts 9:1 NLT). Christ captured Paul's zeal, and after Damascus that zeal led him to "work harder than all the other apostles" (1 Cor. 15:10 NLT).

Desire, a burning passion for more, is at the heart of both saints and sinners. Those who would kill the passion altogether would murder the very essence that makes heroes of the faith.

❖ *THE JOURNEY OF DESIRE, 52–53*

Strike the ground.
—2 KINGS 13:18

I thought of the last story we have from the life of the prophet Elisha. Jehoash was king of Israel at the time, and he went to visit Elisha on his sickbed. He knew that without the help of this great prophet, the future of Israel was looking dim. Enemies were closing in on every side, waiting for the kill. Elisha told the king to take in hand some arrows.

> And the king took them. Elisha told him, "Strike the ground." He struck it three times and stopped. The man of God was angry with him and said, "You should have struck the ground five or six times; then you would have defeated your enemies completely. . . . But now you will defeat them only three times." Elisha died and was buried. (2 Kings 13:18–20)

That's it? What a strange story! Why was the old prophet so angry? Because the king was nonchalant; he was passionless, indifferent. He gave the ground a whack or two. His heart wasn't in it. God says, in effect, "If that is how little you care about the future of your people, that is all the help you will get." In other words, if your heart's not in it, well then, neither is mine. You can't lead a country, let alone flourish in a marriage, with an attitude like that. To abandon desire is to say, "I don't really need you; I don't really want you. But I will live with you because, well, I'm supposed to." It is a grotesque corruption of what was meant to be a beautiful dance between desire and devotion.

❖ *THE JOURNEY OF DESIRE*, 56–57

For everyone who has will be given more, and he will have an
abundance. Whoever does not have, even what he has will be taken
from him.

— MATTHEW 25:29

You may recall the story Jesus told of the man who entrusted three of his servants with thousands of dollars (literally, "talents"), urging them to handle his affairs well while he was away. When he returned, he listened eagerly to their reports. The first two fellows went out into the marketplace and doubled their investment. As a result, they were handsomely rewarded. The third servant was not so fortunate. His gold was taken from him, and he was thrown into "outer darkness, where there will be weeping and gnashing of teeth." My goodness. Why? All he did was bury the money under the porch until his master's return.

Many of us would probably agree with the path he chose— at least the money was safe there. But listen to his reasoning. Speaking to his master, he said, "I know you are a hard man, harvesting crops you didn't plant and gathering crops you didn't cultivate. I was afraid I would lose your money, so I hid it." (See Matt. 25:14–30 NLT.) He was afraid of the master, whom he saw as a hard man. He didn't trust his master's heart.

The issue isn't capital gains—it's what we think of God. When we bury our desires, we are saying the same thing: "God, I don't dare desire because I fear you; I think you are hard-hearted."

❖ *THE JOURNEY OF DESIRE, 57–59*

Be on the alert, stand firm in the faith, act like men, be strong.
—1 CORINTHIANS 16:13 NASB

Our false self demands a formula before it engages; our false self wants a guarantee of success; and mister, you aren't going to get one. So there comes a time in a man's life when he's got to break away from all that and head off into the unknown with God. This is a vital part of our journey, and if we balk here, the journey ends.

Before the moment of Adam's greatest trial, God provided no step-by-step plan, gave no formula for how he was to handle the whole mess. That was not abandonment; that was the way God *honored* Adam. *You are a man; you don't need me to hold you by the hand through this. You have what it takes.* What God *did* offer Adam was friendship. He wasn't left alone to face life; he walked with God in the cool of the day, and there they talked about love and marriage and creativity, what lessons he was learning and what adventures were to come. This is what God is offering to us as well.

The only way to live in this adventure—with all its danger and unpredictability and immensely high stakes—is in an ongoing, intimate relationship with God. The control we so desperately crave is an illusion. Far better to give it up in exchange for God's offer of companionship, set aside stale formulas so that we might enter into an informal friendship.

❀ *WILD AT HEART, 213–14*

Let my lover come into his garden
and taste its choice fruits.
—SONG OF SOLOMON 4:16

A ll God's wildness and all his fierceness are inseparable from his romantic heart. Music, wine, poetry, sunsets . . . those were *his* inventions, not ours. We simply discovered what he had already thought of. Let's bring this a little closer to home. Whose idea was it to create the human form in such a way that a kiss could be so delicious? And he didn't stop there, as only lovers know. Starting with her eyes, King Solomon feasted on his beloved through the course of their wedding night. He cherished her hair, her smile; her lips "drop sweetness as the honeycomb" and "milk and honey are under her tongue." You'll notice he's working his way down:

Your neck is like the tower of David,
   built with elegance . . .
Your two breasts are like two fawns . . .
Until the day breaks
   and the shadows flee,
I will go to the mountain of myrrh
   and to the hill of incense. (Song 4:4–6)

What kind of God would put the Song of Songs in the canon of Holy Scripture? Really, now, is it conceivable that such an erotic and scandalous book would have been placed in the Bible by the Christians *you* know?

❖ WILD AT HEART, 32–33

The father said to his servants, "Quick! Bring the best robe and put it on him. Put a ring on his finger and sandals on his feet. Bring the fattened calf and kill it. Let's have a feast and celebrate. For this son of mine was dead and is alive again; he was lost and is found."
—LUKE 15:22–24

In *The Lion King*, the lion cub Simba is separated in his youth from his father through a murder engineered by his uncle, Scar, the evil one in the story. Scar arranges for the cub to be caught in a stampede of wildebeests, knowing that his father, Mufasa, will risk his life to save his son. He does, and Simba is saved, but Mufasa is killed. Scar then accuses Simba of causing his father's death. Brokenhearted, frightened, racked with guilt, Simba runs away from home.

This is the enemy's one central purpose—to separate us from the Father. He uses neglect to whisper, *You see—no one cares. You're not worth caring about.* He uses a sudden loss of innocence to whisper, *This is a dangerous world, and you are alone. You've been abandoned.* He uses assaults and abuses to scream at a boy, *This is all you are good for.* And in this way he makes it nearly impossible for us to know the Father as Jesus knows him. Satan makes it so very, very hard to come home to the Father, to trust his heart toward us. The details of each story are unique to the boy, but the effect is always a wound in the soul, and with it separation from, and suspicion of the Father.

It's been very effective.

But God is not willing simply to let that be the end of the story. Not in any man's life. He will come for the boy, no matter how old he might now be, and make him his beloved son.

❖ *FATHERED BY GOD, 57–58*

The Son stands first in the line of humanity he restored. We see the original and intended shape of our lives there in him. After God made that decision of what his children should be like, he followed it up by calling people by name. After he called them by name, he set them on a solid basis with himself. And then, after getting them established, he stayed with them to the end, gloriously completing what he had begun.
—ROMANS 8:29–30 *The Message*

God has something in mind. He is deeply and personally committed to restoring humanity. Restoring you. He had a specific man or woman in mind when he made you. By bringing you back to himself through the work of Jesus Christ, he has established relationship with you. He restores you by shaping your life "along the same lines as the life of his Son." By shaping you into the image of Jesus. You can be confident of this. It's a given. Whatever else might be going on in your life, God always has his eye on your transformation.

This is good news, by the way. All of the other things we long for in life—love and friendship, freedom and wholeness, clarity of purpose—it all depends on our restoration. You can't find or keep good friends while you are still an irritating person to be around. And there is no way love can flourish while you are still controlling. You can't find your real purpose in life while you're still slavishly serving other people's expectations of you. You can't find peace while you're ruled by fear. You can't enjoy what you have while you're envying what the other guy has. On and on it goes.

God wants us to be happy. Really. But he knows that in order for us to be truly happy, we have to be whole.

❖ *WALKING WITH GOD, 19–20*

It is for freedom that Christ has set us free. Stand firm, then, and do not let yourselves be burdened again by a yoke of slavery.
—GALATIANS 5:1

The first day of summer vacation. I'm sitting on the porch of our cabin watching the rain fall on all my plans for the day. I cannot hike. I cannot do chores. I cannot fish. The mud is so deep, I cannot drive anywhere. I'm trapped. Pinned down. With myself and God. There is nothing I can do but pay attention to what surfaces inside me when I cannot charge into the day. I begin to write:

I am tweaked again. I'm so tired and wrung, my body hurts from being tired. Or hurts at the first chance to let down and be tired.

I'm tweaked from pushing. Pushing, pushing, always pushing.

This pushing is such a way of life for me, I barely know how to live otherwise. I'm always trying to make life better for me or for someone else. It feels like I heave myself at life. Always looking for some way to improve things. I come up here to the ranch to rest, and in the first ten minutes of quiet, here is where my mind goes: *I ought to teach Sam how to cast a fly rod. We ought to finish that back fence. I ought to work with the horses. I could paint the door now. Make a plan.*

Jesus, have mercy.

❀ WALKING WITH GOD, 25–26

Come to me, all you who are weary and burdened, and I will give you rest. Take my yoke upon you and learn from me, for I am gentle and humble in heart, and you will find rest for your souls. For my yoke is easy and my burden is light.

—MATTHEW 11:28–30

I cannot live my life like this—always working on something. Trying to make life better. Pushing. It's the first day of my vacation, but I can't enjoy it because of the condition I'm in. And I did this to myself. I'm frayed like an old rope because of the way I live my life. And I've got a pretty good sense that this isn't the life God would have me live. I'm pretty sure there isn't a verse that goes, "He leadeth me to utter exhaustion; he runneth me ragged." In fact, doesn't Jesus say something about his yoke is easy and his burden light? Maybe I have some other yoke on me than the yoke of Christ.

Did I really need to take all those trips this year? *Really?* Did I really have to come through for everyone I felt compelled to come through for? *Really?* Here is the embarrassing question: Did I even ask God about those things? Now, I know, I know—our lives seem so inevitable. There's always a reason. There's always a defense. "But I *have* to live like this! If I didn't carry the world on my shoulders—who would?" I also know that I don't want to live like this. The very things I'm doing to try to make life happen—all those things that feel so inevitable and unavoidable—are draining me and preventing me from finding the life God offers.

❖ *WALKING WITH GOD,* 26–27

*I am the good shepherd; I know my sheep and my sheep know me—I
have other sheep that are not of this sheep pen. I must bring them
also. They too will listen to my voice, and there shall be one flock and
one shepherd.*

—JOHN 10:14, 16

We are invited to become followers of Jesus.

Not just believers. *Followers*. There is a difference.

Follower assumes that someone else is doing the leading. As in
"He calls his own sheep by name and leads them out . . . He goes
on ahead of them, and his sheep follow him because they know
his voice" (John 10:3–4). The Bible invites us to an intimacy with
God that will lead us to the life we are meant to live. *If we will
follow him.* "I will instruct you and teach you in the way you
should go; / I will counsel you and watch over you" (Ps. 32:8).
God promises to guide us in the details of our lives. In fact, the
Psalm continues, "Do not be like the horse or the mule, / which
have no understanding / but must be controlled by bit and bridle
/ or they will not come to you" (v. 9).

What would it be like to yield to Christ in the details of our
lives? What would it be like to follow his counsel and instruction
in all the small decisions that add up to the life we find ourselves
living?

It would be . . . amazing.

❧   *WALKING WITH GOD, 28–29*

The LORD said, "Go out and stand on the mountain in the presence
of the LORD, for the LORD is about to pass by." After the wind there
was an earthquake, but the LORD was not in the earthquake. After the
earthquake came a fire, but the LORD was not in the fire. And after the
fire came a gentle whisper.

—1 KINGS 19:11–12

This is step one in learning to listen to the voice of God: ask simple questions. You cannot start with huge and desperate questions, such as, "Should I marry Ted?" or "Do you want me to sell the family business tomorrow?" That's like learning to play the piano by starting with Mozart, learning to ski by doing double black diamonds. There is way too much emotion involved, too much swirling around in our heads. I find that to hear the voice of God, we must be in a posture of quiet surrender. Starting with small questions helps us learn to do that.

Remember the story of the prophet Elijah after his triumph on Mount Carmel? He ran and hid in a cave. And there God spoke to him.

A gentle whisper. "A still small voice," as some translations have it. To hear that gentle whisper, we have to settle down. Shut out all the drama. Quiet our hearts. Now, as we grow in our personal holiness, we can be quiet and surrendered even in the major questions. But that takes time, and maturity. Don't ask that of yourself as you are starting out. Begin with simple questions.

❀ *WALKING WITH GOD, 30*

The Lord who delivered me from the paw of the lion and the paw of the bear will deliver me from the hand of this Philistine.

—1 SAMUEL 17:37

The armies of Israel have drawn up against the armies of the Philistines, but not a single shot has been fired from any bow. The reason is Goliath, a mercenary of tremendous size and strength who has killed many men bare-handed, no one wants to be next. David is barely a teen when he goes to the camp and sees what is going on. He offers to fight the giant and is brought before the king, who in turn attempts to dissuade the lad. Saul says, "You are not able to go out against this Philistine and fight him; you are only a boy, and he has been a fighting man from his youth" (1 Sam. 17:33). Sound advice. David replies:

> Your servant has been keeping his father's sheep. When a lion or a bear came and carried off a sheep from the flock, I went after it, struck it and rescued the sheep from its mouth. When it turned on me, I seized it by its hair, struck it and killed it. . . . The Lord who delivered me from the paw of the lion and the paw of the bear will deliver me from the hand of this Philistine. (vv. 34–37)

There is a settled confidence in the boy—he knows he has what it takes. But it is not an arrogance—he knows that God has been with him.

❖ FATHERED BY GOD, 71–72

Be on the alert, stand firm in the faith, act like men, be strong.
— 1 CORINTHIANS 16:13 NASB

It may take time and require repeated provocation, but eventually a man must come to realize that there are certain things in life worth fighting for. Perhaps, when we appreciate the truth of this, we can better understand the heart of God.

I don't fully understand the modern church's amnesia-plus-aversion regarding one of the most central qualities of God understood for centuries before us:

The LORD is a warrior; the Lord is his name. (Exod. 15:3)
The LORD will march out like a mighty man, like a warrior
    he will stir up his zeal; with a shout he will raise the battle
    cry and will triumph over his enemies. (Isa. 42:13)
But the LORD is with me like a mighty warrior; so my
    persecutors will stumble and not prevail. (Jer. 20:11)
Lift up your heads, O you gates; be lifted up, you ancient
    doors, that the King of glory may come in. Who is this
    King of glory? The LORD strong and mighty, the LORD
    mighty in battle. (Ps. 24:7–8)

Our God is a warrior, mighty and terrible in battle, and he leads armies. It is *this* God that man is made in the image of.

❂ *FATHERED BY GOD*, 88–89

Gird your sword upon your side,
O mighty one.
—PSALM 45:3

Our image of Jesus as a man has suffered greatly in the church, but perhaps no more so than our image of Jesus as a warrior. What was it that made Jesus so outraged that he sat down, and in an act of premeditated aggression, built for himself a whip of cords and then, having built it, used it on the merchants occupying the temple courtyards (John 2:13–17)? "Zeal for your house will consume me" (John 2:17). Is this the kind of behavior you'd expect from the Jesus you were taught, gentle Jesus meek and mild? Yes, Jesus could be immensely kind. But what is this other side to him we see in the Gospels? "Woe to you, teachers of the law and Pharisees, you hypocrites! You travel over land and sea to win a single convert, and when he becomes one, you make him twice as much a son of hell as you are" (Matt. 23:15). Oh, my. Them's fightin' words.

Our God is a warrior because there are certain things in life worth fighting for, must be fought for. He makes man a warrior in his own image because he intends for man to join him in that battle.

❖ *FATHERED BY GOD, 91–92*

O righteous God,
who searches minds and hearts,
bring to an end the violence of the wicked
and make the righteous secure.
—PSALM 7:9

I hope you're getting the picture by now. If a man does not find those things for which his heart is made, if he is never even invited to live for them from his deep heart, he will look for them in some other way. Why is pornography the number one snare for men? A man longs for the beauty, but without his fierce and passionate heart he cannot find her or win her or keep her. Though he is powerfully drawn to the woman, he does not know how to fight for her or even that he *is* to fight for her. Rather, he finds her mostly a mystery that he knows he cannot solve, and so at a soul level he keeps his distance. And privately, secretly, he turns to the imitation. What makes pornography so addictive is that more than anything else in a lost man's life, it makes him *feel* like a man without ever requiring a thing of him. The less a guy feels like a real man in the presence of a real woman, the more vulnerable he is to porn.

And so a man's heart, driven into the darker regions of the soul, denied the very things he most deeply desires, comes out in darker places. Now, a man's struggles, his wounds and addictions, are a bit more involved than that, but those are the core reasons. As the poet George Herbert warned, "He begins to die, that quits his desires." And you know what? We all know it. Every man knows that something's happened, something's gone wrong . . . we just don't know what it is.

❁ *WILD AT HEART, 44*

*When the woman saw that the fruit of the tree was good for food and
pleasing to the eye, and also desirable for gaining wisdom, she took
some and ate it. She also gave some to her husband, who was with her,
and he ate it.*

—GENESIS 3:6

God gives Adam some instructions on the care of creation, and
his role in the unfolding story. It's pretty basic, and very generous (see Gen. 2:16–17). But notice what God *doesn't* tell Adam.

There is no warning or instruction over what is about to occur:
the Temptation of Eve. This is just staggering. Notably missing
from the dialogue between Adam and God is something like this:
"Adam, one more thing. A week from Tuesday, about four in the
afternoon, you and Eve are going to be down in the orchard and
something dangerous is going to happen. Adam, are you listening?
The eternal destiny of the human race hangs on this moment.
Now, here's what I want you to do . . ." He doesn't tell him. He
doesn't even mention it, so far as we know. Good grief—*why not?!*
Because God *believes* in Adam. This is what he's designed to
do—to come through in a pinch. Adam doesn't need play-by-play
instructions because this is what Adam is *for*. It's already there,
everything he needs, in his design, in his heart.

Needless to say, the story doesn't go well. Adam fails; he fails Eve,
and the rest of humanity. And every man after him, every son of
Adam, carries in his heart now the same failure. Every man repeats
the sin of Adam, every day. We truly are a chip off the old block.

❧ WILD AT HEART, 50–51

* I'm indebted to Crabb, Hudson, and Andrews for pointing this out in
The Silence of Adam

*Do not conform any longer to the pattern of this world, but be
transformed by the renewing of your mind. Then you will be able to test
and approve what God's will is–his good, pleasing and perfect will.*

—ROMANS 12:2

Cinderella rises from the cinders to become a queen. The Ugly
Duckling becomes a beautiful swan. Pinocchio becomes a
real boy. The frog becomes a prince. The Cowardly Lion gets his
courage and the Scarecrow gets his brains and the Tin Woodman
gets a new heart. In hope beyond hope, they are all transformed
into the very thing they never thought they could be.

Why are we enchanted by tales of transformation? I can't
think of a movie or novel or fairy tale that doesn't somehow turn
on this. Why is it an essential part of any great story? Because
it is the secret to Christianity, and Christianity is the secret to
the universe. "You must be born again" (John 3:7). You must be
transformed. Keeping the Law, following the rules, polishing up
your manners—none of that will do. "What counts is whether
we really have been changed into new and different people"
(Gal. 6:15). Is this not the message of the gospel? Zacchaeus the
trickster becomes Zacchaeus the Honest One. Mary the whore
becomes Mary the Last of the Truly Faithful. Paul the self-righ-
teous murderer becomes Paul the Humble Apostle.

And we?

❂ *WAKING THE DEAD*, 56–57

*The LORD saw how great man's wickedness on the earth had become,
and that every inclination of the thoughts of his heart was only evil all
the time. The LORD was grieved that he had made man on the earth,
and his heart was filled with pain.*

—GENESIS 6:5–6

Something has gone wrong with the human race, and we know it. Something *within* the human race. Read a newspaper. Spend a weekend with your relatives. Pay attention to the movements of your own heart. Most of the misery we suffer on this planet is the fruit of the human heart gone bad.

Scripture could not be clearer about this. Yes, God created us to reflect his glory, but barely three chapters into the drama we torpedoed the whole project. Sin entered the picture and spread like a computer virus. By the sixth chapter of Genesis, our downward spiral had reached the point where God himself couldn't bear it any longer. His heart is broken because ours is fallen.

Any honest person knows this. We know we are not what we were meant to be. Most of the world religions concur on this point. Something needs to be done.

But the usual remedies involve some sort of shaping up on our part, some sort of face-lift whereby we start behaving as we should. It never works. It never will. Of course, the reason all those treatments ultimately fail is that we quite misdiagnosed the disease. The problem is not in our behavior; the problem is *in us*. As Jesus said, "For out of the heart come evil thoughts, murder, adultery, sexual immorality, theft, false testimony, slander" (Matt. 15:19). We don't need an upgrade. We need transformation.

❈ WAKING THE DEAD, 57–59

> *The king said to Daniel, "Surely your God is the God of gods and the*
> *Lord of kings and a revealer of mysteries, for you were able to reveal*
> *this mystery."*
> —DANIEL 2:47

As Frederick Buechner reminds us in his wonderful book *Telling the Truth: The Gospel as Tragedy, Comedy and Fairy Tale*, the world of the gospel is the world of fairy tale, with one notable exception:

> It is a world of magic and mystery . . . [W]here goodness is pitted against evil, love against hate, order against chaos, in a great struggle where often it is hard to be sure who belongs to which side because appearances are endlessly deceptive. Yet for all its confusion and wildness, it is a world where the battle goes ultimately to the good, who live happily ever after, and where in the long run everybody, good and evil alike, becomes known by his true name . . . That is the fairy tale of the Gospel with, of course, one crucial difference from all other fairy tales . . . that it not only happened once upon a time but has kept on happening ever since.

God has been weaving a drama since before the beginning of time, which he has also placed in our hearts. Who are the main players? What is the plot? How do we fit in? As we rediscover the oldest story in the world, one that is forever young, we journey into the heart of God and toward the recovery of our own hearts.

❖ *THE SACRED ROMANCE, 46*

*The thief comes only to steal and kill and destroy; I have come that
they may have life, and have it to the full.*
—JOHN 10:10

Have you ever wondered why Jesus married those two statements? Did you even know he spoke them at the same
time? I mean, he says them in one breath. And he has his reasons. By all means, God intends life for you. But right now that
life is *opposed*. It doesn't just roll in on a tray. There is a thief. He
comes to steal and kill and destroy. Why won't we face this? I
know so few people who will face this. The offer is life, but you're
going to have to fight for it because there's an Enemy in your life
with a different agenda. There *is* something set against us.

We are at war.

I don't like that fact any more than you do, but the sooner
we come to terms with it, the better hope we have of making it
through to the life we do want. This is not Eden. You probably
figured that out. This is not Mayberry, this is not *Seinfeld*'s world,
this is not *Survivor*. The world in which we live is a combat zone,
a violent clash of kingdoms, a bitter struggle unto the death. I am
sorry if I'm the one to break this news to you: you were born into a
world at war, and you will live all your days in the midst of a great
battle, involving all the forces of heaven and hell and played out
here on earth.

Where *did* you think all this opposition was coming from?

❖ WAKING THE DEAD, *12–13*

May he give you the desire of your heart
and make all your plans succeed.
—PSALM 20:4

In the quiet moments of the day we sense a nagging within, a discontentment, a hunger for something else. But because we have not solved the riddle of our existence, we assume that something is wrong—not with life, but with us. *Everyone else seems to be getting on with things. What's wrong with me?* We feel guilty about our chronic disappointment. *Why can't I just learn to be happier in my job, in my marriage, in my church, in my group of friends?* You see, even while we are doing other things, "getting on with life," we still have an eye out for the life we secretly want. When someone seems to have gotten it together, we wonder, *How did he do it?* Maybe if we read the same book, spent time with him, went to his church, things would come together for us as well. You see, we can never entirely give up our quest. Gerald May reminds us,

> When the desire is too much to bear, we often bury it beneath frenzied thoughts and activities or escape it by dulling our immediate consciousness of living. It is possible to run away from the desire for years, even decades, at a time, but we cannot eradicate it entirely. It keeps touching us in little glimpses and hints in our dreams, our hopes, our unguarded moments. (*The Awakened Heart*)

Even though we sleep, our desire does not. "It is who we are." It is the essence of the human soul, the secret of our existence.

❀ *THE JOURNEY OF DESIRE, 10–11*

The LORD had said to Abram, "Leave your country, your people and your father's household and go to the land I will show you."
—GENESIS 12:1

My gender seems to need little encouragement to go exploring. It comes naturally, like our innate love of maps. In 1260 Marco Polo headed off to find China, and in 1967, when I was seven, I tried to dig a hole straight through from our backyard with my friend Danny Wilson. We gave up at about eight feet, but it made a great fort. Hannibal crosses his famous Alps, and there comes a day in a boy's life when he first crosses the street and enters the company of the great explorers. Scott and Amundsen race for the South Pole, Peary and Cook vie for the North, and when last summer I gave my boys some loose change and permission to ride their bikes down to the store to buy a soda, you'd have thought I'd given them a charter to go find the equator. Magellan sails due west, around the tip of South America—despite warnings that he and his crew will drop off the end of the earth—and Huck Finn heads off down the Mississippi ignoring similar threats. Powell follows the Colorado into the Grand Canyon, even though—no, *because*—no one has done it before and everyone is saying it can't be done.

❀ WILD AT HEART, 4

How beautiful your sandaled feet,
O prince's daughter!
Your graceful legs are like jewels,
the work of a craftsman's hands.
—Song of Solomon 7:1

The desire to be beautiful is an ageless longing. Beauty has been extolled and worshiped and kept just out of reach for most of us. (Do you like having your picture taken? Do you like *seeing* those pictures later? How do you feel when people ask you your age? This issue of beauty runs deep!) For others, beauty has been shamed, used, and abused. Some of you have learned that possessing beauty can be dangerous. And yet— and this is just astounding—*in spite* of all the pain and distress that beauty has caused, the desire remains.

And it's *not* just the desire for an outward beauty, but more—a desire to be captivating in the depths of *who you are*. Cinderella is beautiful, yes, but she is also good. Her outward beauty would be hollow were it not for the beauty of her heart. That's why we love her. Ruth may have been a lovely, strong woman, but it is to her unrelenting courage and vulnerability and faith in God that Boaz is drawn. Esther is the most beautiful woman in the land, but it is her bravery and her cunning, good heart that moves the king to spare her people. This isn't about clothes and grooming . . . We desire to possess a beauty that is worth pursuing, worth fighting for, a beauty that is core to who we *truly* are. We want beauty that can be seen; beauty that can be felt; beauty that affects others; a beauty all our own to unveil.

❀ *Captivating, 16–17*

*Ah, Sovereign LORD . . . I do not know how to speak; I am only a
child. But the LORD said to me, "Do not say, 'I am only a child.' You
must go to everyone I send you to and say whatever I command you.
Do not be afraid of them, for I am with you and will rescue you,"
declares the LORD.*

—JEREMIAH 1:6–8

When God comes to call Jeremiah to be his prophet of hard
sayings to Judah, Jeremiah protests.

God is saying that these things will be done through Jeremiah's
dependence on God's strength and provision, and that God will
rescue him. Yet there is something about God's rescues that make
them a little less timely than dialing 911. He leaves Abraham with
his knife raised and ready to plunge into Isaac's heart, and Isaac
waiting for the knife to descend; he leaves Joseph languishing for
years in an Egyptian prison; he allows the Israelites to suffer four
hundred years of bondage under the Egyptians and leaves those
same Israelites backed against the Red Sea with Pharaoh's chariots
thundering down on them. He abandons Jesus to the cross and
does not rescue him at all. And then there are those of us who,
along with the saints under heaven's very altar, are groaning under
the weight of things gone wrong, waiting for that same Jesus to
return and sweep us up with him in power and glory. "How long,
O Lord?" we whisper in our weariness and pain.

Indeed, God calls us to battles where the deck appears stacked
in favor of those who are his enemies and ours, just to increase the
drama of the play. And there is the clear picture, even from God
himself, that he does so to enhance his own glory.

❖ *THE SACRED ROMANCE*, 55

I am always with you;
you hold me by my right hand.
My flesh and my heart may fail,
but God is the strength of my heart
and my portion forever.
—Psalm 73:23–24, 26

Until we come to terms with *war* as the context of our days, we will not understand life. We will misinterpret 90 percent of what is happening around us and to us. It will be very hard to believe that God's intentions toward us are life abundant; it will be even harder not to feel that somehow we are just blowing it. Worse, we will begin to accept some really awful things about God. That four-year-old little girl being molested by her daddy—that is "God's *will*"? That ugly divorce that tore your family apart—God wanted that to happen too? And that plane crash that took the lives of so many—that was ordained by God?

Most people get stuck at some point because God appears to have abandoned them. A young woman recently said to me, "God rather silent right now." Yes, it's been awful. I don't discount that. She is unloved, unemployed, under a lot. But her attitude strikes me as deeply naive, as someone caught in a cross fire who asks, "God, why won't you make them stop firing at me?" I'm sorry, but that's not where we are right now. It's not where we are in the Story. That day is coming, *later*, when the lion shall lie down with the lamb and we'll beat swords into plowshares. For now, it's bloody battle.

It sure explains a lot, doesn't it?

❧ Waking the Dead, *17–18*

Therefore we do not lose heart. Though outwardly we are wasting away, yet inwardly we are being renewed day by day. For our light and momentary troubles are achieving for us an eternal glory that far outweighs them all. So we fix our eyes not on what is seen, but what is unseen. For what is seen is temporary, but what is unseen is eternal.
—2 CORINTHIANS 4:16–18

The first line grabs me by the throat. "Therefore we do not lose heart." Somebody knows how not to lose heart? I'm all ears. For we *are* losing heart. All of us. Daily. We are losing—or we have already lost—heart. That glorious, resilient image of God in us is fading, fading, fading away. And this man claims to know a way out.

So, how, Paul—*how*? How do we not lose heart?

So we fix our eyes not on what is seen, but on what is unseen. (2 Cor. 4:18)

What? I let out a sigh of disappointment. *Now that's helpful.* "Look at what you cannot see." That sounds like Eastern mysticism, that sort of wispy wisdom dripping in spirituality but completely inapplicable to our lives. Life is an illusion. Look at what you cannot see. *What can this mean?* Remembering that a little humility can take me a long way, I give it another go.

This wise old seer is saying that there is a way of looking at life, and that those who discover it are able to live from the heart no matter what. How do we do this? By seeing with the eyes of the heart. Later in life, writing from prison to some friends he was deeply concerned about, Paul said, "I pray . . . that the eyes of your heart may be enlightened" (Eph. 1:18).

❖ WAKING THE DEAD, 21–23

When he was at the table with them, he took bread, gave thanks, broke it and began to give it to them. Then their eyes were opened and they recognized him, and he disappeared from their sight. They asked each other, "Were not our hearts burning within us while he talked with us on the road and opened the Scriptures to us?"

—LUKE 24:30-32

What do all great stories and myths tell us? What do they have in common? What are they trying to get across? Wherever they may come from, whatever their shape might be, they nearly always speak to us is three eternal truths. The first truth these stories are trying to remind us is that *things are not what they seem.* There is a whole lot more going on here than meets the eye. Much more. After the tornado sets her down, Dorothy wakes and steps out of her old farmhouse to find herself in a strange new world, a land of Munchkins and fairies and wicked witches. The Land of Oz. How brilliant for the filmmakers to have waited for this moment to introduce color in the movie. Up till now the story has been told in black and white; when Dorothy steps out of the house, the screen explodes in color, and she whispers to her little friend, "Toto . . . I don't think we're in Kansas anymore."

Isn't this the very lesson of the Emmaus Road? You recall the story—two followers of Christ are headed out of town after the Crucifixion, as dejected as two people can be. Their hopes have been shattered. They staked it all on the Nazarene, and now he's dead. As they go home, Jesus comes alongside, very much alive but incognito, and joins their conversation.

There is more going on here than meets the eye. Far more.

❧ WAKING THE DEAD, 26–27, 29

*Wake up, O sleeper . . . Be very careful, then, how you live . . .
because the days are evil.*

—EPHESIANS 5:14–16

The second eternal truth brought to us comes like a broken message over the radio or an urgent e-mail from a distant country, telling us that some great struggle or quest or battle is well under way. May even be hanging in the balance.

In C. S. Lewis's *The Lion, the Witch, and the Wardrobe* when the four children stumble into Narnia, the country and all its lovely creatures are imprisoned under the spell of the White Witch and have been for a hundred years. In another story, Jack and his mother are starving and must sell their only cow.

Frodo barely makes it out of the Shire with his life and the ring of power. In the nick of time, he learns that Bilbo's magic ring is the One Ring, that Sauron has discovered its whereabouts, and that the Nine Black Riders are already across the borders searching for the little hobbit with deadly intent. The future of Middle Earth hangs on a thread.

Again, this is *exactly* what the Scriptures have been trying to wake us up to for years. "Wake up, O sleeper . . . Be very careful, then, how you live . . . because the days are evil" (Eph 5:14–16). In effect, the Bible warns, "Use your head. Make the most of every chance you get. These are desperate times!"

Christianity isn't a religion about going to Sunday school, potluck suppers, being nice, holding car washes, sending our secondhand clothes off to Mexico. This is a world at war. Something large and immensely dangerous is unfolding all around us, we are caught up in it, and above all we doubt we have been given a key role to play.

❖ *WAKING THE DEAD*, 29–30

God is love. Whoever lives in love lives in God, and God in him.
—1 JOHN 4:16

W e need one another. God knows that. He will help us. We have only to ask and surrender, to wait, to hope, and, in faith, to love. We must also repent.

For a woman to enjoy relationship, she must repent of her need to control and her insistence that people fill her. Fallen Eve demands that people "come through" for her. Redeemed Eve is being met in the depths of her soul by Christ and is free to offer to others, free to desire, and willing to be disappointed. Fallen Eve has been wounded by others and withdraws in order to protect herself from further harm. Redeemed Eve knows that she has something of value to offer; that she is made for relationship. Therefore, being safe and secure in her relationship with her Lord, she can risk being vulnerable with others and offer her true self.

Nevertheless, love is risky. C. S. Lewis wrote,

To love at all is to be vulnerable. Wrap it carefully round with hobbies and little luxuries; avoid all entanglements; lock it up safe in the casket or coffin of your selfishness. But in that casket—safe, dark, motionless, airless—it will change. It will not be broken; it will become unbreakable, impenetrable, irredeemable . . . The only place outside Heaven where you can be perfectly safe from all the dangers . . . of love is Hell. (*The Four Loves*)

❧ CAPTIVATING, *181–82*

Jesus said, "Peace be with you! As the Father has sent me, I am
sending you."
—JOHN 20:21

Every mythic story *shouts* to us that in this desperate hour *we*
have a crucial role to play. This is the third eternal truth contained in all great stories, and it happens to be the one we most
desperately need if we are ever to understand our days. Frodo, the
little Halfling from the Shire, young and naive in so many ways,
"the most unlikely person imaginable," is the Ring Bearer. He,
too, must learn through dangerous paths and fierce battle that a
task has been appointed to him, and if he does not find a way, no
one will. Dorothy is just a farm girl from Kansas, who stumbled
into Oz not because she was looking for adventure but because
someone had hurt her feelings and she decided to run away from
home. Yet she's the one to bring down the Wicked Witch of the
West. Joan of Arc was also a farm girl, illiterate, the youngest in
her family, when she received her first vision from God. Just about
everyone doubted her; the commander of the French army said
she should be taken home and given a good whipping. Yet she
ended up leading armies to war.

You see this throughout Scripture: a little boy will slay the giant,
a loudmouthed fisherman who can't hold down a job will lead
the church, and a prostitute with a golden heart is the one to per-
form the deed that Jesus asked us all to tell "wherever the gospel is
preached throughout the world" (Mark 14:9). Things are not what
they seem. *We* are not what we seem.

❧ WAKING THE DEAD, 32–33

> *Then Jesus came to them and said, "All authority in heaven and*
> *on earth has been given to me. Therefore, go and make disciples of*
> *all nations . . . And surely I am with you always, to the very end*
> *of the age."*
> —MATTHEW 28:18–20

In this desperate hour we have a crucial role to play. Of all the eternal truths we struggle to believe, this is the one we doubt most of all. Our days are not extraordinary. They are filled with the mundane, with hassles mostly. And we? We are . . . a dime a dozen. Nothing special really. Probably a disappointment to God. But as C. S. Lewis wrote, "The value of . . . myth is that it takes all the things we know and restores to them the rich significance which has been hidden by 'the veil of familiarity.'" You are not what you think you are. There is a glory to your life that your Enemy fears, and he is hell-bent on destroying that glory before you act on it. This part of the answer will sound unbelievable at first; perhaps it will sound too good to be true; certainly, you will wonder if it is true for you. But once you begin to see with those eyes, once you have begun to know it is true from the bottom of your heart, it will change everything.

The story of your life is the story of the long and brutal assault on your heart by the one who knows what you could be and fears it.

❖ WAKING THE DEAD, 33–34

The watchmen found me
as they made their rounds in the city.
"Have you seen the one my heart loves?"
—SONG OF SOLOMON 3:3

I know I am not alone in this nagging sense of failing to measure up, a feeling of not being good enough. Everyone I've ever met feels it—something deeper than just the sense of failing at what he or she does. An underlying, gut feeling of failing at who he or she is. *I am not enough*, and *I am too much* at the same time. Not pretty enough, not strong enough, not kind enough, not gracious enough, not disciplined enough. But too emotional or too aloof, too needy or too isolated, too sensitive or too detached, too strong, too opinionated, too messy. The result is shame, the universal companion, especially of women. It haunts us, nipping at our heels, feeding on our deepest fears and driving us to overcompensate.

We feel *unseen*, even by those who are closest to us. We feel *unsought*—that no one has the passion or the courage to pursue us, to get past our messiness to find the woman deep inside. And we feel *uncertain*—uncertain what it even means to be a woman; uncertain what it truly means to be feminine; uncertain if we are or ever will be.

Aware of our deep failings, we pour contempt on our own hearts for wanting more. Oh, we long for intimacy and for adventure; we long to be the Beauty of some great story. But the desires set deep in our hearts seem like a luxury, granted only to those women who get their acts together. The message to the rest of us—whether from a driven culture or a driven church—is: *Try harder*.

❀ CAPTIVATING, 6–7

Be on your guard; stand firm in the faith; be men of courage; be
strong. Do everything in love.

—1 CORINTHIANS 16:13–14

Every man wants a battle to fight. It's the whole thing with
boys and weapons.

And look at the movies men love—*Braveheart, Gladiator, Top
Gun, High Noon, Saving Private Ryan.* Men are made for battle.
(And ladies, don't you love the heroes of those movies? You might
not want to fight in a war, but don't you long for a man who will fight
for *you?*) Women don't fear a man's strength if he is a good man.

Men also long for adventure. Adventure is a deeply spiritual
longing in the heart of every man. Adventure requires something
of us, puts us to the test. Though we may fear the test, at the same
time we yearn to be tested, to discover that we have what it takes.

Finally, every man longs for a Beauty to rescue. He really does.
Where would Robin Hood be without Marian, or King Arthur
without Guinevere? Lonely men fighting lonely battles. You see,
it's not just that a man needs a battle to fight. He needs someone to
fight *for.* There is nothing that inspires a man to courage so much
as the woman he loves. Most of the daring (and okay, sometimes
ridiculous) things young men do are to impress the girls. Men go
to war carrying photos of their sweethearts in their wallets—that is
a metaphor of this deeper longing, to fight for the Beauty. This is
not to say that a woman is a "helpless creature" who can't live her
life without a man. I'm saying that men long to offer their strength
on behalf of a woman.

She inspires him to be a hero.

❖ CAPTIVATING, *17–18*

Count yourselves dead to sin but alive to God in Christ Jesus.
—ROMANS 6:11

The new covenant has two parts to it: "I will give you a new heart and put a new spirit in you; I will remove from you your heart of stone and give you a heart of flesh" (Ezek. 36:26). God removed your old heart when he circumcised your heart; he gives you a new heart when he joins you to the life of Christ. That's why Paul can say "count yourselves dead to sin" *and* "alive to God in Christ Jesus" (Rom. 6:11).

The Resurrection affirms the promise Christ made. For it was *life* he offered to give us: "I have come that they may have life, and have it to the full" (John 10:10). We are saved by his life when we find that *we are able to live* the way we've always known we should live. We are free to be what he meant when he made us. If you are a believer, you have a new life—the life of Christ. And you have a new heart. Do you know what this means? Your heart is good.

❁ WAKING THE DEAD, 66–67

Do you not know that your body is a temple of the Holy Spirit, who is in you, whom you have received from God?

—1 CORINTHIANS 6:19

Each person knows that his or her *body* is the temple of God. "Don't you know that you yourselves are God's temple and that God's Spirit lives in you?" (1 Cor. 3:16). Okay—each of us is now the temple of God. So where, then, is the Holy of Holies?

Your heart.

That's right—your heart. Paul teaches us in Ephesians that "Christ may dwell in your hearts by faith" (3:17). God comes down to dwell in us, *in our hearts*. Now, we know this: evil cannot dwell where God is. "You are not a God who takes pleasure in evil; with you the wicked cannot dwell" (Ps. 5:4). Something pretty dramatic must have happened in our hearts, then, to make them fit to be the dwelling place of a holy God.

Of course, none of this can happen for us until we give our lives back to God. We cannot know the joy or the life or the freedom of heart I've described here until we surrender our lives to Jesus and surrender them totally. Renouncing all the ways we have turned from God in our hearts, we forsake the idols we have worshiped and given our hearts over to. We turn and give ourselves body, soul, and spirit back to God, asking him to cleanse our hearts and make them new.

❧ WAKING THE DEAD, 68

The good man brings good things out of the good stored up in his heart, and the evil man brings evil things out of the evil stored up in his heart.

—LUKE 6:45

It's undeniable: the new covenant, accomplished through the work of Christ, means that we have new hearts. Our hearts *are* good. Or God's a liar.

Until we embrace that stunning truth, we will find it really hard to make decisions, because we can't trust what our hearts are saying. In fact, we won't find our calling, our place in God's kingdom, because that is written on our hearts. We'll have a really hard time hearing God's voice in a deeply intimate way, because God speaks to us in our hearts. We'll live under guilt and shame for all sorts of evil thoughts and desires that the Enemy has convinced us were ours. God will seem aloof. Worship and prayer will feel like chores.

Of course, I just described the life most Christians feel doomed to live. Explaining the parable of the sower and the seed, Jesus says, "The seed on good soil stands for those *with a noble and good heart*, who hear the word, retain it, and by persevering produce a crop" (Luke 8:15, emphasis added).

Jesus himself teaches that the heart can be good and even noble. That somebody is you, if you are his. God kept his promise. We have new hearts. Do you know what this means? Your heart is good. Let that sink in for a moment. Your heart is *good*.

What would happen if you believed it, if you came to the place where you *knew* it was true? Your life would never be the same.

❖ WAKING THE DEAD, 69–70

The LORD God formed the man from the dust of the ground and breathed into his nostrils the breath of life, and the man became a living being.
—GENESIS 2:7

God sets his own image on the earth. He creates a being like himself. He creates a son. Nothing in creation even comes close. Picture Michelangelo's *David*. He is . . . magnificent. Truly, the masterpiece seems complete. And yet, the Master says that something is not good, not right. Something is missing . . . and that something is Eve.

> The Lord God cast a deep slumber on the human, and he slept, and He took one of his ribs and closed over the flesh where it had been, and the Lord God built the rib He had taken from the human into a woman and He brought her to the human. (Gen. 2:21–23)

She is the crescendo, the final, astonishing work of God. Woman. In one last flourish creation comes to a finish not with Adam, but with *Eve*. She is the Master's finishing touch. How we wish this were an illustrated book, and we could show you now some painting or sculpture that captures this. Eve is . . . breathtaking.

Given the way creation unfolds, how it builds to ever higher and higher works of art, can there be any doubt that Eve is the crown of creation? She is God's final touch. She fills a place in the world nothing and no one else can fill.

❀ CAPTIVATING, *24–25*

Zion said, "The LORD has forsaken me, the Lord has forgotten me."
Can a mother forget the baby at her breast and have no compassion on
the child she has borne? Though she may forget, I will not forget you!
—ISAIAH 49:14–15

The vast desire and capacity a woman has for intimate relation-ships tell us of God's vast desire and capacity for intimate relationships. In fact, this may be *the* most important thing we ever learn about God—that he yearns for relationship with us. "Now this is eternal life: that they may know you, the only true God" (John 17:3). The whole story of the Bible is a love story between God and his people. He yearns for us. He *cares*. He has a tender heart.

I will give them a heart to know me, that I am the LORD.
They will be my people, and I will be their God, for they
will return to me with all their heart. (Jer. 24:7)
O Jerusalem, Jerusalem . . . how often I have longed to gather
your children together, as a hen gathers her chicks under
her wings, but you were not willing. (Matt. 23:37)

What a comfort to know that this universe we live in is rela-tional at its core, that our God is a tenderhearted God who yearns for relationship with us. If you have any doubt about that, simply look at the message he sent us in Woman. Amazing. Not only does God long *for* us, but he longs to be loved *by* us. Oh, how we've missed this. How many of you see God as longing to be loved by you? We see him as strong and powerful, but not as need-ing us, vulnerable to us, yearning to be desired.

❀ CAPTIVATING, 28–29

He has rescued us from the dominion of darkness and brought us into the kingdom of the Son he loves, in whom we have redemption, the forgiveness of sins.

—COLOSSIANS 1:13–14

Being unable to defeat God through raw power, Satan's legions decide to wound God as deeply as possible by stealing the love of his beloved through seduction. And having "seduced them to his party," to ravish them body and soul; and having ravished them, to mock them even as they are hurled to the depths of hell with God himself unable to save them because of their rejection of him. This is Satan's motivation and goal for every man, woman, and child into whom God ever breathed the breath of life. Like a roaring lion, he "hungers" for us.

> Be self-controlled and alert. Your enemy the devil prowls around like a roaring lion looking for someone to devour. Resist him, standing firm in the faith, because you know that your brothers throughout the world are undergoing the same kind of sufferings. (1 Peter 5:8–9)

God could have given up on the love affair with mankind. He could have resorted to power and demanded our loyalty, or given us a kind of spiritual lobotomy that would take away our choice to love him. Even now, he could easily obliterate our enemy and demand the allegiance of our hearts, but the love affair that began in the laughter of the Trinity would be over, at least for us. And Satan's accusation that the kingdom of God is established only through raw power would be vindicated.

❖ *THE SACRED ROMANCE, 104–5*

I belong to my lover,
and his desire is for me.
—SONG OF SOLOMON 7:10

Have you ever had to literally turn a lover over to a mortal enemy to allow her to find out for herself what his intentions toward her really were? Have you ever had to lie in bed knowing she was believing his lies and was having sex with him every night? Have you ever sat helplessly by in a parking lot, while your enemy and his friends took turns raping your lover even as you sat nearby, unable to win her heart enough so she would trust you to rescue her? Have you ever called this one you had loved for so long, even the day after her rape, and asked her if she was ready to come back to you only to have her say her heart was still captured by your enemy? Have you ever watched your lover's beauty slowly diminish and fade in a haze of alcohol, drugs, occult practices, and infant sacrifice until she is no longer recognizable in body or soul? Have you ever loved one so much that you even send your only son to talk with her about your love for her, knowing that he will be killed by her? (And in spite of knowing all of this, he was willing to do it because he loved her, too, and believed you were meant for each other.)

All this and more God has endured because of his refusal to stop loving us. The depth and faithfulness of his love for us!

❖ *THE SACRED ROMANCE, 106*

But in your hearts set apart Christ as Lord. Always be prepared to give an answer to everyone who asks you to give the reason for the hope that you have.

—1 PETER 3:15

A curious warning is given to us in Peter's first epistle. There he tells us to be ready to give the reason for the hope that lies within us to everyone who asks (3:15). Now, what's strange about that passage is this: no one ever asks. When was the last time someone stopped you to inquire about the reason for the hope that lies within you? You're at the market, say, in the frozen food section. A friend you haven't seen for some time comes up to you, grasps you by both shoulders and pleads, "Please, you've got to tell me. How can you live with such hope? Where does it come from? I must know." In talking with hundreds of Christians, I've met only one or two who have experienced something like this.

Yet God tells us to be ready, so what's wrong? To be blunt, nothing about our lives is worth asking about. There's nothing intriguing about our hopes, nothing to make anyone curious. Not that we don't have hopes; we do. We hope we'll have enough after taxes this year to take a summer vacation. We hope our kids don't wreck the car. We hope our favorite team goes to the World Series, and so on. Nothing wrong with any of those hopes; nothing unusual, either. Everyone has hopes like that, so why bother asking us? It's life as usual. Sanctified resignation has become the new abiding place of contemporary Christians. No wonder nobody asks. Do *you* want the life of any Christian you know?

❖ *THE JOURNEY OF DESIRE, 64*

Be still, and know that I am God.
—PSALM 46:10

I find that to hear the voice of God, we must be in a posture of quiet surrender.

I am not desperately hoping to hear what I secretly want to hear. Am I willing to hear whatever it is God wants to say? That is absolutely critical. If I can only hear an answer that agrees with what I want to hear, then I am not in a posture of surrender to God's will, and it will be hard for me to hear him at all—or to trust what I *do* hear, especially if it is the answer I'm looking for.

There is no more decisive issue when it comes to hearing the voice of God than the issue of surrender. Which is beautiful, really. We are drawn to God in search of guidance, but we come away with a deeper holiness because we are learning surrender. Sometimes I will even say as I'm listening, *Lord—I will accept whatever it is you want to say to me.* It helps me bring my soul to a posture of quiet surrender.

So there are the basics: Start with small questions. Repeat the question quietly in your heart to God. Bring yourself to a posture of quiet surrender. And let me add this—I am assuming we are talking about matters of counsel or guidance that are not directly addressed by Scripture. You don't need to ask God whether or not to commit murder or to run off with your neighbor's television.

❖ WALKING WITH GOD, *31*

*May he strengthen your hearts so that you will be blameless and holy
in the presence of our God and Father when our Lord Jesus comes with
all his holy ones.*

—1 THESSALONIANS 3:13

Things may not unfold the way you think they will when you're following God. Remember—he is after both our transformation *and* our joy. The one hangs upon the other.

Pause. You *do* know what he is after in your own life, don't you? Maybe that's why we stay so busy—to avoid knowing, so we can avoid dealing with it. And you do know that the "quick fix" doesn't ever work. Simply telling myself, "You are too busy, John. You've got to slow down," is about as effective as telling an addict to quit. (Has it worked for you?)

There are forces driving the way I live, reasons and compulsions written deep in my soul. I know where my pushing and striving come from. They come from unbelief, from some deep fear that it's all up to me. Life is up to me. I've got to make as much headway as I can before the bottom drops out. Make hay while the sun shines 'cause it isn't always going to shine and what's *that* underlying dread? God is not just after behavior modification (as in, stop it), but real and deep and lasting change.

❧ *WALKING WITH GOD, 32–33*

Long before be laid down earth's foundations, be had us in mind, had settled on us as the focus of his love, to be made whole and holy by his love.

—EPHESIANS 1:4 *The Message*

Whole and holy. The two go hand in hand. Oh, how important this is. You can't find the holiness you want without deep wholeness. And you can't find the wholeness you want without deep holiness. You can't simply tell the meth addict to quit. She does *need to* quit, but she requires profound healing *to be able to* quit. You can't just tell a raging man to stop losing his temper. He would love to stop. He'd give anything to stop. He doesn't know how. He doesn't know all the forces within him that swell up and overwhelm him with anger.

For too long, there have been two camps in Christendom. One is the holiness or "righteousness" crowd. They are the folks holding up the standard, preaching a message of moral purity. The results have been . . . mixed. Some morality, and a great deal of guilt and shame. Very little lasting change comes from this approach. Hey, I'm all for purity. It's just that you can't get there without the healing of your soul.

God disciplines us for our good, that we may share in his holiness. "Make level paths for your feet" so that the lame may not be disabled but rather healed (Hebrews 12:10–13). Healed. As in fixed. Restored. Made whole. The Bible says we can't hope to walk the path God would have us walk without the healing of our souls.

❖ WALKING WITH GOD, 34–35

For sin shall not be your master, because you are not under law, but under grace.
—ROMANS 6:14

The Bible says we can't hope to walk the path God would have us walk without the healing of our souls. Now, the other major camp in Christendom is the "grace" camp. Their message is that we can't hope to satisfy a holy God, but we are forgiven. We are under grace. And praise the living God, we are under grace. But what about holiness? What about deep personal change? Paul says, "For sin shall not be your master." He's assuming that a certain kind of grace will set us free from sin's power over our daily lives. My drivenness and compulsion will ruin me if they continue. God knows that. He also knows what I need.

I know, at least in part, what my drivenness is rooted in. Early on in my life, I found myself alone. It was a deep and profound wounding. No boy is meant to be on his own. But that wounding led to a sinful resolution—*I will make it on my own*. I felt that life was up to me (that was my wounding). I resolved to live as though life were up to me (that was my sin).

The path to freedom from all this pushing and striving involves *both* repentance and healing so that I can be made whole and holy by his love.

❁ *WALKING WITH GOD*, 36

For this people's heart has become calloused;
they hardly hear with their ears,
and they have closed their eyes.
Otherwise they might see with their eyes,
hear with their ears,
understand with their hearts
and turn, and I would heal them.
—MATTHEW 13:15

Heal them. Jesus yearned for his people to turn back to him *so that* he could heal them! The "otherwise" means that if they weren't so hardheaded, they would turn to him and he would heal them. This truth is essential to your view of the gospel. It will shape your convictions about nearly everything else.

God wants to restore us. Our part is to "turn," to repent as best we can. But we also need his healing. As Ephesians 1:4 teaches, God chose us to make us whole and holy through his love. God will make known to us the path of life if we will follow him. And as we do, we will find along that path our need for wholeness and holiness.

Jesus, forgive me. I ask your forgiveness of this deep commit-
ment to make life work on my own—for all my striving and
pushing and for all the unbelief that propels me. Forgive me.
And I ask you to heal me of this. Heal the places in my soul
that have so long felt alone, felt that life was up to me.

❦ WALKING WITH GOD, 36

Then Jesus said to him, "Go, Satan!" . . . Then the devil left Him;
and behold, angels came and began to minister to Him.

—MATTHEW 4:10–11 NKJV

The warrior must learn to yield his heart to nothing. Not to kill his heart for fear of falling into temptation, but to protect his heart for nobler things, to keep the integrity of his heart as a great reservoir of passionate strength and holy desire. That was Jesus' battle in the wilderness, as Satan tried this way and that to get him to surrender his integrity. *You don't need to trust God to meet your needs—make these stones become bread. Prove God cares for you—throw yourself off this building. You don't need to go the way of the cross—worship me and I'll give you the kingdoms of this world.* Jesus will not give in. This is no easy thing to do, as the history of man attests. As your own history attests.

And notice—at the end of the battle, "angels came and ministered to Him" (Matt. 4:11 NKJV). There is something for us to see here, or it would not have been included in the record. Jesus needs some ministering to, which gives us the sense that he was sorely taxed by the event. I take some comfort from this, both because it is a reminder of the human side of the incarnation mystery—Jesus really was a man—and because that sure has been my experience of these battles. When they are over, I am utterly drained and need some ministering myself.

It's not all trial and test and battle, not by any means. It's just that most often, good comfort comes *after* the fight and is so much more enjoyable in this way. One of the spoils of war.

❀ *FATHERED BY GOD, 106*

I will not speak with you much longer, for the prince of this world is coming. He has no hold on me.

—JOHN 14:30

The enemy is coming, Jesus told his disciples, but "he has no hold on me" (John 14:30). I love that; I just love it. Jesus is so clean, they've got nothing on him. It tells us something vital about warfare. First, that holiness is your best weapon. Spiritual warfare will make you holy. Trust me. Why is the enemy using that particular angle on you at this particular moment? Invite Christ in. Is it an occasion for repentance? Deeper healing? Strengthening feeble places? Good! That's good. You'll be a better person for it. The battle we find ourselves in gives a whole new purpose to holiness. The call is not "become a moral man because it's decent." The call is "become a holy man and a warrior, for you are needed in this battle, and if you do not become that man, you will be taken out."

The recovery of the warrior is absolutely crucial to the recovery of a man. All else rests on this, for you will have to fight, my brothers, for everything you desire and everything you hold dear in this world. Despite what you feel, or what you may have been told, you have a warrior's heart because you bear the image of God. And he will train you to become a great warrior, if you'll let him.

❖ *FATHERED BY GOD, 121–22*

Look at the lilies of the field and how they grow . . . yet Solomon in all his glory was not dressed as beautifully as they are.
— Matthew 6:28–29 nlt

We've heard ad infinitum that men are rational beings, along with the supporting evidence that our brains work differently than do women's, and this is true. Spatial abstractions, logic, analysis — men tend to excel in these because we are more left- than right-brained, and the commissural fibers that connect the two hemispheres appear in women in ratios far higher than in men. Women have an interstate uniting both sides of their brains. Men have a game trail. Thus men tend to compartmentalize, a capacity that allows men to handle the atrocities of war, and administrate justice. It also makes them excellent chess players and auto mechanics. And yet . . .

I don't buy it. Too many men hide behind reason and logic. A man must grow beyond mere reason, or he will be stunted as a man, certainly as a lover. No woman wants to be analyzed, and many marriages fail because the man insists on treating her as a problem to be solved, rather than a mystery to be known and loved. David was a cunning tactician as a warrior, but he was also a poet of the first order. And when Jesus says, "Consider the lilies of the field," he does not mean analyze them but rather, *behold* them, take them in, let their beauty speak, for "Solomon in all his glory was not dressed as beautifully as they are" (Matt. 6:29 nlt). He appeals to their beauty to show us the love of God. The lover is awakened when a man comes to see that the poetic is far truer than the propositional and the analytical.

❀ *Fathered by God, 131–32*

I found the one my heart loves.
—SONG OF SOLOMON 3:4

John Wesley was thirty-five when he experienced the now famous "warming" of his heart—not his mind—toward Christ, and he knew in that moment he had become not merely a Christian, but something more—a lover of God. Shortly after, he penned the hymn "Jesus, Lover of My Soul," whose first verse goes like this: "Jesus, Lover of my soul / Let me to thy bosom fly."

David would have had no problem at all understanding this. The poetry that flowed from the heart of this passionate lover is filled with unapologetic emotion toward God. He speaks of drinking from God's "river of delights," how his lover has filled his heart "with greater joy" than all the wealth other men have found, and he writes in many of his love songs how his heart sings to God. He cries through the night, aches to be with God, for he has found, really found, his life in God: "You have made known to me the path of life; you will fill me with joy in your presence" to such a degree that his heart and soul "pant for you, O God. My soul thirsts for God," his body even longing for God. These are not the words of a dry theologian or moralist. These are not the words of even your average pastor. For him, God's love "is better than life." David is captivated by the Beauty he finds in God. On and on it goes. The man is undone. He is as smitten as any lover might be, only—can we begin to accept this? do we even have a category for it?—his lover is God.

❧ *FATHERED BY GOD, 136–37*

Oh, my dear friend! You're so beautiful!
And your eyes so beautiful—like doves!
—SONG OF SOLOMON 1:15 *The Message*

Falling in love with a woman is a manly thing, so not only *can* we speak of falling in love, we *must*. God said of the first man that his life was not good without her (Gen. 2:18), so for most men, no matter how bold an adventurer or brave a warrior, he is not living as a man should live unless he makes room for a woman in his life. And, in most cases at this stage, it usually is a woman who comes to awaken the heart of a man.

The awakening of his heart is essential if a man would truly love a woman. Look at things from her point of view. What does she long for in a man? Every little girl dreams of the day her prince will come. Look at the movies women love—the hero is a *romancer*. He pursues her, wins her heart, takes her into a great adventure and love story. And notice—what is the great sorrow of every woman in a disappointing marriage? Isn't it that he no longer pursues, no longer romances her? Life has been reduced to function and problem solving. What she longs for is what you are is meant to become.

❧ FATHERED BY GOD, *140–42*

For you have been called to live in freedom, my brothers and sisters.
But don't use your freedom to satisfy your sinful nature. Instead, use
your freedom to serve one another in love.

—GALATIANS 5:13 NLT

So when it comes to loving a woman, the great divide lies between men as lovers and men as consumers. Does he seek her out, long for her, because really he yearns for her to meet some need in his life—a need for validation (she makes him feel like a man), or mercy, or simply sexual gratification? That man is a Consumer, as my friend Craig calls him. The lover, on the other hand, wants to fight for *her*—he wants to protect her, make her life better, wants to fill her heart in every way he can. It is no chore for him to bring flowers, or music, spend hours talking together. Having his own heart awakened, he wants to know and love and free her heart. The sexual difference between lover and consumer is revealing—read *Song of Songs* and ask yourself, "Does this sound like our bedroom?" The lover wants to "make love" to her. The consumer—well, there are any number of crass phrases men use to talk about getting into bed with her.

Of course the stage of the lover brings with it great pain and suffering, because we are speaking of the heart, and the heart, as we all know, is vulnerable like nothing else. Resilient, thank God, but vulnerable. The heights of joy this stage ushers in are greater than any other, but with them comes the potential for sorrow as deep as the heights are high. That is why he must also be a warrior, and that is why he must find his greatest love in God.

❧ FATHERED BY GOD, 142–43

There is no one like the God of Jeshurun,
who rides on the heavens to help you.
—Deuteronomy 33:26

E ve is given to Adam as his *ezer kenegdo*—or as many translations have it, his "help meet" or "helper." Doesn't sound like
much, does it? It makes me think of Hamburger Helper. But
Robert Alter says this is "a notoriously difficult word to translate."
It means something far more powerful than just "helper"; it can
also mean "*lifesaver.*" The phrase is only used elsewhere of God,
when you need him to come through for you desperately. Eve is
a life giver; she is Adam's ally, his "essential other." It is to *both* of
them that the charter for adventure is given. It will take both of
them to sustain life. And they will both need to fight together.

Eve is deceived . . . and rather easily, as my friend Jan Meyers
points out. In *The Allure of Hope*, Jan writes, "Eve was convinced
that God was withholding something from her." Not even the
extravagance of Eden kept her from doubting that God's heart is
good. "When Eve was deceived, the artistry of being a woman took
a fateful dive into the barren places of control and loneliness."
Now every daughter of Eve wants to "control her surrounding, her
relationships, her God." No longer is she vulnerable; now she will
be grasping. No longer does she want simply to share in the adventure; now, she wants to control it. And as for her beauty, she either
hides it in fear and anger, or she uses it to secure her place in the
world. Fallen Eve either becomes rigid or clingy." Put simply, Eve
is no longer simply *inviting.*

❖ *Wild at Heart, 51–52*

Therefore, since we have such a hope, we are very bold. We are not like Moses, who would put a veil over his face to keep the Israelites from gazing at it while the radiance was fading away . . . And we, who with unveiled faces all reflect the Lord's glory, are being transformed into his likeness with ever-increasing glory, which comes from the Lord, who is the Spirit.

—2 CORINTHIANS 3:12–13, 18

Moses put a veil over his face, first to hide his glory, then to hide the fact that it was fading away. That, too, was a picture of a deeper reality. We all do that. We all have veiled our glory, or someone has veiled it for us. Usually some combination of both. But the time has come to set all veils aside.

We are in the process of being unveiled. Created to reflect God's glory, born to bear his image, we are ransomed back to God to reflect that glory again. Every heart was given a mythic glory, and that glory is being *restored*. Remember the mission of Christ, said in effect, "I have come to give you back your heart and set you free." For as Saint Irenaeus said, "The glory of God is man fully alive." Our destiny is to come fully alive. To live with ever-*increasing* glory. As you may recall, this is the third eternal truth every good myth has been trying to get across to us: *your heart bears a glory, and your glory is needed* . . . now.

❖ WAKING THE DEAD, 74–75

"Of all the commandments, which is the most important?" "The most important one," answered Jesus, "is this: 'Hear, O Israel, the Lord our God, the Lord is one. Love the Lord your God with all your heart and with all your soul and with all your mind and with all your strength.'"
—MARK 12:28–30

Can there be any doubt that God wants to be sought after? The first and greatest of all commands is to love him (Matt. 22:36–38). He *wants* us to love him. To seek him with all our heart. A woman longs to be sought after, too, with the whole heart of her pursuer. God longs to be *desired*. Just as a woman longs to be desired. This is not some weakness on the part of a woman, that deep yearning to be desired. God feels the same way.

Life changes dramatically when romance comes into our lives. Christianity changes dramatically when we discover that it, too, is a great romance. That God yearns to share a life of beauty, intimacy, and adventure with us. "I have loved you with an everlasting love" (Jer. 31:3). This whole world was made for romance—the rivers and the glens, the meadows and the beaches. Flowers, music, a kiss. But we have a way of forgetting all that, losing ourselves in work and worry. Eve—God's message to the world in feminine form—invites us to romance. Through her God makes romance a priority of the universe.

God endows womankind with qualities that are essential to relationship, qualities that speak of God. She is inviting, vulnerable. She embodies mercy. She is and fierce and fiercely devoted. Oh yes, our God has a passionate, romantic heart. Just look at Eve.

❂ CAPTIVATING, *29–30*

One thing I ask of the LORD,
this is what I seek:
that I may dwell in the house of the LORD
all the days of my life,
to gaze upon the beauty of the LORD
and to seek him in his temple.
—PSALM 27:4

Beauty is powerful. It may be the most powerful thing on earth. It is dangerous. Because it *matters*. Let us try to explain why.

First, beauty *speaks*. Oxford bishop Richard Harries wrote, "It is the beauty of the created order which gives an answer to our questionings about God." And we do have questions. Augustine said he found answers in the beauty of the world:

I said to all these things, "Tell me of my God who you are not, tell me something about him." And with a great voice they cried out: "He made us" (Ps. 99:3). My question was the attention I gave to them, and their response was their beauty.

What does beauty say to us? Think of what it's like to be caught in traffic for more than an hour. Horns blaring, people shouting obscenities. Then remember what it's like to come into a beautiful place, a garden or a meadow or a quiet beach. There is room for your soul. You can rest. All is well. I sit outside on a summer evening and just listen and behold, and peace begins to come into my soul.

That is what beauty says: *All shall be well.*

❖ CAPTIVATING, 37–38

For since the creation of the world God's invisible qualities—his eternal power and divine nature—have been clearly seen.
—ROMANS 1:20

Beauty is *transcendent*. It is our most immediate experience of the eternal. Think of what it's like to behold a gorgeous sunset or the ocean at dawn. Remember the ending of a great story. We yearn to linger, to experience it all our days. Sometimes the beauty is so deep it pierces us with longing. For what? For life as it was meant to be. Beauty reminds us of an Eden we have never known, but somehow know our hearts were created for. Beauty speaks of heaven to come, when all shall be beautiful. It haunts us with eternity. Beauty says, *There is a glory calling to you.* And if there is a glory, there is a source of glory. What great goodness could have possibly created this? Beauty draws us to God.

All these things are true for any experience of Beauty. Beauty is, without question, the most *essential* and the most *misunderstood* of all God's qualities—of all feminine qualities, too. We know it has caused untold pain in the lives of women. But even there something is speaking. Why so much heartache over beauty? We don't ache over being geniuses, or fabulous hockey players. Women ache over the issue of beauty—they ache to be beautiful, to believe they are beautiful, and they worry over keeping it if ever they can find it.

❂ *CAPTIVATING, 40–41*

Those who see you stare at you Satan,
they ponder your fate:
"Is this the man who shook the earth
and made kingdoms tremble,
the man who made the world a desert,
who overthrew its cities
and would not let his captives go home?"

—ISAIAH 14:16–17

I ndeed, part of God's victory over the enemy of our souls, which we will be invited to take part in, will be an open mocking of Satan and his forces in view of all the peoples of the earth along with the angelic hosts. We are given a picture of the enemy's defeat, which is the culmination of Act III of the Sacred Romance, by Isaiah.

"You're the one we've been scared of all this time? You're the one we've been believing?" we will ask incredulously. And we will turn and walk away in the embrace of the Prince, never to speak Satan's name again. But in the meantime, our adversary will continue to use our Message of the Arrows, along with doubts about the goodness of the Prince, to lure us to spend our lives with less-wild lovers than God.

❀ *THE SACRED ROMANCE, 121*

This is what the LORD *says:*
"What fault did your fathers find in me,
that they strayed so far from me?
—JEREMIAH 2:5

The story of Eden is not over. Every day we reenact the Fall as we turn in our desire to the very things that will destroy us. As Gerald May reminds us,

Addiction exists wherever persons are internally compelled to give energy to things that are not their true desires . . . We succumb because the energy of our desire becomes attached, nailed, to specific behaviors, objects or people. (*Addiction and Grace*)

Addiction may seem too strong a term to some of you. The woman who is serving so faithfully at church—surely, there's nothing wrong with that. And who can blame the man who stays long at the office to provide for his family? Sure, you may look forward to the next meal and your hobbies can be a nuisance, but to call any of this an addiction seems a stretch.

I have one simple response: give it up. You will soon discover the tentacles of attachment deep in your soul. Remember, we will make an idol of anything, especially a good thing. So distant now from Eden, we are desperate for life, and we come to believe that we must arrange for it as best we can, or no one will. God must thwart us to save us.

❖ *THE JOURNEY OF DESIRE,* 92–93

Cursed is the ground because of you;
through painful toil you will eat of it
all the days of your life.
It will produce thorns and thistles for you.
—GENESIS 3:17–18

God *promises* every man futility and failure; he *guarantees* every woman relational heartache and loneliness. We spend most of our waking hours attempting to end-run the curse. We will fight this truth with all we've got. Sure, other people suffer defeat. Other people face loneliness. But not me. I can beat the odds. We see the neighbor's kids go off the deep end, and we make a mental note: *they didn't pray for their kids every day.* And we make praying for our kids every day part of our plan. It doesn't have to happen to us.

Isn't there something defensive that rises up in you at the idea that you cannot make life work out? Isn't there something just a little bit stubborn, an inner voice that says, *I can do it?* Thus Blaise Pascal writes, "All men seek happiness. This is without exception. Whatever different means they employ, they all tend to this end . . . This is the motive of every action of every man."

It can't be done. No matter how hard we try, no matter how clever our plan, we cannot arrange for the life we desire. Stop reading for a moment and ask yourself this question: Will life ever be what I so deeply want it to be, in a way that cannot be lost? This is the second lesson we must learn, and in many ways the hardest to accept. We must have life; we cannot arrange for it.

❧ *THE JOURNEY OF DESIRE*, 96–97

In this world you will have trouble.
— JOHN 16:33

No kidding. Jesus, the master of understatement, captures in one sentence the story of our lives. He adds, "But take heart! I have overcome the world" (John 16:33). Why aren't we more encouraged? (Sometimes we'll try to *feel* encouraged when we hear a "religious" passage like this, but it never really lasts.) The reason is that we are still committed to arranging for life now. Be honest. Isn't there a disappointment when you realize that I'm not going to offer you the seven secrets of a really great life today? If I wanted to make millions, that's the book I would write. The only thing is, I would have to lie. It can't be done. Not *yet*. And that *yet* makes all the difference in the world, because desire cannot live without hope. But hope in what? *For* what?

> Set your hope *fully* on the grace to be given you when Jesus Christ is revealed. (1 Peter 1:13, emphasis added)

I read passages like this, and I don't know whether to laugh or to cry. Fully? We don't even set our hope *partially* on the life to come. Not really, not in the desires of our hearts. Heaven may be coming. Great. But it's a long way off and who really knows, so I'm getting what I can now. For most Christians, heaven is a backup plan. Our primary work is finding a life we can at least get a little pleasure from here.

❁ *THE JOURNEY OF DESIRE*, 98–99

When Abram was ninety-nine years old, the LORD appeared to him and said, "I am God Almighty; walk before me and be blameless . . ." Abram fell facedown, and God said to him, "As for me, this is my covenant with you: You will be the father of many nations. No longer will you be called Abram; your name will be Abraham, for I have made you a father of many nations."

—GENESIS 17:1, 3–5

The history of a man's relationship with God is the story of how God calls him out, takes him on a journey, and gives him his true name. He created Adam for adventure, battle and beauty. So God calls Abram out from Ur of the Chaldeans to a land he has never seen and along the way he gets a new name. He becomes Abraham. God takes Jacob off into Mesopotamia somewhere, to learn things he has to learn and cannot learn at his mother's side. When he rides back into town, he has a limp and a new name as well.

Even if your father did his job, he can only take you partway. There comes a time when you have to leave all that is familiar and go on into the unknown with God.

Saul was a guy who really thought he understood the story and very much liked the part he had written for himself. He was the hero of his own little miniseries, *Saul the Avenger*. After that little matter on the Damascus road he becomes *Paul*; and rather than heading back into all of the old and familiar ways, he is led out into Arabia for three years to learn directly from God. Jesus shows us that initiation can happen even when we've lost our father or grandfather.

❖ *WILD AT HEART, 103–4*

My heart leaps for joy
and I will give thanks to him in song.
—PSALM 28:7

A few years ago a woman with a sensitive spirit and a keen eye for what God is up to pulled me aside to offer this warning: "The battle in your life is against your joy."

It hit me like a Mack truck.

But of course. Suddenly life made sense. The hassles. The battles. The disappointments. The losses. The resignation. Why hadn't I seen it before? I mean, I face a lot of different skirmishes day to day, but now the plot, the diabolical plot behind them all came into view. I began to see how the enemy was first trying to take away all joy from my life. Wear me down. Then, weary and thirsty, I would be quite vulnerable to some counterfeit joy. It would start with mild addictions, then build to something worse. Thus he would destroy all that God has done in and through me. It was so obvious. Of course.

Her observation became a revelation became a rescue. The smoke alarm sounding off before the house goes up in flames. Joy as a category had seemed . . . irrelevant. Nice but unessential. Like owning a hot tub. And distant too. The hot tub is in Fiji. Wouldn't it be nice. Ain't going to happen. Life's not really about joy. I've got all this *stuff* that has to get done. The mail is stacking up, and I haven't paid the bills in two months. Life's about surviving—and getting a little pleasure. That's what seemed true.

Really now—how much do you think about joy? Do you see it as essential to your life, something God insists on?

❀ WALKING WITH GOD, 37–38

The joy of the Lord is your strength.
—NEHEMIAH 8:10

I began to realize that what I've done for most of my life is resign myself to this idea: *I'm really not going to have any lasting joy.* And from that resignation, I've gone on to try and find what I could have. And soon, joy isn't even a consideration because I've settled for relief.

Now, to be fair, joy isn't exactly falling from the sky these days. We don't go out to gather it each morning like manna. It's hard to come by. Joy seems more elusive than winning the lottery. We don't like to think about it much, because it hurts to allow ourselves to feel how much we long for joy, and how seldom it drops by.

But joy *is* the point. I know it is. God says that joy is our strength. "The joy of the Lord is your strength" (Neh. 8:10). I think, *My strength? I don't even think of it as my occasional boost.* But yes, now that I give it some thought, I can see that when I have felt joy I have felt more alive than at any other time in my life. Pull up a memory of one of your best moments. The day at the beach. Your eighth birthday. Remember how you felt. Now think what life would be like if you felt like that on a regular basis. Maybe that's what being strengthened by joy feels like. It would be good.

❀ *WALKING WITH GOD, 39–40*

Splendor and majesty are before him;
strength and joy in his dwelling place.
—1 CHRONICLES 16:27

I take up a concordance and begin to read a bit on joy. "My heart leaps for joy" (Ps. 28:7). When was the last time my heart leapt for joy?

"You have filled my heart with greater joy than when their grain and new wine abound" (Psalms 4:7). I believe David when he says this. I believe God does this. I just don't know firsthand. I turn to the Gospels. What does Jesus have to say about joy?

I have told you this so that my joy may be in you and that your joy may be complete (John 15:11).

I am coming to you now, but I say these things while I am still in the world, so that they may have the full measure of my joy within them (17:13).

Joy complete? The full measure of his joy? That's what Jesus wants for us? I'm almost stunned. It's so obvious now, yet it makes me uncomfortable. Probably because it's too close to my heart, to what I long for. We avoid it, because it feels too vulnerable to admit the joy we long for but do not have.

Jesus, I have no idea where to go from here. But I invite you in. Take me where I need to go. I know this is connected to the life you want me to live.

❖ WALKING WITH GOD, *40–41*

One thing I ask of the LORD,
this is what I seek:
that I may dwell in the house of the LORD
all the days of my life,
to gaze upon the beauty of the LORD.
—PSALMS 27:4

We cannot control what the Romancer is up to, but there is a *posture* we can take. There is an openness that will enable us to recognize and receive the wooing. So let me ask—are you willing to let go of your insistence to control, meaning, to allow for a life that exists beyond the realm of analysis, to let some portions of your life be impractical, to cease evaluating all things based on their utility and function? Coming closer to the heart, are you willing to let passion rise in you, though undoubtedly it may unnerve you? To permit the healing of some of your deepest wounds? To let yourself be run through as with a rapier by Beauty itself? Are you willing, at some level, to be undone?

Then we may proceed.

To enter into the Romance we must slow down, or we will miss the wooing. Turn off the news and put on some music. Take a walk. Take up painting, or writing or reading poetry. Better still, what was it that stirred *your* heart over the years? *Go and get it back.*

This is hard to do, especially for men who are out conquering the world. But remember—what the evil one does to a good warrior if he cannot keep him in the battle is to bury him with battles. Wear him down with fight after fight. But life is *not* all about the battle. The Romance is always central.

❖ FATHERED BY GOD, 146–147

Your love is better than life.
—PSALM 63:3

L isten to King David:

> *Though an army besiege me,*
>   *my heart will not fear;*
> *though war break out against me,*
>   *even then will I be confident.*
> *One thing I ask of the Lord,*
>   *this is what I seek:*
> *that I may dwell in the house of the Lord*
>   *all the days of my life,*
> *to gaze upon the beauty of the LORD. (Ps. 27:3–4)*

He knows battle, knows what it is to have God come through for him. He does not fear it; he is confident as a seasoned warrior is confident. But, he does not make it his heart's desire. What he *seeks* is not battle—what he seeks is the romance with God. "To gaze upon the beauty of the Lord." For we must remember: the battle is for the Romance. What we fight for is the freedom and healing that allow us to have the intimacy with God we were created to enjoy. To drink from his river of delights.

❖ FATHERED BY GOD, *147–148*

Be imitators of God . . . and live a life of love.
—EPHESIANS 5:1–2

We must open our hearts to all the other ways God is bringing beauty into our lives. The beauty of a flower garden or moonlight on water, the beauty of music or a written word. Our souls crave Beauty, and if we do not find it we will be famished. We must take in Beauty, often, or we will be taken out by Beauty.

Learning to be loved, and learning to love, learning to be romanced, and learning to romance. Not duty. Not merely discipline. But an awakening of our hearts to the Beauty and Love of God, and at the same time (we cannot wait until some later time), we offer our hearts as well—to God, to the women in our lives, to our sons and daughters, to others. This is a love story, after all. As William Blake said, "And we are put on earth a little space / To learn to bear the beams of love." Or, in Paul's words, "Be imitators of God . . . and live a life of love" (Eph. 5:1–2). He is a great Romancer, and you shall be also.

❦ *FATHERED BY GOD, 153–54*

*Be strong and courageous, because you will lead these people to
inherit the land I swore to their forefathers to give them. Be strong
and very courageous . . . Have I not commanded you? Be strong and
courageous. Do not be terrified; do not be discouraged, for the LORD
your God will be with you wherever you go.*

—JOSHUA 1:6–7, 9

Joshua knew what it was to be afraid. For years he had been second in command, Moses' right-hand man. But now it was his turn to lead. The children of Israel weren't just going to waltz in and pick up the Promised Land like a quart of milk; they were going to have to fight for it. And Moses was not going with them. If Joshua was completely confident about the situation, why would God have had to tell him over and over and over again not to be afraid? In fact, God gives him a special word of encouragement: "As I was with Moses, so I will be with you; I will never leave you nor forsake you" (Josh. 1:5).

How was God "with Moses"? As a mighty warrior. Remember the plagues? Remember all those Egyptian soldiers drowned with their horses and chariots out there in the Red Sea? It was after that display of God's strength that the people of Israel sang, "The LORD is a warrior; the LORD is his name" (Ex. 15:3). God fought for Moses and for Israel; then he covenanted with Joshua to do the same and they took down Jericho and every other enemy.

❖ *WILD AT HEART, 167*

Be strong and courageous. Do not be afraid or terrified because of them, for the LORD your God goes with you; he will never leave you nor forsake you.

—DEUTERONOMY 31:6

The most dangerous man on earth is the man who has reckoned with his own death. All men die; few men ever really *live*. Sure, you can create a safe life for yourself . . . and end your days in a rest home babbling on about some forgotten misfortune. I'd rather go down swinging. Listen to G. K. Chesterton on courage:

> Courage is almost a contradiction in terms. It means a strong desire to live taking the form of a readiness to die. "He that will lose his life, the same shall save it," is not a piece of mysticism for saints and heroes. It is a piece of everyday advice for sailors or mountaineers. It might be printed in an Alpine guide or a drill book. The paradox is the whole principle of courage; even of quite earthly or quite brutal courage. . . . He can only get away from death by continually stepping within an inch of it. A soldier surrounded by enemies, if he is to cut his way out, needs to combine a strong desire for living with a strange carelessness about dying. He must not merely cling to live, for then he will be a coward, and will not escape. He must not merely wait for death, for then he will be a suicide, and will not escape. He must seek his life in a spirit of furious indifference to it; he must desire life like water and yet drink death like wine.

❖ WILD AT HEART, 169

He heals the brokenhearted
and binds up their wounds.
—Psalm 147:3

I expect that all of us at one time or another have said, "Well, part of me wants to, and another part of me doesn't." You know the feeling—part of you pulled one direction, part of you the other. Part of me loves writing and genuinely looks forward to a day at my desk. But not all of me. Sometimes I'm also afraid of it. Part of me fears that I will fail—that I am simply stating what is painfully obvious, or saying something vital but incoherent. I'm drawn to it, and I also feel ambivalent about it. Come to think of it, I feel that way about a lot of things. Part of me wants to go ahead and dive into friendship, take the risk. *I'm tired of living alone.* Another part says, *Stay away—you'll get hurt. Nobody really cares anyway.* Part of me says, *Wow! Maybe God really is going to come through for me.* Another voice rises up and says, *You are on your own.*

Don't you feel sometimes like a house divided?

Take your little phobias. Why are you afraid of heights or intimacy or public speaking? All the discipline in the world wouldn't get you to go skydiving or share something personal in a small group. Why do you hate it when people criticize you? Why do you bite your nails? Why do you work so many hours? Why do you get irritated at these questions? You won't go out unless your makeup is perfect—why is that? Something in you "freezes" when your dad calls—what's that all about? You clean and organize; you demand perfection—did you ever wonder *why*?

❊   Waking the Dead, *128–30*

When I want to do good, evil is right there with me.
— ROMANS 7:21

There is a civil war waged between the new heart and the old nature. Romans 7–8 describes it quite well. Part of me doesn't want to love my neighbor — not when his son just backed his car into my Jeep and smashed it up. I want to take the little brat to court. Part of me knows that prayer is essential; another part of me would rather turn on the TV and check out. And that whole bit about long-suffering — no way. Part of me wants to just get drunk. And that is the part I must crucify daily, give no ground to, make no alliance with. It's not the true me (Rom. 7:22). It's my battle with the flesh. We all know that battle well. But that is not what I'm wanting to explore here.

No, there's something else we are describing when we say, "Well, part of me wants to and part of me doesn't." It's more than a figure of speech. We might not know it, but something really significant is being revealed in those remarks. There are these places that we cannot seem to get beyond. Everything is going along just fine, and then — boom. Something suddenly bring you to tears or makes you furious, depressed, or anxious, and you cannot say why. I'll tell you why.

We are not wholehearted.

❖ WAKING THE DEAD, *130*

Scorn has broken my heart
and has left me helpless;
I looked for sympathy,
but there was none,
for comforters, but I found none.
—PSALM 69:20

When Isaiah promised that the Messiah will come to heal the brokenhearted, he was not speaking poetically. The Hebrew is *leb shabar* (*leb* for "heart," *shabar* for "broken"). Isaiah uses the word *shabar* to describe a bush whose "twigs are dry, they are broken off" (27:11); to describe the idols of Babylon lying "shattered on the ground" (21:9), as a statue shatters into a thousand pieces when you knock it off the table. God is speaking literally here. He says, "Your heart is now in many pieces. I want to heal it."

The heart can be broken—literally. Just like a branch or a statue or a bone. Can you name any precious thing that *can't*? Certainly, we've seen that the mind can be broken—or what are all those mental institutions for? The will can be broken too. Have you seen photos of concentration camp prisoners? But somehow we have overlooked the fact that this treasure called the heart can also be broken, *has* been broken, and now lies in pieces down under the surface. When it comes to "habits" we cannot quit, anger that flies out of nowhere, fears we cannot overcome, or weaknesses we hate to admit—much of what troubles us comes out of the broken places in our hearts crying out for relief.

Jesus speaks as though we are the brokenhearted.

❖ WAKING THE DEAD, *131–34*

I tell you the truth, no one who has left home or wife or brothers or
parents or children for the sake of the kingdom of God will fail to receive
many times as much in this age and, in the age to come, eternal life.
—LUKE 18:29–30

Okay . . . I know this whole question of "what has God promised us in *this* life?" is fraught with problems. It's a question
that's got heresy on both sides. So, let me make a few things clear:

I am not advocating a "name it and claim it" theology, whereby
we can have anything and everything we want if we just claim it
in Jesus' name. After all, Jesus said, "In this world you will have
trouble" (John 16:33).

Nor am I advocating a "prosperity" doctrine that claims God
wants everyone to be rich and healthy. "The poor you will always
have with you" (Matt. 26:11).

What I *am* saying is that Christ does not put his offer of Life to
us totally in the future. That's the other mistake. "'I tell you the
truth,' Jesus said to them, 'no one who has left home or wife or
brothers or parents or children for the sake of the kingdom of God
will fail to receive many times as much *in this age* and, in the age
to come, eternal life'" (Luke 18:29–30, emphasis added).

Jesus doesn't locate his offer to us only in some distant future,
after we've slogged our way through our days here on earth.
He talks about a life available to us *in this age*. So does Paul:
"Godliness has value for all things, holding promise *for both the
present life* and the life to come" (1 Tim. 4:8, emphasis added).

There is a Life available to us now. Let's find it.

❖ *WAKING THE DEAD, 13*

It is the glory of God to conceal a matter;
to search out a matter is the glory of kings.
—PROVERBS 25:2

One of the deepest ways a woman bears the image of God is in her mystery. By mystery we don't mean "forever beyond your knowing," but "something to be explored." God yearns to be known. But he wants to be *sought after* by those who would know him. He says, "You will seek me and find me when you seek me with all your heart" (Jer. 29:13). There is dignity here; God does not throw himself at any passerby. If you would know him you must love him; you must seek him with your whole heart. This is crucial to any woman's soul. "You cannot simply have me. You must seek me, pursue me. I won't let you in unless I know you love me."

Is not the Trinity a great mystery? Not something to be solved, but to be known with ever-deepening pleasure and awe, something to be enjoyed. Just like God, a woman is not a problem to be solved, but a vast wonder to be enjoyed. This is so true of her sexuality. Few women can or even want to "just do it." Foreplay is crucial to her heart, the whispering and loving and exploring of each other that culminates in intercourse. That is a picture of what it means to love her *soul*. She yearns to be known, and that takes time and intimacy. It requires an unveiling. As she is sought after, she reveals more of her beauty. As she unveils her beauty, she draws us to know her more deeply.

Whatever else it means to be feminine, it is depth and mystery and complexity, with beauty as their very essence.

❀ *CAPTIVATING, 41–42*

You are no longer a slave, but a son.
—GALATIANS 4:7

Life on the road takes us into our heart, for *only when we are present in the deep sentences can God speak to them.* That's why the story is a journey; it has to be lived, it cannot simply be talked about. When we face trials, our most common reaction is to ask God, "Why won't you relieve us?" And when he doesn't, we resignedly ask, "What do you want me to do?" Now we have a new question: "Where is the Romance headed?"

There is another great "revealing" in our life on the road. We run our race, we travel our journey, in the words of Hebrews, before "a great cloud of witnesses" (12:1). When we face a decision to fall back or press on, the whole universe holds its breath—angels, demons, our friends and foes, and the Trinity itself—watching with bated breath to see what we will do. We are still in the drama of Act III and the heart of God is still on trial. The question that lingers from the fall of Satan and the fall of man remains: Will anyone trust the great heart of the Father, or will we shrink back in faithless fear?

As we grow into the love of God and the freedom of our own hearts, we grow in our ability to cast our vote on behalf of God. Our acts of love and sacrifice, the little decisions to leave our false loves behind and the great struggles of our heart reveal to the world our true identity: We really are the sons and daughters of God.

❁ *THE SACRED ROMANCE, 154–55*

*So the men Moses had sent to explore the land, who returned and
made the whole community grumble against him by spreading a bad
report about it.*

—NUMBERS 14:36

It's better to stay in the safety of the camp than venture forth on
a wing and a prayer. Who knows what dangers lie ahead? This
was the counsel of the ten faithless spies sent in to have a look at
the Promised Land when the Jews came out of Egypt. Only two of
the twelve, Joshua and Caleb, saw things differently. Their hearts
were captured by a vision of what might be and they urged the
people to press on. But their voices were drowned by the fears of
the other ten spies and Israel wandered for another forty years.
Without the anticipation of better things ahead, we will have no
heart for the journey.

One of the most poisonous of all Satan's whispers is simply,
"Things will never change." That lie kills expectation, trapping
our hearts forever in the present. To keep desire alive and flourishing, we must renew our vision for what lies ahead. Things will
not always be like this. Jesus has promised to "make all things
new." Eye has not seen, ear has not heard all that God has in
store for his lovers, which does not mean "we have no clue so
don't even try to imagine," but rather, *you cannot outdream God.*
Desire is kept alive by imagination, the antidote to resignation.
We will need imagination, which is to say, we will need *hope.*

As the road grows long we grow weary; impatience and discouragement tempt us to forsake the way for some easier path.
These shortcuts never work, and the guilt we feel for having chosen them only compounds our feelings of despair.

❁ *THE SACRED ROMANCE, 156–57*

For whoever wants to save his life will lose it, but whoever loses his life for me will find it.

—MATTHEW 16:25

Faith looks back and draws courage; hope looks ahead and keeps desire alive. And meantime? In the meantime we need one more item for our journey. To appreciate what it may be, we have to step back and ask, what is all this for? The resurrection of our heart, the discovery of our role in the Larger Story, entering into the Sacred Romance—why do we pursue these things? If we say we seek all of this for our own sake, we're right back where we started: lost in our own story.

Jesus said that when a person lives merely to preserve his life, he eventually loses it altogether. Rather, Jesus encouraged us to give our lives away and discover life as it was always meant to be. Self-preservation, the theme of every small story, is so deeply wrong because it violates the Trinity, whose members live to bring glory *to the others*. The road we travel will take us into the battle to restore beauty in all things, chief among them the hearts of those we know. We grow in glory so that we might assist others in doing so; we give our glory to increase theirs. In order to fulfill the purpose of our journey, we will need a passion to increase glory; we will need *love*.

The road is not entirely rough. There are oases along the way. It would be a dreadful mistake to assume that our Beloved is only waiting for us at the end of the road. Our communion with him sustains us along our path.

❂ THE SACRED ROMANCE, 158

For great is his love toward us,
and the faithfulness of the LORD endures forever.
Praise the Lord.
—PSALM 117:2

Every courtship, at least every healthy one, is moving toward a deeper heart intimacy that is the ground for the consummation of the relationship spiritually, emotionally, and physically. The first question in the orthodox confessions of faith tests our awareness of this wonderful truth when it asks, "What is the chief end and purpose of man?" And the answer: "To know God and to enjoy knowing him forever." Listen with me to excerpts from a conversation between two lovers:

Lover: "How beautiful you are, my darling! Oh, how beautiful! Your eyes are doves."

Beloved: "How handsome you are, my lover! Oh, how charming! And our bed is verdant."

Lover: "Show me your face, let me hear your voice; for your voice is sweet, and your face is lovely . . . Your mouth is like the best wine."

(Song of Solomon 1:15–16; 2:14)

This is not a conversation from the latest dime-store romance but a glimpse through the bedroom window at the love affair between Solomon and his queen. As we turn from the window and look into God's eyes, we realize that this is the kind of passion he feels for us and desires from us in return—an intimacy much more sensuous, much more exotic than sex itself.

❧ *THE SACRED ROMANCE, 159–61*

*For this reason a man will leave his father and mother and be united
to his wife, and they will become one flesh. The man and his wife were
both naked, and they felt no shame.*

—GENESIS 2:24–25

The older Christian wedding vows contained these amazing words: "With my body, I thee worship." Maybe our forefathers weren't so prudish after all; maybe they understood sex far better than we do. To give yourself over to another, passionately and nakedly, to adore that person body, soul, and spirit—we know there is something special, even sacramental about sex. It requires trust and abandonment, guided by a wholehearted devotion. What else can this be but worship? After all, God employs explicitly sexual language to describe faithfulness (and unfaithfulness) to him. For us creatures of the flesh, sexual intimacy is the closest parallel we have to real worship. Even the world knows this. Why else would sexual ecstasy become the number one rival to communion with God? The best impostors succeed because they are nearly indistinguishable from what they are trying to imitate. We worship sex because we don't know how to worship God. But we will.

God's design was that the two shall become one flesh. The physical oneness was meant to be the expression of a total interweaving of being. Is it any wonder that we crave this? Our alienation is removed, if only for a moment, and in the paradox of love, we are at the same time known and yet taken beyond ourselves.

❖ *THE JOURNEY OF DESIRE, 134–35*

So God created man in his own image, in the image of God he created
him; male and female he created them.
—GENESIS 1:27

It is a mystery almost too great to mention, but God is the expression of the very thing we seek in each other. For do we not bear God's image? Are we not a living portrait of God? Indeed we are, and in a most surprising place—in our *gender*. Follow me closely now. Gender—masculinity and femininity—is how we bear the image of God. "I thought that there was only one kind of soul," said a shocked friend. "And God sort of poured those souls into male or female bodies." Many people believe something like that. But it contradicts the Word of God. We bear his image as men and women, and God does not have a body. So it must be at the level of the soul—the eternal part of us—that we reflect God. The text is clear; it is *as a man* or *as a woman* that the image is bestowed.

God wanted to show the world something of his strength. Is he not a great warrior? Has he not performed the daring rescue of his beloved? And this is why he gave us the sculpture that is man. Men bear the image of God in their dangerous, yet inviting strength. Women, too, bear the image of God, but in a much different way. Is not God a being of great mystery and beauty? Is there not something tender and alluring about the essence of the Divine? And this is why he gave us the sculpture that is woman.

❂ *THE JOURNEY OF DESIRE, 136*

For with you is the fountain of life;
in your light we see light.
—Psalm 36:9

God is the source of all masculine power; God is also the fountain of all feminine allure. Come to think of it, he is the wellspring of everything that has ever romanced your heart. The thundering strength of a waterfall, the delicacy of a flower, the stirring capacity of music, the richness of wine. The masculine and the feminine that fill all creation come from the same heart. What we have sought, what we have tasted in part with our earthly lovers, we will come face-to-face with in our True Love. For the incompleteness that we seek to relieve in the deep embrace of our earthly love is never fully healed. The union does not last, whatever the poets and pop artists may say. Morning comes and we've got to get out of bed and off to our day, incomplete once more. But oh, to have it healed forever, to drink deeply from that fount of which we've had only a sip, to dive into that sea in which we have only waded.

And so Catherine of Siena can pray, "O fire surpassing every fire because you alone are the fire that burns without consuming! . . . Yet your consuming does not distress the soul but fattens her with insatiable love." The French mystic Madam Guyon can write, "I slept not all night, because Thy love, O my God, flowed in me like delicious oil, and burned as a fire . . . I love God far more than the most affectionate lover among men loves his earthly attachment."

❖ *The Journey of Desire, 137–38*

On this mountain the LORD *Almighty will prepare*
a feast of rich food for all peoples.
—ISAIAH 25:6

Imagine the stories that we'll hear. And all the questions that shall finally have answers. "What were you thinking when you drove the old Ford out on the ice?" "Did you hear that Betty and Dan got back together? But of course you did—you were probably involved in that, weren't you?" "How come you never told us about your time in the war?" "Did you ever know how much I loved you?" And the answers won't be one-word answers, but story after story, a feast of wonder and laughter and glad tears.

The setting for this will be a great party, the wedding feast of the Lamb. Now, you've got to get images of Baptist receptions entirely out of your mind—folks milling around in the church gym, holding Styrofoam cups of punch, wondering what to do with themselves. You've got to picture an Italian wedding or, better, a Jewish wedding. They roll up the rugs and push back the furniture. There is *dancing*: "Then maidens will dance and be glad, young men and old as well" (Jer. 31:13). There is *feasting*: "On this mountain the LORD Almighty will prepare a feast of rich food for all peoples" (Isa. 25:6). (Can you imagine what kind of cook God must be?) And there is *drinking*—the feast God says he is preparing includes "a banquet of aged wine—the best of meats and the finest of wines." In fact, at his Last Supper our Bridegroom said he will not drink of "the fruit of the vine until the kingdom of God comes" (Luke 22:18). Then he'll pop a cork.

❖ THE JOURNEY OF DESIRE, *141–42*

For you created my inmost being;
you knit me together in my mother's womb.
I praise you because I am fearfully and wonderfully made;
your works are wonderful,
I know that full well.

—PSALM 139:14–15

"Somehow," notes Os Guinness, "we human beings are never happier than when we are expressing the deepest gifts that are truly us." Now, some children are gifted toward science, and others are born athletes. But whatever their specialty, *all* children are inherently creative. Give my sons a barrel of Legos and a free afternoon, and they will produce an endless variety of spaceships and fortresses and who knows what. It comes naturally to children; it's in their *nature*, their design as little image bearers.

This is precisely what happens when God shares with mankind his own artistic capacity and then sets us down in a paradise of unlimited potential. It is an act of creative *invitation*, like providing Monet with a studio for the summer, stocked full of brushes and oils and empty canvases. Or like setting Martha Stewart loose in a gourmet kitchen just before the holidays. You needn't provide instructions or motivation; all you have to do is release them to be who they are, and remarkable things will result.

Our creative nature is essential to who we are as human beings— as image bearers—and it brings us great joy to live it out with freedom and skill.

❖ *THE JOURNEY OF DESIRE, 152–54*

Blessed are they whose ways are blameless,
who walk according to the law of the LORD.
Blessed are they who keep his statutes
and seek him with all their heart.

—PSALM 119:1–2

Against the flesh, the traitor within, a warrior uses discipline. We have a two-dimensional version of this now, which we call a "quiet time." But most men have a hard time sustaining any sort of devotional life because it has no vital connection to recovering and protecting their strength; it feels about as important as flossing. But if you saw your life as a great battle and you *knew* you needed time with God for your very survival, you would do it. Maybe not perfectly—nobody ever does and that's not the point anyway—but you would have a reason to seek him. We give a half-hearted attempt at the spiritual disciplines when the only reason we have is that we "ought" to. But we'll find a way to make it work when we are convinced we're history if we don't.

Time with God each day is not about academic study or getting through a certain amount of Scripture or any of that. It's about connecting with God. We've got to keep those lines of communication open, so use whatever helps. Sometimes I'll listen to music; other times I'll read Scripture or a passage from a book; often I will journal; maybe I'll go for a run; then there are days when all I need is silence and solitude and the rising sun. The point is simply to do *whatever brings me back to my heart and the heart of God.*

The discipline, by the way, is never the point. The whole point of a "devotional life" is *connecting with God.* This is our primary antidote to the counterfeits the world holds out to us.

❖ WILD AT HEART, 171–72

Be strong and let us fight bravely for our people and the cities of our God.

—1 CHRONICLES 19:13

Once upon a time (as the story goes) there was a beautiful maiden, an absolute enchantress. She might be the daughter of a king or a common servant girl, but we know she is a princess at heart. She is young with a youth that seems eternal. Her flowing hair, her deep eyes, her luscious lips, her sculpted figure—she makes the rose blush for shame; the sun is pale compared to her light. Her heart is golden, her love as true as an arrow. But this lovely maiden is unattainable, the prisoner of an evil power who holds her captive in a dark tower. Only a champion may win her; only the most valiant, daring, and brave warrior has a chance of setting her free.

Against all hope he comes; with cunning and raw courage he lays siege to the tower and the sinister one who holds her. Much blood is shed on both sides; three times the knight is thrown back, but three times he rises again. Eventually the sorcerer is defeated; the dragon falls, the giant is slain. The maiden is his; through his valor he has won her heart. On horseback they ride off to his cottage by a stream in the woods for a rendezvous that gives passion and romance new meaning.

From ancient fables to the latest blockbuster, the theme of a strong man coming to rescue a beautiful woman is universal to human nature. It is written in our hearts, one of the core desires of every man and every woman.

❖ *WILD AT HEART, 180–81*

Give us aid against the enemy,
for the help of man is worthless.
—PSALM 60:11

Why does every story have a villain?
Little Red Riding Hood is attacked by a wolf. Dorothy must face and bring down the Wicked Witch of the West. Qui-Gon Jinn and Obi-Wan Kenobi go hand to hand against Darth Maul. Frodo is hunted by the Black Riders. (The Morgul blade that the Black Riders pierced Frodo with in the battle on Weathertop—it was aimed at his heart). Beowulf kills the monster Grendel, and then he has to battle Grendel's mother. Saint George slays the dragon. The children who stumbled into Narnia are called upon by Aslan to battle the White Witch and her armies so that Narnia might be free.

Every story has a villain because *yours* does. You were born into a world at war. When Satan lost the battle against Michael and his angels, "he was hurled to the earth, and his angels with him" (Rev. 12:9). That means that right now, on this earth, there are hundreds of thousands, if not millions, of fallen angels, foul spirits, bent on our destruction. And what is Satan's mood? "He is filled with fury, because he knows that his time is short" (v. 12). So what does he spend every day and every night of his sleepless, untiring existence doing? "Then the dragon was enraged at the woman and went off to make war against . . . those who obey God's commandments and hold to the testimony of Jesus" (v. 17). He has you in his crosshairs, and he isn't smiling.

You have an enemy. He is trying to steal your freedom, kill your heart, destroy your life.

❖ WAKING THE DEAD, *150–51*

Jesus said to them, "You belong to your father, the devil, and you want to carry out your father's desire. He was a murderer from the beginning, not holding to the truth, for there is no truth in him. When he lies, he speaks his native language, for he is a liar and the father of lies."

—JOHN 8:44

Satan is called in Scripture the father of lies (John 8:44). His very first attack against the human race was to lie to Eve and Adam about God, and where life is to be found, and what the consequences of certain actions would and would not be. He is a master at this. He suggests to us—as he suggested to Adam and Eve—some sort of idea or inclination or impression, and what he is seeking is a sort of "agreement" on our part. He's hoping we'll buy into whatever he's saying, offering, insinuating. Our first parents bought into it, and look what disaster came of it. The Evil One is still lying to us, seeking our agreement every single day.

Your heart is good. Your heart matters to God. Those are the two hardest things to hang on to. I'm serious—try it. Try to hold this up for even a day. *My heart is good. My heart matters to God.* You will be amazed at how much accusation you live under. You have an argument with your daughter on the way to school; as you drive off, you have a nagging sense of, *Well, you really blew that one.* If your heart agrees—*Yeah, I really did*—without taking the issue to Jesus, then the Enemy will try to go for more. *You're always blowing it with her.* Another agreement is made. *It's true. I'm such a lousy parent.* It moves from *You did a bad thing* to *You are bad.* After a while, it just becomes a cloud we live under, accept as normal.

148 | ❖ WAKING THE DEAD, 152–53

Satan rose up against Israel and incited David to take a census of Israel.
—1 Chronicles 21:1

Any movement toward freedom and life, any movement toward God or others, *will be opposed*. Marriage, friendship, beauty, rest—the thief wants it all.

> So, it becomes the devil's business to keep the Christian's spirit imprisoned. He knows that the believing and justified Christian has been raised up out of the grave of his sins and trespasses. From that point on, Satan works that much harder to keep us bound and gagged, actually imprisoned in our own grave clothes. He knows that if we continue in this kind of bondage . . . we are not much better off than when we were spiritually dead. (A.W. Tozer)

Sadly, many of these accusations will actually be spoken by Christians. Having dismissed a warfare worldview, they do not know who is stirring them to say certain things. "Satan rose up against Israel and incited David to take a census of Israel" (1 Chron. 21:1). The Enemy used David, who apparently wasn't watching for it, to do evil. He tried to use Peter too. (Matt. 16:21–23).

Heads up—these words will come from anywhere. Be careful what or whom you are agreeing with.

When we make those agreements with the demonic forces, we come under their influence. It becomes a kind of permission we give the Enemy, sort of like a contract.

❀ Waking the Dead, 154–55

"Be careful," Jesus said to them. "Be on your guard against the yeast of the Pharisees and Sadducees."
—MATTHEW 16:6

I was reading the prophet Jeremiah a few weeks ago when I ran across a passage that referred to God as "the LORD Almighty." To be honest, it didn't resonate. There's something too religious about the phrase; it sounds churchy, sanctimonious. The *Lawd Almiiiighty.* It sounds like something your grandmother would say when you came into her kitchen covered in mud. I found myself curious about what the *actual* phrase means in Hebrew. Might we have lost something in the translation? So I turned to the front of the version I was using for an explanation. Here is what the editors said:

> Because for most readers today the phrases "the Lord of hosts" and "God of hosts" have little meaning, this version renders them "the Lord Almighty" and "God Almighty." These renderings convey the sense of the Hebrew, namely, "he who is sovereign over all the 'hosts' (powers) in heaven and on earth, especially over the 'hosts' (armies) of Israel."

No, they don't. They don't even come close. The Hebrew means "the God of angel armies," "the God of the armies who fight for his people." *The God who is at war.* Does "Lord Almighty" convey "the God who is at war"? Not to me, it doesn't. Not to anyone I've asked. It sounds like "the God who is up there but still in charge." Powerful, in control. The God of angel armies sounds like the one who would roll up his sleeves, take up sword and shield to break down gates of bronze, and cut through bars of iron to rescue me.

❖ WAKING THE DEAD, 160

No eye has seen, no ear has heard, no mind has conceived what God has prepared for those who love him.
—1 CORINTHIANS 2:9

The crisis of hope that afflicts the church today is a crisis of *imagination.* Catholic philosopher Peter Kreeft writes:

Medieval imagery (which is almost totally biblical imagery) of light, jewels, stars, candles, trumpets, and angels no longer fits our ranch-style, supermarket world. Pathetic modern substitutes of fluffy clouds, sexless cherubs, harps and metal halos (not halos of *light*) presided over by a stuffy divine Chairman of the Bored are a joke, not a glory. . . . Our pictures of Heaven simply do not move us; they are not moving pictures. It is this aesthetic failure rather than intellectual or moral failures in our pictures of Heaven and of God that threatens faith most potently today. Our pictures of Heaven are dull, platitudinous and syrupy; therefore, so is our faith, our hope, and our love of Heaven . . . It doesn't matter whether it's a dull lie or a dull truth. Dullness, not doubt, is the strongest enemy of faith, just as indifference, not hate, is the strongest enemy of love. (*Everything You Wanted to Know About Heaven*)

If our pictures of heaven are to move us, they must be moving pictures. So go ahead—dream a little. Use your imagination. Picture the best possible ending to your story you can. If that isn't heaven, something better is.

❖ *THE SACRED ROMANCE, 180–81*

The shepherd calls his own sheep by name and leads them out. When he has brought out all his own, he goes on ahead of them, and his sheep follow him because they know his voice.

—JOHN 10:4

I love this passage and have spent a good deal of time here. But today I'm struck by the phrase "he goes on ahead of them." It's almost as if I'd never noticed it before, never given it my heart's attention. Jesus goes ahead of us. That is so reassuring, and that is *such* a different view than the one with which I approach each day. Or better, it reveals to me the way that I see each day. Here's what happens.

I connect with God in the morning in prayer and sometimes through reading of some sort. But then a shift occurs. Somewhere between prayer, and having breakfast, and getting the boys off to school, and getting to work myself, and beginning to answer e-mails and tackle projects, a subtle parting occurs. I don't feel as though I am following Jesus going ahead of me. I just sort of take it for granted that I am blazing the trail. Until this morning I never would have put it into those words. But this passage makes me realize that I don't see our relationship as God going on ahead of me. But I want to. Oh, how I want to. My heart is engaged. This is no intellectual exercise, but a living and immediate conversation with God through his Word.

Do you really, Jesus? Do you really go on ahead of me? That is such a better view of God, a view where he is engaged with us and intimately involved in the world and in our lives.

❖ *WALKING WITH GOD, 44-45*

I will instruct you and teach you in the way you should go;
I will counsel you and watch over you.
—PSALM 32:8

Hearing from God *flows out of* our relationship. That relationship was established for us by Jesus Christ. (Romans 5:1). Whatever we might be feeling, we do have relationship with God now, because we belong to him. And our relationship is secure:

I am convinced that neither death nor life, neither angels nor demons, neither the present nor the future, nor any powers, neither height nor depth, nor anything else in all creation, will be able to separate us from the love of God that is in Christ Jesus our Lord. (Romans 8:38–39)

I am God's. He is mine.

Because we *do* have relationship with God secured for us by Jesus Christ and all he has done, we can now grow in *developing* that relationship. We can, on the basis of what is objectively true, move into an experience of God in our lives that deepens over time. And that includes learning to hear his voice. Prayer, not as making speeches to God, a one-sided conversation, but as the act of talking to and hearing from God. A two-sided conversation. It is a rich inheritance we have.

❈ WALKING WITH GOD, 48–49

*I am convinced that neither death nor life, neither angels nor demons,
neither the present nor the future, nor any powers, neither height nor
depth, nor anything else in all creation, will be able to separate us
from the love of God that is in Christ Jesus our Lord.*
— ROMANS 8:38–39

My ability to hear God's voice on any given day does not change my position in Christ one bit. I share this because the last thing I want to introduce into your faith is shame or doubt or some other attack because you're not hearing clearly right now.

Taking the journey toward an intimacy with God that includes conversational intimacy is a beautiful thing, full of surprises and gifts from him.

But it can also send us reeling if we are basing our relationship with God on our ability to hear from him in this moment or on this particular issue. I know that's happened to me. Our faith is based on something much more solid than today's episode. We have the Scriptures, given to us by God, and they are the bedrock of everything else. They tell us that because we have placed our faith in God, we belong to him and are completely secure. They tell us that he is involved in our lives today, whether we feel it or not. They tell us he will never, ever abandon us. So, if you're not yet hearing, don't worry. It's okay. Keep praying. Keep listening. Notice what God might be up to other than answering the immediate question.

❖ WALKING WITH GOD, 49–50

But seek first his kingdom and his righteousness, and all these things will be given to you as well.
—MATTHEW 6:33

God wants us to be happy, but he knows that we cannot be truly happy until we are completely his and until he is our all. And the weaning process is hard.

The sorrows of our lives are in great part his weaning process. We give our hearts over to so many things other than God. We look to so many other things for life. I know I do. Especially the very gifts that he himself gives to us—they become more important to us than he is. That's not the way it is supposed to be. As long as our happiness is tied to the things we can lose, we are vulnerable. This truth is core to the human condition and to understanding what God is doing in our lives. We really believed that God's primary reason for being is to provide us with happiness, give us a good life. It doesn't occur to us that our thinking is backwards. It doesn't even occur to us that God is meant to be our all, and that until he is our all, we are subhuman. The first and greatest command is to love God with our whole being. Yet, it is rare to find someone who is completely given over to God. And so normal to be surrounded by people who are trying to make life work. We think of the few who are abandoned to God as being sort of odd. The rest of the world—the ones trying to make life work—seem perfectly normal to us.

❂ *WALKING WITH GOD*, 85–86

*Command those who are rich in this present world not to be arrogant
nor to put their hope in wealth, which is so uncertain, but to put their
hope in God, who richly provides us with everything for our enjoyment.*
—1 TIMOTHY 6:17

I am just stunned by this propensity I see in myself—and in everyone I know—this stubborn inclination to view the world in one
and only one way: as the chance to live a happy little life.

Now don't get me wrong. There is so much about the world
that is good and beautiful even though it is fallen. And there is so
much good in the life that God gives us. As Paul said, God "richly
provides us with everything for our enjoyment" (1 Timothy 6:17).
In Ecclesiastes, Solomon wrote that to enjoy our work and our
food each day is a gift from God (Ecclesiastes 2:24). We are created to enjoy life. But we end up worshiping the gift instead of
the Giver. We seek for life and look to God as our assistant in the
endeavor. We are far more upset when things go wrong than we
ever are when we aren't close to God. And so God must, from time
to time, and sometimes very insistently, disrupt our lives *so that* we
release our grasping of life here and now. Usually through pain.

God is asking us to let go of the things we love and have given
our hearts to, so that we can give our hearts even more fully to
him. He thwarts us in our attempts to make life work so that our
efforts fail, and we must face the fact that we don't really look to
God for life.

❖ WALKING WITH GOD, 86–87

The king's heart is in the hand of the LORD;
he directs it like a watercourse wherever he pleases.
—PROVERBS 21:1

There are many *offices* a man might fulfill as a king—father of a household, manager of a department, pastor of a church, coach of a team, prime minister of a nation—but the *heart* required is the same. "The king's heart is in the hand of the Lord; he directs it like a watercourse wherever he pleases" (Prov. 21:1). The passage is often used to explain the sovereignty of God, in that he can do with a man whatever he well pleases. Certainly, God is that sovereign. But I don't think that's the spirit of this passage. God rarely forces a man to do something against his will because God would far and above prefer that he didn't have to, that the man *wills* to do the will of God. "Choose for yourselves this day whom you will serve" (Josh. 24:15).

What God is after is a man so *yielded* to him, so completely surrendered, that his heart is easily moved by the Spirit of God to the purposes of God.

That kind of heart makes for a good king.

❀   *FATHERED BY GOD, 162*

*Whoever wants to become great among you must be your servant, and
whoever wants to be first must be your slave—just as the Son of Man
did not come to be served, but to serve.*

—MATTHEW 20:26–28

Too many men, finding themselves Kings even though they
have *not* taken the masculine journey—seize the opportu-
nity to make life good . . . *for themselves.* This is not why a man is
given power and property.

Jesus called them together and said, "You know that the
rulers of the Gentiles lord it over them, and their high officials exercise authority over them. Not so with you. (Matt.
20:25–26)

That is the true test of a king.

Simply put, the test is this: *What is life like for the people under
his authority?* Really. It's that simple. What is life like for the people in his kingdom? Have a look at his wife—is she tired, stressed
out, overlooked? What about his children—are they flourishing?
Talk to the people who work for him—do they feel they are simply building *his* kingdom, or that he is serving them? Are they
growing in their own talents and abilities, joyful because they are
cared for, given a place in the kingdom? If he is a pastor, look at
his congregation—are they enjoying the genuine freedom and
life Christ promised? Or is the unspoken system of the church
one of fear, guilt, and performance?

❖ *FATHERED BY GOD, 168, 167*

What do you think? If a man owns a hundred sheep, and one of them wanders away, will he not leave the ninety-nine on the hills and go to look for the one that wandered off?
—MATTHEW 18:12

The gospel says that we, who are God's beloved, created a cosmic crisis. It says we, too, were stolen from our True Love and that he launched the greatest campaign in the history of the world to get us back. God created us for intimacy with him. When we turned our back on him he promised to come for us. He sent personal messengers; he used beauty and affliction to recapture our hearts. After all else failed, he conceived the most daring of plans. Under the cover of night he stole into the enemy's camp incognito, the Ancient of Days disguised as a newborn. The Incarnation, as Phil Yancey reminds us, was a daring raid into enemy territory. The whole world lay under the power of the Evil One and we were held in the dungeons of darkness. God risked it all to rescue us. Why? What is it that he sees in us that causes him to act the jealous lover, to lay siege both on the kingdom of darkness and on our own idolatries as if on Troy—not to annihilate, but to win us once again for himself?

This fierce intention, this reckless ambition that shoves all conventions aside, willing literally to move heaven and earth—what does he want from us?

❂ *THE SACRED ROMANCE, 91*

Lift up your heads, O you gates;
be lifted up, you ancient doors,
that the King of glory may come in.
Who is this King of glory?
The LORD strong and mighty,
the LORD mighty in battle.
— PSALM 24:7–8

If the way to avoid the murderous rage and deceptive allures of desire is to kill it, if deadness is next to godliness, then Jesus had to be the deadest person ever. But he is called the *living* God. "It is a dreadful thing," the writer of Hebrews says, "to fall into the hands of the living God . . . For our 'God is a consuming fire'" (10:31; 12:29). And what is this consuming fire? His jealous love (Deut. 4:24).

God is a deeply, profoundly passionate person. Zeal consumes him. It is the secret of his life, the writer of Hebrews says. The "joy set before him" enabled Jesus to endure the agony of the Cross (Heb. 12:2). In other words, his profound desire for something greater sustained him at the moment of his deepest trial.

We cannot hope to live like him without a similar depth of passion. Many people find that the dilemma of desire is too much to live with, and so they abandon, they disown their desire. This is certainly true of a majority of Christians at present. Somehow we believe that we can get on without it. We are mistaken.

❖ *THE JOURNEY OF DESIRE, 54–55*

For Zion's sake I will not keep silent,
for Jerusalem's sake I will not remain quiet,
till her righteousness shines out like the dawn,
her salvation like a blazing torch . . .
As a bridegroom rejoices over his bride,
so will your God rejoice over you.
—ISAIAH 62:1, 5

God is a romantic at heart, and he has his own bride to fight for. He is a jealous lover, and his jealousy is for the hearts of his people and for their freedom.

Though she has committed adultery, fallen captive to his enemy, God is willing to move heaven and earth to win her back:

Who is this coming from Edom,
*   from Bozrah, with his garments stained crimson?*
Who is this, robed in splendor,
*   striding forward in the greatness of his strength?*
"It is I, speaking in righteousness,
*   mighty to save."*
Why are your garments red,
*   like those of one treading the winepress?*
"I have trodden the winepress alone;
*   from the nations no one was with me.*
For the day of vengeance was in my heart,
* and the year of my redemption has come." (Isa. 63:1–4)*

This is the God of heaven and earth. The Lion of Judah.

❀ WILD AT HEART, 34–35

The LORD God called to the man, "Where are you?"
—GENESIS 3:9

The thought of *me* being called out of hiding is unnerving. I don't think I want to be seen. Many years ago, during my life in the theater, I received a standing ovation for a performance. The audience was literally on its feet, cheering. What actor doesn't crave a standing ovation? So you know what I did? I *ran*. Literally. As soon as the curtain went down I bolted for the door, so I wouldn't have to talk to anyone. I didn't want to be seen. I know, it's weird, but I'll bet you feel the same about being unveiled.

There's the beautiful scene toward the end of Joseph's life where he, too, is unveiled. The very brothers who sold him into slavery as a boy are standing before what they believe is an angry Egyptian lord, equal in power to Pharaoh himself, their knees knocking. The silver cup of this dreaded lord was found stashed away in their luggage as they headed out of town—placed there by Joseph himself as a ruse. Now Joseph interrogates them till they squirm, deepening the plot by using an interpreter as if he doesn't understand Hebrew, pressing them hard. Finally, unable to hold back his tears, he *reveals* himself: "I am Joseph; does my father still live? . . . So you shall tell my father of all my glory in Egypt . . . and you shall hurry and bring my father down here" (Gen. 45:3, 13 NKJV). This is who I really am! Tell him about my glory! Amazing.

❧ WAKING THE DEAD, 72–73

"Can I not, O house of Israel, deal with you as this potter does?"
declares the LORD. "Behold, like the clay in the potter's hand, so are
you in My hand, O house of Israel."
—JEREMIAH 18:6

The Scriptures employ a wide scale of metaphors to capture the many facets of our relationship with God. If you consider them in a sort of ascending order, there is a noticeable and breathtaking progression. Down near the bottom of the totem pole we are the clay and he is the Potter. Moving up a notch, we are the sheep and he is the Shepherd, which is a little better position on the food chain but hardly flattering. Moving upward, we are the servants of the Master, which at least lets us into the house, even if we have to wipe our feet, watch our manners. Most Christians never get past this point, but the ladder of metaphors is about to make a swift ascent. God also calls us his children and himself our heavenly Father, which brings us into the possibility of real intimacy. Friendship opens a level of communion that a five-year-old doesn't know with his mother and father. And "friends" are what he calls us.

But there is still a higher and deeper level of intimacy and partnership awaiting us at the top of this metaphorical ascent. We are lovers. The courtship that began with a honeymoon in the Garden culminates in the wedding feast of the Lamb. "I will take delight in you," he says to us, "as a bridegroom rejoices over his bride, so will I rejoice over you," so that we might say in return, "I am my beloved's and his desire is for me."

❖ *THE SACRED ROMANCE,* 96

You said in your heart,
"I will ascend to heaven;
I will raise my throne
above the stars of God . . .
I will ascend above the tops of the clouds;
I will make myself like the Most High."
—ISAIAH 14:13–14

Our enemy is the angel Lucifer, one of the first and highest angels God created. He is the antagonist in the sacred romance, the great villain. All other villains are only a shadow of him. He is the one God gave a place of honor and trust "among the fiery stones" of the courts of heaven and who sees God face-to-face even to this day. He is one who spurned God's love and lost everything good through the sin of presumption. His desire was, and still is, to possess everything that belongs to God, including the worship of all those whom God loves. And God, as the Author of the great Story in which we are all living, has mysteriously allowed him a certain freedom to harass and oppress the other characters in the play, sometimes in a severe manner.

In some ways, Satan knows us better than we know ourselves. The one purpose of his heart is the destruction of all that God loves. He stalks us day and night, as the Lord tells us through Peter: "Your enemy the devil prowls around like a roaring lion looking for someone to devour" (1 Peter 5:8). Peter makes it clear he is talking especially to believers, saying in verse 9, "Resist him, standing firm in the faith, because you know that *your brothers* throughout the world are undergoing the same kind of sufferings" (emphasis mine).

　❖ *THE SACRED ROMANCE, 101–2*

*And He said to him, "What is written in the Law? How do you read
it?" And he answered, 'Love the Lord your God with all your heart
and with all your soul and with all your strength and with all your
mind'; and, 'Love your neighbor as yourself.'"*
—LUKE 10:26–27

The core of Satan's plan for each of us is not found in tempting us with obvious sins like shoplifting or illicit sex. His grand tactic in separating us from our heart is to sneak in as the Storyteller through our fears and the wounds we have received from life's arrows. He weaves a story that becomes our particular "Message of the Arrows." Counting on our vanity and blindness, he seduces us to try to control life by living in the smaller stories we all construct to one degree or another. He accuses God to us and us to God. He accuses us through the words of parents and friends and God himself. He calls good evil and evil good and always helps us question whether God has anything good in mind in his plans for us. He steals our innocence as children and replaces it with a blind naïveté or cynicism as adults.

At the same time Satan is at work reinterpreting our own individual stories in order to make God our enemy, he is also at work dismantling the Sacred Romance—the larger story God is telling—so that there is nothing visible to take our breath away. He replaces the love affair with a religious system of do's and don'ts that parches our hearts and replaces our worship and communion services with entertainment. Our experience of life deteriorates from the passion of a grand love affair, in the midst of a life-and-death battle, to an endless series of chores and errands, a busyness that separates us from God, each other, and even from our own thirstiness.

❖ *THE SACRED ROMANCE, 107–9*

It is for freedom that Christ has set us free.
— GALATIANS 5:1

Having abandoned desire, we have lost hope. C. S. Lewis summed it up: "We can only hope for what we desire." No desire, no hope. Now, desire doesn't always translate into hope. There are many things I desire that I have little hope for. I desire to have lots more money than I do, but I see little reason to think it will come. But there isn't one thing I hope for that I don't *also* desire. This is Lewis's point. Bland assurances of the sweet by-and-by don't inflame the soul. Our hopes are deeply tied to our real desires, and so killing desire has meant a hopeless life for too many. It's as if we've already entered Dante's *Inferno*, where the sign over hell reads, "Abandon hope, all ye who enter here."

The effect has been disastrous, not only for individual Christians, but also for the message of the gospel as a whole. People aren't exactly ripping the roofs off churches to get inside. We see the Enemy's ploy: drain all the life and beauty and adventure from the gospel, bury Christians in duty, and nobody will want to take a closer look. It's so very unappealing.

The danger of disowning desire is that it sets us up for a fall. We are unable to distinguish real life from a tempting imitation. We are fooled by the impostors. Eventually, we find some means of procuring a taste of the life we were meant for.

❂ *THE JOURNEY OF DESIRE, 64–66*

Remain in me, and I will remain in you.
—JOHN 15:4

Remain in me, and I will remain in you," Jesus said. A simple command, it seems. And yet, we overlook it. If Jesus must tell us to remain in him, then he seems to be assuming that it is quite possible *not* to remain in him. The common life is, in fact, a life lived separate from him. And that is a dangerous place to live. We cannot enjoy the fellowship of God, or his protection, or all the benefits of his kingdom unless we remain in him—that is, live in him—in our day-to-day lives. Vine and branches, Shepherd and sheep. *Stay close. Stay with me*, Jesus is saying. An old saint said to me years ago that the devil doesn't so much care what particular thing he gets us to fall prey to. His primary aim is simply to get us to do something outside of Christ, for then we are vulnerable.

I want two things that are mutually opposed—I want to live a nice little life, and I want to play an important role in God's kingdom. And it's in those times that I am trying to live a nice little life that I make decisions and choices that cause me in small and subtle ways to live outside of Jesus. The Shepherd is headed one direction, and I am headed another. Not to some flagrant sin—that's too easy to recognize. Instead, I'm simply wandering off looking for the pasture I deem best. I don't even think to ask God about it.

❖ WALKING WITH GOD, 88–90

Then the LORD said to Joshua, "See, I have delivered Jericho into your hands, along with its king and its fighting men."
—JOSHUA 6:2

There's something we need to be honest about: part of us doesn't really *want* to hear what God has to say. Really. Even after years of God's rescues and surprises and blessing upon blessing, there's a part of me that gets irritated when someone says, "Let's ask God." The act itself is a disruption. Sometimes it feels like grinding the gears. Stop? Now? Ask God? I'm bugged. That's part of it. And the other part is, if we do hear something, we'll have to obey.

I was reading the story of Joshua, and it stopped me in my tracks. My goodness, the Israelites received specific instructions from God all the way through the battle of Jericho—when to cross the river, how to cross the river, when to take Jericho, how to take Jericho. And it worked! *It worked.* You'd think they would have been convinced. This is how to follow God. But the next day comes and here they are, ready to take city number two, and you know what—they don't ask! It's not that they don't ask the second question, they don't even ask the first. They just charge ahead. And they pay for it. Dearly.

I know something of this. I don't ask because I don't want to know. If I know what God thinks, then I'm faced with the decision of whether to follow his counsel or not. What was initially just a quandary or a moment of confusion becomes an issue of obedience.

❂ WALKING WITH GOD, 90–91

Keep me as the apple of your eye.
—PSALM 17:8

Every woman is haunted by Eve in the core of her being. She knows, if only when she passes a mirror, that she is not what she was meant to be. We are more keenly aware of our own short-comings than anyone else. Remembering the glory that was once ours awakens my heart to an ache that has long gone unfulfilled. It's almost too much to hope for, too much to have lost.

You see, every little girl—and every little boy—is asking one fundamental question. But they are very different questions, depending on whether you are a little boy or a little girl. Little boys want to know, *Do I have what it takes*? All that rough-and-tumble, all that daring and superhero dress-up, all of that is a boy seeking to prove that he does have what it takes. He was made in the image of a warrior God. Nearly all a man does is fueled by his search for validation, that longing he carries for an answer to his question.

Little girls want to know, *Am I lovely*? The twirling skirts, the dress-up, the longing to be pretty and to be seen—that is what that's all about. We are seeking an answer to our question. For most of us, the answer to our question when we were young was, "No, there is nothing captivating about you." Get off the coffee table. Nearly all a woman does in her adult life is fueled by her longing to be delighted in, her longing to be beautiful, to be irreplaceable, to have her question answered, "Yes!"

Why does the question linger so?

❧ CAPTIVATING, *46*

For I am afflicted and needy,
and my heart is wounded within me.
—PSALM 109:22

The wounds that we received as young girls did not come alone. They brought messages with them, messages that struck at the core of our hearts, right in the place of our question. Our wounds strike at the core of our *femininity*. The damage done to our feminine hearts through the wounds we received is made much worse by the horrible things we believe about ourselves as a result. As children, we didn't have the faculties to process and sort through what was happening to us. Our parents were godlike. We believed them to be right. If we were overwhelmed or belittled or hurt or abused, we believed that somehow it was because of *us*— the problem was with *us*.

We can't put words to it, but down deep we fear there is something terribly wrong with us. If we were the princess, then our prince would have come. If we were the daughter of a king, he would have fought for us. We can't help but believe that if we were different, if we were *better*, then we would have been loved as we so longed to be. It must be us.

❀ CAPTIVATING, *68–71*

He heals the brokenhearted
and binds up their wounds.
—PSALM 147:3

As a result of the wounds we receive growing up, we come to believe that some part of us, maybe every part of us, is marred. Shame enters in and makes its crippling home deep within our hearts. Shame is what makes us look away, so we avoid eye contact with strangers and friends. Shame is that feeling that haunts us, the sense that if someone really knew us, they would shake their heads in disgust and run away. Shame makes us feel, no, *believe*, that we do not measure up—not to the world's standards, the church's standards, or our own.

Others seem to master their lives, but shame grips our hearts and pins them down, ever ready to point out our failures and judge our worth. We are lacking. We know we are not all that we long to be, all that God longs for us to be, but instead of coming up for grace-filled air and asking God what he thinks of us, shame keeps us pinned down and gasping, believing that we deserve to suffocate. If we were not deemed worthy of love as children, it is incredibly difficult to believe we are worth loving as adults. Shame says we are unworthy, broken, and beyond repair.

Shame causes us to hide. We are afraid of being truly seen, and so we hide our truest selves and offer only what we believe is wanted. We refuse to bring the weight of our lives, who God has made us to be, to bear on others out of a fear of being rejected.

❀ CAPTIVATING, 73–74

> *God took the man and put him in the Garden of Eden to work it and*
> *take care of it. And the* LORD *God commanded the man, "You are free*
> *to eat from any tree in the garden."*
> —GENESIS 2:15–16

God begins our courtship with a surprise. Taking the blindfold off, he turns us around and reveals his handmade wedding present. "Here," he says. "It's yours. Enjoy yourselves. Do you like it? Take it for a spin." A lavish gift indeed. What's he up to? Flowers, chocolates, exotic vacations, dinners at the finest restaurants—any person would feel pursued. But what are his intentions? Surprisingly, we see in the first glimpse of God's wildness the goodness of his heart—he gives us our freedom. In order for a true romance to occur, we had to be free to reject him. In *Disappointment with God*, Philip Yancey reminds us that the powers of the Author aren't sufficient to win our hearts.

Power can do everything but the most important thing: it cannot control love . . . In a concentration camp, the guards possess almost unlimited power. By applying force, they can make you renounce your God, curse your family, work without pay, eat human excrement, kill and then bury your closest friend or even your own mother. All this is within their power. Only one thing is not: they cannot force you to love them. This fact may help explain why God sometimes seems shy to use his power. He created us to love him.

The wildness of giving us freedom is even more staggering when we remember that God has already paid dearly for giving freedom to the angels. But because of his grand heart he goes ahead and takes the risk, an enormous, colossal risk. The reason he didn't make puppets is because he wanted lovers.

❧ *THE SACRED ROMANCE*, 77–78

Then a great and powerful wind tore the mountains apart and
shattered the rocks before the LORD, but the LORD was not in the wind.
After the wind there was an earthquake, but the LORD was not in the
earthquake. After the earthquake came a fire, but the LORD was not in
the fire. And after the fire came a gentle whisper.
—1 KINGS 19:11

When we first think of being in a relationship with God, we probably picture him as somewhat flashy. He gave Jacob visions of angels descending and ascending to heaven; he parted the Red Sea for Moses, and made the sun stand still for a day so the Israelites could win a battle. He definitely makes an impression. But you kind of wonder what he's like when you're alone with him. Would he just stay the life of the party, still playing to the crowd?

An image from the Scriptures shows us a very different side of God. A picture of the way God desires to commune with us is found in 1 Kings 19, where we find the prophet Elijah worn out and afraid, fleeing from Jezebel. She has been trying to kill him ever since he did the same to her prophets. God tenderly ministers to Elijah, twice bringing him food and water. Elijah, strengthened, travels forty days and forty nights until he reaches Mt. Horeb, where he goes to sleep in a cave. The Lord wakes him and listens to his lament about what it is like to be God's prophet. Elijah is worn out from "doing" and badly in need of restoration of spirit. A great wind strikes the mountain, followed by an earthquake and a fire. And God is in none of these. Finally, Elijah hears a "gentle whisper." And it is in the gentle whisper that he finds God.

❖ *THE SACRED ROMANCE, 162*

I have been hurt by their adulterous hearts which turned away from Me, and by their eyes which played the harlot after their idols.
—EZEKIEL 6:9

In order to learn who we really are, we must have a place in our lives where removed from the materialism, entertainment, diversion, and busyness of our Vanity Fair society. The things sold at the booths in the Fair are tranquilizers that separate us, and protect us, from the emptiness and need of our heart. As we leave these less-wild lovers behind and enter into solitude and silence in our own desert place, the first thing we encounter is not rest, but fear and a compulsion to return to activity. In *The Ascent to Truth*, Thomas Merton says:

> We look for rest and if we find it, it becomes intolerable. Incapable of the divine activity which alone can satisfy rest . . . fallen man flings himself upon exterior things, not so much for their own sake as for the sake of agitation which keeps his spirit pleasantly numb . . . The distraction diverts us aside from the one thing that can help us to begin our ascent to truth . . . the sense of our own emptiness.

But what do we do with our emptiness if we stay with our heart? If we try to pray, our minds fill with busy, disconnected petitions that start with the words "God, help me to do this or that better, have more faith, read the Bible more." The busy petitions of our minds seem to leave something inside our chest cavity unexpressed, something that is trying to tell us about the way things are.

❧ *THE SACRED ROMANCE, 172*

Be strong and let your heart take courage,
All you who hope in the LORD.
—PSALM 21:24

Astory is only as good as its ending. Without a happy ending that draws us on in eager anticipation, our journey becomes a nightmare of endless struggle. Is this all there is? Is this as good as it gets? On a recent flight I was chatting with one of the attendants about her spiritual beliefs. A follower of a New Age guru, she said with all earnestness, "I don't believe in heaven. I believe life is a never-ending cycle of birth and death." *What a horror*, I thought to myself. *This Story had better have a happy ending.* Paul felt the same. If this is as good as it gets, he said, you may as well stop at a bar on the way home and tie one on; go to Nordstrom and max out all your credit cards; bake a cake and eat the whole thing. "Let us eat and drink, for tomorrow we die" (1 Cor. 15:32).

Our hearts cannot live without hope. Gabriel Marcel says that "hope is for the soul what breathing is for the living organism." In the trinity of Christian graces—faith, hope, and love—love may be the greatest but hope plays the deciding role. The apostle Paul tells us that faith and love depend on hope, our anticipation of what lies ahead: "Faith and love . . . spring from the hope that is stored up for you in heaven" (Col. 1:5). Our courage for the journey so often falters because we've lost our hope of heaven—the consummation of our Love Story. The reason most men, to quote Thoreau, "live lives of quiet desperation" is that they live without hope.

❧ *THE SACRED ROMANCE, 177–78*

Husbands, love your wives, just as Christ loved the church and gave himself up for her.
—EPHESIANS 5:25

There is something mythic about the way a man is with a woman. Our sexuality offers a parable of amazing depth when it comes to being masculine and feminine. The man comes to offer his strength and the woman invites the man into herself, acts that require courage and vulnerability and selflessness for both of them. Notice first that if the man will not rise to the occasion, nothing will happen. He must move; his strength must swell before he can enter her. But neither will the love consummate unless the woman opens herself in stunning vulnerability. When both are living as they were meant to live, the man enters his woman and offers her his strength. He *spills himself there*, in her, for her; she draws him in, embraces and envelops him. When all is over he is spent; but ah, what a sweet death it is.

And that is how life is created. The beauty of a woman arouses a man to play the man; the strength of a man, offered tenderly to his woman, allows her to be beautiful; it brings life to her and to many. This is far, far more than sex and orgasm. It is a reality that extends to every aspect of our lives. When a man withholds himself from his woman, he leaves her without the life only he can bring. This is never more true than how a man offers—or does not offer—his words. Life and death are in the power of the tongue says Proverbs (18:21). She is made for and craves words from him.

❖ *WILD AT HEART, 185*

Trust in the LORD with all your heart,
and lean not on your own understanding.
—PROVERBS 3:5

Where would we be today if Abraham had carefully weighed the pros and cons of God's invitation and decided that he'd rather hang on to his medical benefits, three weeks paid vacation, and retirement plan in Ur? What would have happened if Moses had listened to his mother's advice to "never play with matches" and lived a careful, cautious life steering clear of all burning bushes? You wouldn't have the gospel if Paul had concluded that the life of a Pharisee, while not everything a man dreams for, was at least predictable and certainly more stable than following a voice he heard on the Damascus road. After all, people hear voices all the time, and who really knows whether it's God or just one's imagination. Where would we be if Jesus was not fierce and wild and romantic to the core? Come to think of it, we wouldn't *be* at all if God hadn't taken that enormous risk of us in the first place.

Most men spend the energy of their lives trying to eliminate risk, or squeezing it down to a more manageable size. Their children hear "no" far more than they hear "yes"; their employees feel chained up and their wives are equally bound. If it works, if a man succeeds in securing his life against all risk, he'll wind up in a cocoon of self-protection, wondering why he's suffocating. If it doesn't work, he curses God, redoubles his efforts and his blood pressure. When you look at the structure of the false self men tend to create, it always revolves around two themes: seizing upon some sort of competence and rejecting anything that cannot be controlled.

❖ *WILD AT HEART, 202–3*

Jesus knew that the Father had put all things under his power, and that he had come from God and was returning to God; so he got up from the meal, took off his outer clothing, and wrapped a towel around his waist. After that, he poured water into a basin and began to wash his disciples' feet, drying them with the towel that was wrapped around him.

—JOHN 13:3–5

To live as authentic, ransomed, and redeemed means to be real and present in this moment. If we continue to hide, much will be lost. We cannot have intimacy with God or anyone else if we stay hidden and offer only who we think we ought to be or what we believe is wanted. We cannot play the role we were meant to play if we remain bound by shame and fear, presenting only to the world the face we have learned is safe. *You have only one life to live. It would be best to live your own.*

What have we to offer, really, other than who we are and what God has been pouring into our lives? It was not by accident that you were born; it was not by chance that you have the desires you do. The Victorious Trinity has planned on your being here now, "for such a time as this" (Esth. 4:14). We need you.

Jesus knew who he was. God really does want you to know who *you* are. So, are you willing to take a moment and allow him to remind you who you truly are?

❧ CAPTIVATING, *216*

Not everyone who says to me, 'Lord, Lord,' will enter the kingdom of heaven, but only he who does the will of my Father who is in heaven.
—MATTHEW 7:21

Who has kept the new covenant so effectively under wraps that most Christians still believe their hearts are evil? To say your heart is good still sounds like heresy. Who convinced the church to stay so focused on the Cross that we know next to nothing about the power of the Resurrection and the Ascension? Is it any wonder that we think Christianity is primarily about not sinning and waiting to die to go to heaven? What happened to the *life*, the glory of God as man fully alive?

Let me ask you another question: whom did Jesus tangle with more than any other group or type of person? Who started the rumors about him to try to discredit his ministry? Who kept trying to put him on the spot with their loaded questions? And when it became clear they could not shame or intimidate him back into place, where did the open opposition to Christ come from? Who paid Judas the thirty pieces of silver? Who got the crowd to yell for Barabbas when Pilate was ready to let Jesus go?

Religion and its defenders have always been the most insidious enemy of the true faith precisely because they are not glaring opponents; they are *impostors*. A raving pagan is easier to dismiss than an elder in your church. Before Jesus came along, the Pharisees ran the show. Everybody took what they said as gospel—even though it didn't sound like good news at all. The Pharisees and their brethren down through the ages have merely acted—unknowingly, for the most part—as puppets, the mouthpiece of the Enemy.

❖ WAKING THE DEAD, *161*

You are worthy, our Lord and God,
to receive glory and honor and power,
for you created all things,
and by your will they were created
and have their being.

—REVELATION 4:11

When the biblical writers speak of heaven, they use the most beautiful imagery they can. In the book of Revelation, John uses the word *like* again and again. "And He who was sitting was like a jasper stone and a sardius in appearance; and there was a rainbow around the throne, like an emerald in appearance" (4:3, 6 NASB).

I believe the beauty of heaven is why the Bible says we shall be "feasted." It's not merely that there will be no suffering, though that will be tremendous joy in itself, to have every wound dressed with the leaves from the tree of life (Rev. 22:2). But there is more. We will have glorified bodies with which to partake of all the beauty of heaven. As C. S. Lewis wrote,

> We do not want merely to *see* beauty, though, God knows, even that is bounty enough. We want something else which can hardly be put into words—to be united with the beauty we see, to pass into it, to receive it into ourselves, to bathe in it, to become part of it. (*The Weight of Glory*)

And so we shall.

❖ *THE SACRED ROMANCE, 186–87*

They devoted themselves to the apostles' teaching and to the fellowship, to the breaking of bread and to prayer. Everyone was filled with awe, and many wonders and miraculous signs were done by the apostles.

—ACTS 2:42–43

Dorothy takes her journey with the Scarecrow, the Tin Woodman, the Lion, and of course, Toto. Maximus in the movie *Gladiator* rallies his little band and triumphs over the greatest empire on earth. When Captain John Miller is sent deep behind enemy lines to save Private Ryan, he goes in with a squad of eight rangers. And, of course, Jesus had the Twelve. This is written so deeply on our hearts: *You must not go alone.* The Scriptures are full of such warnings, but until we see our desperate situation, we hear it as an optional religious assembly for an hour on Sunday mornings.

Think again of Frodo or Neo or Caspian or Jesus. Imagine you are surrounded by a small company of friends who know you well (characters, to be sure, but they love you, and you have come to love them). They understand that we all are at war, know that the purposes of God are to bring a man or a woman fully alive, and are living by sheer necessity and joy in fellowship with God. They fight for you, and you for them. Imagine you *could* have a little fellowship of the heart. Would you want it if it were available?

❀ WAKING THE DEAD, 187–88

*Aquila and Priscilla greet you warmly in the Lord, and so does the
church that meets at their house.*

—1 CORINTHIANS 16:19

Jesus didn't march around Israel with his multitudes of followers
in tow. He had twelve men—knuckleheads, every last one of
them, but they were a band of brothers. This is the way of the
kingdom of God. Though we are part of a great company, we are
meant to live in little platoons. The little companies we form
must be small enough for each of the members to know one
another as friends and allies. Is it possible for five thousand people
who gather for an hour on a Sunday morning to really and truly
know one another? Okay, how about five hundred? One hundred
and eighty? It can't be done. They can't possibly be intimate
allies. It can be inspiring and encouraging to celebrate with a big
ol' crowd of people, but who will fight for your heart?

Who will fight for your heart?

How can we offer the stream of counseling to one another
unless we actually *know* one another, know one another's stories?
Counseling became a hired relationship between two people
primarily because we couldn't find it anywhere else; we haven't
formed the sort of small fellowships that would allow the stream
to flow quite naturally. Is it possible to offer rich and penetrating
words to someone you barely know, in the lobby of your church,
as you dash to pick up the kids? And what about warfare? Would
you feel comfortable turning to the person in the pew next to you
and, as you pass the offering plate, asking him to bind a demon
that is sitting on your head?

❖ WAKING THE DEAD, *190–91*

They broke bread in their homes and ate together with glad and sincere hearts.

—ACTS 2:46

The abundant life of fellowship with God is something we learn, and grow into, and offer one another, within a small fellowship. We hear each other's stories. We discover each other's glories. We learn to walk with God together. We pray for each other's healing. We cover each other's backs. This small core fellowship is the essential ingredient for the Christian life. Jesus modeled it for us *for a reason*. Sure, he spoke to the masses. But he *lived* in a little platoon, a small fellowship of friends and allies. His followers took his example and lived this way too. "Aquila and Priscilla greet you warmly in the Lord, and so does the church that meets at their house" (1 Cor. 16:19); "Give my greetings to the brothers at Laodicea, and to Nympha and the church in her house" (Col. 4:15).

Church is not a building. Church is not an event that takes place on Sundays. I know, it's how we've come to think of it. "I go to First Baptist." "We are members of St. Luke's." "Is it time to go to church?" Much to our surprise, that is *not* how the Bible uses the term. Not at all. When the Scripture talks about church, it means *community*. The little fellowships of the heart that are outposts of the kingdom. A shared life. They worship together, eat together, pray for one another, go on quests together. They hang out together, in each other's homes. When Peter was sprung from prison, "he went to the house of Mary the mother of John" where the church had gathered to pray for his release (Acts 12:12).

❖ *WAKING THE DEAD, 191–92*

Give my greetings to the brothers at Laodicea, and to Nympha and the church in her house.

—COLOSSIANS 4:15

Of course, small groups have become a part of the programming most churches offer their people. For the most part, they are disappointing and short-lived—by the very admission of those who try them. There are two reasons. One, you can't just throw a random group of people together for a twelve-week study of some kind and expect them to become intimate allies. The sort of devotion we want and need takes place within a shared life. Over the years our fellowship has gone camping together. We play together; help one another move; paint a room; find work. We throw great parties. We fight for each other. And we live in the abundant life of fellowship with God. This is how it was meant to be.

I love this description of the early church: "All the believers were one in heart" (Acts 4:32). A camaraderie was being expressed there, a bond, an esprit de corps. It means they all loved the same thing, they all wanted the same thing, and they were bonded together to find it, come hell or high water. And hell or high water *will* come, friends, and this will be the test of whether or not your band will make it: if you are one in heart. Judas betrayed the brothers because his heart was never really with them, just as Cipher betrays the company on the *Nebuchadnezzar* and as Boromir betrays the fellowship of the Ring. My goodness—churches split over the size of the parking lot or what instruments to use during worship. Most churches are *not* "one in heart."

❖ WAKING THE DEAD, 193

Bear with each other and forgive whatever grievances you may have against one another. Forgive as the Lord forgave you.
—COLOSSIANS 3:13

G. K. Chesterton wrote, "The family is . . . like a little kingdom, and, like most other little kingdoms, is generally in a state of something resembling anarchy." He could have been describing a little fellowship (our *true* family, because it is the family of God). It is a royal mess. I will not whitewash this. It is *disruptive*. Going to church with hundreds of other people to sit and hear a sermon doesn't ask much of you. It certainly will never expose you. Community will. It will reveal where *you* have yet to become holy, right at the very moment you are so keenly aware of how *they* have yet to become holy. It will bring you close and you will be *seen* and you will be *known*, and therein lies the power and therein lies the danger.

We've experienced incredible disappointments in our fellowship. We have—every last one of us—hurt one another. Sometimes deeply. One night, Stasi and I laid out a vision for where we thought things should be going—our lifelong dream for redemptive community. We hoped the company would leap to it with loud hurrahs. Far from it. Their response was more on the level of blank stares. Our dream was mishandled—badly. I was . . . stunned. Disappointed. I felt the dive toward a total loss of heart. The following day I could feel my heart being pulled toward resentment. Moments like that usually toll the beginning of the end for most attempts at community.

❖ *WAKING THE DEAD, 197–98*

Jesus said, "And when you pray, do not be like the hypocrites, for they love to pray standing in the synagogues and on the street corners to be seen by men. I tell you the truth, they have received their reward in full. But when you pray, go into your room, close the door and pray to your Father, who is unseen. Then your Father, who sees what is done in secret, will reward you. And when you pray, do not keep on babbling like pagans, for they think they will be heard because of their many words. Do not be like them, for your Father knows what you need before you ask him."

—MATTHEW 6:5–8

Remember the disciples asking Jesus, "Teach us to pray"? Too many times we just jump in and start praying (making prayer speeches to God), and it doesn't have much effect. We just sort of swing our sword around in the air randomly. Do this for a while and you'll get the impression that prayer doesn't really work. Or that God isn't in it.

Oh, it works, and he's in it. When we pray effectively. John says, "This is the confidence we have in approaching God: that if we ask anything according to his will, he hears us. And if we know that he hears us—whatever we ask—we know that we have what we asked of him" (1 John 5:14–15).

That's an awesome promise. If we pray according to God's will, he hears us all right. And he answers our prayers. Isn't that what you want? I sure do. I want to see my prayers work! I want to pray according to God's will. But I don't always know what that is, so, *I ask*.

❖ WALKING WITH GOD, *104*

Your enemy the devil prowls around like a roaring lion looking for someone to devour.

—1 PETER 5:8

We must be aware of this—Satan is an opportunist. He is always looking for open doors, opportunities, a chink in the armor. He'll seize what might otherwise simply be an event—an argument, an emotion, a loss like this—and he'll use it as an entrée for his lies, deceits, and oppression. I've felt it around someone else's bad news. I'll be doing fine, and then someone will tell me a story of some hardship or loss that a friend is undergoing, and *boom*—a sense of lingering darkness will creep over me, not strong at first, just that sense of, *Right, this is what life is really like—it's hard and unpredictable.* It feels like an assault against my faith. Sure, some of this is my own weirdness and paranoia. But not all of it.

What I'm warning you about is that when you are in a vulnerable place, realize that you are in a vulnerable place, and remember that all predators look for the vulnerable one in the herd. Once we are in the kingdom that is yet to come, once the world has been restored to all it was meant to be, then we will be able to live without interruption, without assault. Then we can drop our guard. But not until then. Not even in moments of tenderness and sorrow. I know it seems unfair, but the enemy does not play fair. He is an opportunist.

❖ WALKING WITH GOD, *127–28, 129*

*Therefore I am now going to allure her;
I will lead her into the desert
and speak tenderly to her.*
—HOSEA 2:14

We construct a life of safety and find some place to get a taste of being enjoyed or at least of being "needed." Our journey toward healing begins when we repent of those ways, lay them down, let them go. As Frederick Buechner says,

The trouble with steeling yourself against the harshness of reality is that the same steel that secures your life against being destroyed secures your life also against being opened up and transformed. (*The Sacred Journey*)

God comes to us and asks, "Will you let me come for you?" Not only does he thwart, but at the same time he calls to us, "Set it down. Set it down. Turn from your ways to me. I want to come for you."

To enter the journey toward the healing of your feminine heart, all it requires is a "Yes. Okay." A simple turning in the heart. Like the Prodigal, we wake one day to see that the life we've constructed is no life at all. We let desire speak to us again; we let our hearts have a voice, and what the voice usually says is, *This isn't working. My life is a disaster. Jesus—I'm sorry. Forgive me. Please come for me.*

❀ CAPTIVATING, 98–99

Do not give way to fear.
—1 PETER 3:6

Of course this is scary. Responding to the invitations of Jesus often feels like the riskiest thing we've ever done. Just ask Rahab, Esther, Ruth, and Mary.

Webster defines "risk" as exposing one's life to the possibility of injury, damage, or loss. The life of the friends of God is a life of profound risk. The risk of loving others. The risk of stepping out and offering, speaking up and following our God-given dreams. The risk of playing the irreplaceable role that is ours to play. Of course it is hard. If it were easy, you'd see lots of women living this way.

So come back then to what Peter said when he urged women to offer their beauty to others in love. This is the secret of femininity unleashed: "Do not give way to fear" (1 Peter 3:6).

The reason we fear to step out is because we know that it might not go well (is that an understatement?). We have a history of wounds screaming at us to play it safe. We feel so deeply that if it doesn't go well, if we are not received well, their reaction becomes the verdict on our lives, on our very beings, on our hearts. We fear that our deepest doubts about ourselves as women will be confirmed. Again. That is why we can *only* risk stepping out when we are resting in the love of God. When we have received his verdict on our lives—that we are chosen and dearly loved. That he finds us captivating. Then we are free to offer.

❖ *CAPTIVATING, 213–14*

Whoever has my commands and obeys them, he is the one who loves me.

—JOHN 14:21

H e wants the same thing that you want. He wants to be loved. He wants to be known as only lovers can know each other. He wants intimacy with you. Yes, yes, he wants your obedience but only when it flows out of a heart filled with love for him. Following hard after Jesus is the heart's natural response when it has been captured and fallen deeply in love with him.

Reading George MacDonald several years ago, I came across an astounding thought. You've probably heard that there is in every human heart a place that God alone can fill. (Lord knows we've tried to fill it with everything else, to our utter dismay.) But what the old poet was saying was that there is *also* in God's heart a place that you alone can fill. "It follows that there is also a chamber in God himself, into which none can enter but the one, the individual." You. You are meant to fill a place in the heart of God no one and nothing else can fill. Whoa. He longs for *you*.

God wants to live this life together with you, to share in your days and decisions, your desires and disappointments. He wants intimacy with you in the midst of the madness and mundane, the meetings and memos, the laundry and lists, the carpools and conversations and projects and pain. He wants to pour his love into your heart and he longs to have you pour yours into his. He is not interested in intimacy with the person you think you are supposed to be. He wants intimacy with the real you.

❂ *CAPTIVATING, 120–21*

And he took bread, gave thanks and broke it, and gave it to them,
saying, "This is my body given for you; do this in remembrance of me."
—LUKE 22:19

If we choose the way of desire, our greatest enemy on the road ahead is not the Arrows, nor Satan, nor our false lovers. The most crippling thing that besets the pilgrim heart is simply forgetfulness. You *will* forget; this isn't the first book you've read in search of God. What do you remember from the others? I have had enough encounters with God to provide a lifetime of conviction—why don't I live more faithfully? Because I forget.

I am humbled by the story of the golden calf. These people, the Jews God has just delivered from Egypt, have seen an eyeful. First came the plagues, then the Passover, then the escape from Pharaoh's armies and last-minute rescue straight through the Red Sea. After that came the manna: breakfast in bed, so to speak, every morning for months. They drank water from a rock. They heard and saw the fireworks at Mount Sinai and shook in their sandals at the presence of God. I think it's safe to say that this band of ransomed slaves had reasons to believe. Then their leader, Moses, disappears for forty days into the "consuming fire" that enveloped the top of the mountain, which they could see with their own eyes. While he's up there, they blow the whole thing off for a wild bacchanalian party in honor of an idol made from their earrings.

My first reaction is arrogant: How could they possibly be so stupid? How could they forget everything they've received straight from the hand of God?

My second is a bit more honest: That's me; I forget all the time.

❀ THE SACRED ROMANCE, 202

When I saw their fear, I rose and spoke to the nobles, the officials and
the rest of the people: "Do not be afraid of them; remember the Lord
who is great and awesome, and fight for your brothers, your sons,
your daughters, your wives and your houses."

—NEHEMIAH 4:14

We were meant to remember together, in community. We need to tell our stories to others and to hear their stories told. We need to help each other with the interpretation of the Larger Story and our own. Our regular times of coming together to worship are intended to be times of corporate remembrance. "This, God has done," we say; "this, he will do." How different Sunday mornings would be if they were marked by a rich retelling of the Sacred Romance in the context of real lives.

One of the reasons modern evangelicalism feels so thin is because it is merely modern; there is no connection with the thousands of years of saints who have gone before. Our community of memory must include not only saints from down the street, but also those from down the ages. Let us hear the stories of John and Teresa from last week, but also those of St. John of the Cross and Teresa of Avila, to name only two. Let us draw from that "great cloud of witnesses" and learn from their journeys.

Remembering is not mere nostalgia; it is an act of survival, our way of "watching over our hearts with all diligence." In *The Brothers Karamazov*, the gentle Alyosha says, "And even if only one good memory remains with us in our hearts, that alone may serve some day for our salvation."

❖ *THE SACRED ROMANCE, 207–8*

> *You must no longer live as the Gentiles do, in the futility of their thinking. They are darkened in their understanding and separated from the life of God because of the ignorance that is in them due to the hardening of their hearts.*
>
> —EPHESIANS 4:17–18

The loss of sensitivity that Paul is referring to here is the dullness that most people accept as normal. It actually leads us into sin, to sensuality and lust. The deadened soul requires a greater and greater level of stimulation to arouse it. This is, of course, the downward spiral of any addiction. Just look at the progression of television drama over the past thirty years. What we have now would have been considered shocking, even repulsive, to an earlier audience. This is why holiness is not numbness; it is sensitivity. It is being *more* attuned to our desires, to what we were truly made for and therefore what we truly want. Our problem is that we've grown quite used to seeking life in all kinds of things other than God.

> [W]e seek perfection in human relationships and are disappointed when our lovers cannot love us perfectly. . . . [W]e seek our safety in power and possessions and then we find we must continually worry about them. . . . (Gerald G. May, *Addiction and Grace*)

And so, May says, "the more we become accustomed to seeking spiritual satisfaction through things other than God, the more abnormal and stressful it becomes to look for God directly." Our instrument is out of tune from years of misuse.

❖ *THE JOURNEY OF DESIRE, 175–76*

*We are the true circumcision, who worship in the Spirit of God and
glory in Christ Jesus and put no confidence in the flesh.*
—Philippians 3:3 NASB

Henri Nouwen once asked Mother Teresa for spiritual direction. "Spend one hour each day in adoration of your Lord,"
she said, "and never do anything you know is wrong. Follow this,
and you'll be fine."

Such simple yet profound advice. Worship is the act of the abandoned heart adoring its God. It is the union that we crave. Few of us
experience anything like this on a regular basis, let alone for an hour
each day. But it is what we need. Desperately. Simply showing up
on Sunday is not even close to worship. Neither does singing songs
with religious content pass for worship. What counts is *the posture
of the soul* involved, the open heart pouring forth its love toward
God and communing with him. It is a question of desire.

Worship occurs when we say to God, from the bottom of our
hearts, "You are the One whom I desire." As Thomas à Kempis
prayed, "There is nothing created that can fully satisfy my desires.
Make me one with You in a sure bond of heavenly love, for You
alone are sufficient to Your lover, and without You all things are
vain and of no substance."

In the most often quoted phrase from Augustine, he says, "Our
hearts are restless until they find their rest in Thee." He is referring
to desire. Our only hope for rest from the incessant craving of our
desire is in God, and us united to him. The full union, of course, is
coming. We rehearse for the wedding now through worship.

❧ *The Journey of Desire, 177–78*

Brothers, I do not consider myself yet to have taken hold of it. But one thing I do: Forgetting what is behind and straining toward what is ahead, I press on toward the goal to win the prize for which God has called me heavenward in Christ Jesus.

—PHILIPPIANS 3:13–14

There is a widespread belief in the church that being a Christian somehow satisfies our every desire. As one camp song has it, "I'm inright, outright, upright, downright happy all day long." What complete nonsense! Augustine emphasized, "The whole life of the good Christian is a holy longing. What you desire ardently, as yet you do not see." So, "let us long because we are to be filled . . . That is our life, to be exercised by longing." There's the mystery again. Longing leads to fullness somewhere down the road. Meanwhile, being content is not the same thing as being full.

Paul said he had "learned the secret of being content" (Phil. 4:12), and many Christians assume he no longer experienced the thirst of his soul. But earlier in the same epistle, the old saint said that he had *not* obtained his soul's desire or "already been made perfect." Quite the contrary. He described himself as pressing on, "straining toward what is ahead" (3:12–14). These are not the words of a man who no longer experienced longing because he had arrived. They are the account of a man propelled on his life quest by his desire.

Contentment is not freedom *from* desire, but freedom *of* desire. Being content is not pretending that everything is the way you wish it would be; it is not acting as though you have no wishes. Rather, it is no longer being *ruled* by your desires.

❖ *THE JOURNEY OF DESIRE, 181–82*

You open your hand
and satisfy the desires of every living thing.
—PSALM 145:16

The French mathematician, philosopher, and devout believer, Blaise Pascal, wrote:

> What can this incessant craving, and this impotence of attainment mean, unless there was once a happiness belonging to man, of which only the faintest traces remain, in that void which he attempts to fill with everything within his reach? . . . [B]ecause, in a soul that will live forever, there is an infinite void that nothing can fill, but an infinite unchangeable being.

You can be satisfied, says Pascal; you just can't be sated. There is great joy in a glass of cabernet; the whole bottle is another story. The Israelites tried to hoard the manna—and it crawled with maggots. Our soul's insatiable desire becomes the venom Pascal warns of when it demands its fill here and now, through the otherwise beautiful and good gifts of our lives.

God grants us so much of our heart's desire as we delight in him. Not always, not on demand, but certainly more than we deserve. God delights to give good gifts to his beloved. But that old root would have us shift once more from giver to gift, and seek our rest through being full. This is the turn we must be vigilant to see, watching over our hearts with loving care.

❖ *THE JOURNEY OF DESIRE, 182–83*

*A new commandment I give to you, that you love one another, even as
I have loved you, that you also love one another."*
—JOHN 13:34

Caring for our own hearts isn't selfishness; it's how we begin
to love.

Yes, we care for our hearts for the sake of others. Does that
sound like a contradiction? Not at all. What will you bring to
others if your heart is empty, dried up, pinned down? Love is the
point. And you can't love without your heart, and you can't love
well unless your heart is well.

When it comes to the whole subject of loving others, you must
know this: how you handle your own heart is how you will handle
theirs. This is the wisdom behind Jesus' urging us to love others *as
we love ourselves* (Mark 12:31). "A horrible command," as C. S.
Lewis points out, "if the self were simply to be hated." If you dismiss
your heart, you will end up dismissing theirs. If you expect perfection of your heart, you will raise that same standard for them. If
you manage your heart for efficiency and performance, that is what
you'll pressure them to be.

"But," you protest, "I have lots of grace for other people. I'm
just hard on myself." I tried the same excuse for years. It doesn't
work. Even though we may try to be merciful toward others while
we neglect or beat up ourselves, they can *see* how we treat our own
hearts, and they will always feel the treatment will be the same
for them. They are right. Eventually, inevitably, we will treat them
poorly too.

❖ *WAKING THE DEAD, 211–12*

If your sons are careful of their way, to walk before Me in truth with all their heart and with all their soul, you shall not lack a man on the throne of Israel.

—1 KINGS 2:4 NASB

Caring for your heart is how you protect your relationship with God.

Now there's a new thought. But isn't our heart the new dwelling place of God? It is where we commune with him. It is where we hear his voice. Most of the folks I know who have never heard God speak to them are the same folks who live far from their hearts; they practice the Christianity of principles. Then they wonder why God seems distant. *I guess all that intimacy with God stuff is for others, not me.* It's like a friend who hates the telephone. He neglects to pay the bills, couldn't care less when the phone company disconnects the service. Then he wonders why "nobody ever calls." You cannot cut off your heart and expect to hear from God.

Clairvaux describes Christian maturity as the stage where "we love ourselves for God's sake," meaning that because he considers our hearts the treasures of the kingdom, we do too. We care for ourselves in the same way a woman who knows she is deeply loved cares for herself, while a woman who has been tossed aside tends to "let herself go," as the saying goes. God's friends care for their hearts because they matter to *him*.

❖ WAKING THE DEAD, *213*

We have the word of the prophets made more certain, and you will do well to pay attention to it, as to a light shining in a dark place, until the day dawns and the morning star rises in your hearts.

—2 PETER 1:19

We now are going to war. This is the beginning of the end. The hour is late, and you are needed. We need your heart.

We are now far into this epic story that every great myth points to. We have reached the moment where we, too, must find our courage and rise up to recover our hearts and fight for the hearts of others. The hour is late, and much time has been wasted. Aslan is on the move; we must rally around him at the stone table. We must find Gepetto lost at sea. We must ride hard, ride to Helm's Deep and join the last great battle for Middle Earth. Grab everything God sends you. You'll need everything that helps you see with the eyes of your heart, including those myths, and the way they illumine for us the words God has given in Scripture, to which "you will do well to pay attention . . . as to a light shining in a dark place, until the day dawns and the morning star rises in your hearts" (2 Peter 1:19).

❋ *WAKING THE DEAD, 220–21*

I, the prisoner of the Lord, implore you to walk in a manner worthy of the calling with which you have been called.

—Ephesians 4:1 NASB

We are living somewhere toward the end of Act Three. We have a future, but this tale is not over yet. We now live between the beaches of Normandy and the end of the war. Between Paradise lost and Paradise regained.

We live in a far more dramatic, far more dangerous Story than we ever imagined. The reason we love *The Chronicles of Narnia* or *The Matrix* or *The Lord of the Rings* is because they are telling us something about our lives that we never, ever get on the evening news. Or from most pulpits. They are reminding us of the Epic we are created for. *This* is the sort of tale you've fallen into. How would you live differently if you believed it to be true?

The final test of any belief or faith that claims to provide an answer to our lives is this: Does the one explain the other? Does it explain the longing in your heart for a life you haven't yet found? Does it explain the evil cast around us? Most of all, does it give you back your heart, lead you to the Source of life?

Something has been calling to you all the days of your life. You've heard it on the wind and in the music you love, in laughter and in tears, and most especially in the stories that have ever captured your heart. There *is* a secret written on your heart. A valiant Hero-Lover and his Beloved. An Evil One and a great battle to fight. A Journey and a Quest, more dangerous and more thrilling than you could imagine.

❖ *Epic, 99–100*

Walk in a manner worthy of the God who calls you into His own kingdom and glory.

—1 THESSALONIANS 2:12 NASB

The Story God is telling—like every great story that echoes it—reminds us of three eternal truths it would be good to keep in mind as we take the next step out the door.

First, *things are not what they seem.* Where would we be if Eve had recognized the serpent for who he really was? And that carpenter from Nazareth—he's not what he appears to be, either. There is far more going on around us than meets the eye. We live in a world with two halves, one part that we can see and another part that we cannot. We must live as though the unseen world (the rest of reality) is weightier and more real and more dangerous than the part of reality we can see.

Second, *we are at war.* Our life on earth is a love story, set in the midst of a life-and-death battle. Just look around you. Look at all the casualties strewn across the field. The lost souls, the broken hearts, the captives. We must take this battle seriously.

Third, *you have a crucial role to play.* That is the third eternal truth spoken by every great story, and it happens to be the one we most desperately need if we are ever to understand our days. Frodo underestimated who he was. As did Neo. As did Wallace. As did Peter, James, and John. It is a dangerous thing to underestimate your role in the Story. You will lose heart, and you will miss your cues.

This is our most desperate hour. You are needed.

❁ *EPIC, 100–102*

The Son of God came to give his life as a ransom for many.
— MATTHEW 20:28

Jesus was sentenced to death by a vain puppet of the Roman government. He was nailed to a cross by a handful of Roman soldiers who happened to be on duty, and left there to die. He died sometime around three o'clock in the afternoon on a Friday. Of a broken heart, by the way. And we call it Good Friday, of all strange things, because of what it affected. An innocent man, the Son of God, bleeding for the sins of the world. We rebelled, and the penalty for our rebellion was death. To lose us was too great a pain for God to bear, and so he took it upon himself to rescue us.

You have been ransomed by Christ. Your treachery is forgiven. You are entirely pardoned for every wrong thought and desire and deed. This is what the vast majority of Christians understand as the central work of Christ for us. And make no mistake about it—it is a deep and stunning truth, one that will set you free and bring you joy. For a while.

But the joy for most of us has proved fleeting, because we find that we need to be forgiven again and again and again. Christ has died for us, but we remain (so we believe) deeply marred. It actually ends up producing a great deal of guilt. "After all that Christ has done for you . . . and now you're back here asking forgiveness *again*?" To be destined to a life of repeating the very things that sent our Savior to the cross can hardly be called *salvation*. Think of it.

❀ *WAKING THE DEAD, 61–62*

Your desire will be for your husband, and he will rule over you.
—GENESIS 3:16

The curse upon Eve affects women, yes. But her struggle belongs to all of humanity. There is an ache in Eve now that she tries to get Adam to fill. There is an emptiness given to her to drive her back to God, but she takes it to Adam instead. It makes a mess of many good relationships. You know all about this. No matter how much another person pours into your aching soul, it's never enough. No mere human can fill you. People know this, so they'll pull away because they sense you're asking them to fill you. Every woman—indeed *everyone*—has to reckon with this ache she tries to get her man to fill. In order to learn how to love him, she *must* first stop insisting that he fill her.

We say all this as a sort of prologue, because we cannot talk about loving others well—whoever they might be in your life—until we see that we cannot look to people for things they cannot give.

Ask Jesus to show you what you've been doing with your ultimate questions and how you've related to others. Only then can we talk about loving well.

❀ *CAPTIVATING, 153*

My lover is like a gazelle or a young stag. Look!
—SONG OF SOLOMON 2:9

Sex has a lot to teach us about the relationship between femininity and masculinity. It is a beautiful and rich metaphor, a very passionate and heightened picture for a much broader reality. The question before us is, "How does a woman best love a man?" The answer is simple: Seduce him.

Think of a woman on her wedding night. She dims the lights and puts on a silky something that accentuates the loveliness of her body, reveals the beauty of her naked form, yet also leaves something yet to be unveiled. She puts on perfume and lipstick and checks her hair. She *allures* her man. She hopes to arouse him and invite him to come to her and enter her. In an act of stunning vulnerability she takes life's greatest risk—offering her unveiled beauty to him, opening herself up to him in every way.

And as for her man, if he does not rise to the occasion, nothing will happen. There will be no consummation of love, no life conceived unless the man is able to offer his strength to his woman. That is how we make love. Femininity is what arouses his masculinity. His strength is what makes a woman yearn to be beautiful.

It's that simple, that beautiful, that mysterious, and incredibly profound.

The beauty of a woman is what arouses the strength of a man. He *wants* to play the man when a woman acts like that. You can't hold him back. He *wants* to come through.

❖ CAPTIVATING, *154*

May God himself . . . sanctify you through and through. May your whole spirit, soul and body be kept blameless at the coming of our Lord Jesus Christ.

—1 THESSALONIANS 5:23

We human beings are made up of three interwoven parts. We are body, soul, and spirit. Each part affects the others in a mysterious interplay of life. When Stasi sought healing through counseling, God was addressing her soul. God's provision of the help of antidepressants was a tremendous help to her body. She made real progress. But it was not enough. God wanted her to engage my spirit.

A foul spirit of depression had its bloody claws in Stasi's life. It often works like that—the Enemy knows our weaknesses, and he preys upon them. Paul warns about this in Ephesians when, *writing to Christians*, he warns us not to "give the devil a foothold" in our lives through unhealed and mishandled emotions (4:26–27).

James and Peter both exhort us to *resist* our Enemy (James 4:7; 1 Peter 5:8–9). Jesus said he has given us his authority to overcome the spiritual attacks against us (Luke 10:18–19). Stasi prayed. I as the husband, the head, prayed as well. We commanded this foul spirit to leave me by the authority given to believers in Jesus Christ. Deliverance came. Victory. Release. Healing. Restoration. It was the final key. We need to address all three aspects—body, soul, and spirit—in order to come more fully into healing. Far too many people will focus only on one or two aspects and do not engage in the spiritual warfare that is swirling around us.

But if we would be free, we must.

❖ CAPTIVATING, 192–93

I tell you the truth, whoever hears my word and believes him who sent me has eternal life and will not be condemned; he has crossed over from death to life.

—JOHN 5:24

Life is a journey of the heart that requires the mind—not the other way around. The church sometimes gets this backward and makes knowing the right things the center of life. It's not; the heart is the center of life. Desire is always where the action is. However, staying alive to our desire is not enough; we know that only too well. We must bring the *truth* into our hearts to guard and to guide our desire; this is the other half of our mission. With a recovery of heart and soul taking place in many quarters, my fear now is that we will abandon the pursuit of truth and try to base our journey on our feelings and intuition. We must cling to the truth for dear life.

Most of us were raised in the modern era, the age of reason and science. We came to believe that truth is best discovered in the scientific method.

What is the truth of a kiss? Technically, in a modernistic sense, it is two sets of mandibles pressing together for a certain duration of time. Those of you who have experienced the wonders of a kiss will know that while true, this description is so untrue. It takes away everything beautiful and mysterious and passionate and intimate and leaves you with an icy cold fact. Those who know kissing feel robbed; those who don't are apt to say, "If that's what kissing is all about, I think I'd rather not."

We've done the same thing to theology.

❖ *THE JOURNEY OF DESIRE, 202–3*

You diligently study the Scriptures because you think that by them you possess eternal life. These are the Scriptures that testify about me, yet you refuse to come to me to have life.

—JOHN 5:39

We have dissected God, and man, and the gospel, and we have thousands, if not millions, of facts—all of them quite dead. It's not that these insights aren't true; it's that they no longer speak. I could tell you a few facts about God, for example. He is omniscient, omnipotent, and immutable. There—don't you feel closer to him? All our statements about God forget that he is a person, and as Tozer says, "In the deep of His mighty nature He thinks, wills, enjoys, feels, loves, desires and suffers as any other person may." How do we get to know a person? Through stories. All the wild and sad and courageous tales that we tell—they are what reveal us to others. We must return to the Scriptures for the story that it is and stop approaching it as if it is an encyclopedia, looking for "tips and techniques."

Reminders of the Story are everywhere—in film and novels, in children's fairy tales, in the natural world around us, and in the stories of our own lives. In fact, every story or movie or song or poem that has ever stirred your soul is telling you something you need to know about the Sacred Romance. Even nature is crying out to us of God's great heart and the drama that is unfolding. Sunrise and sunset tell the tale every day, remembering Eden's glory, prophesying Eden's return. These are the trumpet calls from the "hid battlements of eternity." We must capture them like precious treasures, and hold them close to our hearts.

❖ THE JOURNEY OF DESIRE, 203–4

O Jerusalem, Jerusalem . . . how often I have longed to gather your children together, as a hen gathers her chicks under her wings, but you were not willing.

—MATTHEW 23:37

Any parent or lover knows this: love is chosen. You cannot, in the end, force anyone to love you.

So if you are writing a story where love is the meaning, where love is the highest and best of all, where love is the *point*, then you have to allow each person a choice. You have to allow freedom. You cannot force love. God gives us the dignity of freedom, to choose for or against him (and friends, to ignore him is to choose against him).

This is the reason for what Lewis called the Problem of Pain. Why would a kind and loving God create a world where evil is possible? Doesn't he care about our happiness? Isn't he good? Indeed, he does and he is. He cares so much for our happiness that he endows us with the capacity to love and to be loved, which is the greatest happiness of all. He endows us with a dignity that is almost unimaginable. For this creator God is no puppeteer.

"Trust me in this one thing," God says to us. "I have given the entire earth to you, for your joy. Explore it; awaken it; take care of it for me. And I have given you one another, for love and romance and friendship. You shall be my intimate allies. But on this one matter, you must trust me. Trust that my heart for you is good, that I am withholding this for a reason. Do not eat of the fruit of the Tree of the Knowledge of Good and Evil . . . or you will die."

And this is where our Story takes its tragic turn.

❦ EPIC, 52–54

Be strong and courageous, because you will lead these people to inherit the land I swore to their forefathers to give them. Be strong and very courageous. Be careful to obey all the law my servant Moses gave you; do not turn from it to the right or to the left, that you may be successful wherever you go.

—Joshua 1:6–7

"The spiritual life cannot be made suburban," said Howard Macey. "It is always frontier and we who live in it must accept and even rejoice that it remains untamed." The greatest obstacle to realizing our dreams is the false self's hatred of mystery. That's a problem, you see, because *mystery is essential to adventure.* More than that, mystery is the heart of the universe and the God who made it. The most important aspects of any man's world—his relationship with his God and with the people in his life, his calling, the spiritual battles he'll face—every one of them is fraught with mystery. But that is not a bad thing; it is a joyful, rich part of reality and essential to our soul's thirst for adventure.

There are no formulas with God. Period. God is a Person, not a doctrine. He operates not like a system—not even a theological system—but with all the originality of a truly free and alive person. Take Joshua and the Battle of Jericho. The Israelites are staged to make their first military strike into the Promised Land. This is their D-Day, so to speak, and word is going to get around. How does God get the whole thing off to a good start? He has them march around the city blowing trumpets for a week; on the seventh day he has them do it seven times and then give a big holler. It works marvelously, of course. And you know what? It never happens again. Israel never uses that tactic again.

❧ *Wild at Heart,* 208–9

*Whoever believes in me, as the Scripture has said, streams of living
water will flow from within him.*
—John 7:38

The early church father, Irenaeus, wrote, "The glory of God is
man fully alive."

When I first stumbled across this quote my initial reaction
was . . . *You're kidding me. Really?* I mean, is that what you've
been told? That the purpose of God—the very thing he's staked
his reputation on—is your coming fully alive? Huh. Well, that's
a different take on things. It made me wonder, *What are God's
intentions toward me? What is it I've come to believe about that?*
Yes, we've been told any number of times that God does care, and
there are some pretty glowing promises given to us in Scripture
along those lines. But on the other hand, we have the days of our
lives, and they have a way of casting a rather long shadow over our
hearts when it comes to God's intentions toward *us* in particular.
I read the quote again, "The glory of God is man fully alive," and
something began to stir in me. *Could it be?*

I turned to the New Testament to have another look, read for
myself what Jesus said he offers. "I have come that they may have
life, and have it to the full" (John 10:10). Wow. That's different
from saying, "I have come to forgive you. Period." Forgiveness is
awesome, but Jesus says here he came to give us *life*. Hmmm.
Sounds like ol' Irenaeus might be on to something. "I am the
bread of life" (John 6:48). The more I looked, the more this whole
theme of life jumped off the pages. I mean, it's *everywhere*.

❀ Waking the Dead, *10–11*

It is done. I am the Alpha and the Omega, the Beginning and the End. To him who is thirsty I will give to drink without cost from the spring of the water of life. He who overcomes will inherit all this, and I will be his God and he will be my son.

—REVELATION 21:6–7

Life," as a popular saying goes, "is not a dress rehearsal. Live it to the fullest." What a setup for a loss of heart. No one gets all he desires; no one even comes close. If this is it, we are lost. But what if life *is* a dress rehearsal? What if the real production is about to begin? That is precisely what Jesus says; he tells us that we are being shaped, prepared, groomed for a part in the grand drama that is coming.

How many of your plans take an unending future into account? "Let's see, I'm going to be alive forevermore, so . . . if I don't get this done now, I'll get to it later." This is so important, for no human life reaches its potential here.

I was talking with a playwright several years ago. His career was not panning out the way he deeply wanted it to, and he was becoming rather depressed. It wasn't a matter of being unqualified; he was, and is, a very gifted writer. But few playwrights achieve anything like success. Life wasn't inviting him to be who he was—yet. He had never once considered that he would be a great writer in the coming kingdom, and that he was merely in training now. His day was yet to come. Understanding that put his life in an entirely new light.

❀ *THE JOURNEY OF DESIRE, 158–59*

For his anger lasts only a moment,
but his favor lasts a lifetime;
weeping may remain for a night,
but rejoicing comes in the morning.
—PSALM 30:5

Do we form no friendships because our friends might be taken from us? Do we refuse to love because we may be hurt? Do we forsake our dreams because hope has been deferred? To desire is to open our hearts to the possibility of pain; to shut down our hearts is to die altogether. The full proverb reads this way: "Hope deferred makes the heart sick, *but when dreams come true, there is life and joy.*" The road to life and joy lies through, not around, the heartsickness of hope deferred. A good friend came to this realization recently. As we sat talking over breakfast, he put words to our dilemma:

I stand at the crossroads, and I am afraid of the desire. For forty-one years I've tried to control my life by killing the desire, but I can't. Now I know it. But to allow it to be, to let it out is frightening because I know I'll have to give up the control of my life. Is there another option?

The option most of us have chosen is to reduce our desire to a more manageable size. We allow it out only in small doses—just what we can arrange for. Dinner out, a new sofa, a vacation to look forward to, a little too much to drink. It's not working. The tremors of the earthquake inside are beginning to break out.

❂ *THE JOURNEY OF DESIRE, 23–24*

Do not deceive yourselves. If any one of you thinks he is wise by the standards of this age, he should become a "fool" so that he may become wise.

—1 CORINTHIANS 3:18

We live now in a culture of *expertise*, so completely second nature to us that we don't give it a second thought. Cutting-edge advances in science and technology are now available to anyone. Businesses regularly hire consultants to help edge out their competitors. In business circles experts are sometimes even called sages.

They are worlds apart. A sage differs from an expert the way a lover differs from an engineer. To begin with, expertise quite often has nothing to do with walking with God, may in fact lead us farther from him. For the expertise of the specialist gives us the settled assurance that he has matters under control, and that we will also, as soon as we put our trust in him. That is why we love him.

The psychology of expertise comes indistinguishably close to the psychology of the Tower of Babel. "We have matters under our control now. Expertise has given us power over our destinies."

Now of course, there is nothing wrong with expertise. I'd be the first one to find the best heart surgeon should my son need heart surgery. But what are we to make of the passage that tells us, "Everything that does not come from faith is sin" (Rom. 14:23)? Whatever, whenever, wherever we place our hopes and confidence in something other than God, that is sin. Given mankind's nearly limitless ability to rely on anything else, can you see how the culture of expertise actually plays into our godlessness?

❁ *FATHERED BY GOD, 196–197*

It is the Father, living in me, who is doing his work.
—JOHN 14:1

The Sage communes with God—an existence entirely different from and utterly superior to the life of the expert. Whatever
counsel the Sage offers, it draws you to God, not to self-reliance.
Oh, yes, the sage has wisdom, gleaned from years of experience,
and that wisdom is a great offerings. But he has learned not to lean
upon his wisdom, knowing that often God is asking things of us
that seem counterintuitive, and thus the sage's wisdom (and expertise) are fully submitted to his God. Humility might be one of the
great dividing lines between the expert and the Sage, for the Sage
doesn't think he is one. "Do you see a man wise in his own eyes?
There is more hope for a fool than for him" (Prov. 26:12). Thus we
might not know we have a sage at the table, for he will remain
silent while the "experts" prattle on and on. The experts impress.
The Sage draws us to God. He offers a gift of presence, the richness of a soul that has lived long *with God*.

❧ FATHERED BY GOD, 197–98

*Therefore we do not lose heart. Though outwardly we are wasting
away, yet inwardly we are being renewed day by day.*
—2 CORINTHIANS 4:16

We are not what we were meant to be, and we know it. If,
when passing a stranger on the street, we happen to meet
eyes, we quickly avert our glance. Cramped into the awkward community of an elevator, we search for something, anything to look at
instead of each other. We sense that our real self is ruined, and we
fear to be seen. But think for a moment about the millions of tour-
ists who visit ancient sites like the Parthenon, the Colosseum, and
the Pyramids. Though ravaged by time, the elements, and vandals
through the ages, mere shadows of their former glory, these ruins
still awe and inspire. Though fallen, their glory cannot be fully
extinguished. There is something at once sad and grand about
them. And such we are. Abused, neglected, vandalized, fallen—we
are still fearful and wonderful. We are, as one theologian put it,
"glorious ruins." But unlike those grand monuments, we who are
Christ's have been redeemed and are being renewed as Paul said,
"day by day," restored in the love of God.

Could it be that we, all of us, the homecoming queens and
quarterbacks and the passed over and picked on, really possess
hidden greatness? Is there something in us worth fighting over?
The fact that we don't see our own glory is part of the tragedy of
the Fall; a sort of spiritual amnesia has taken all of us.

❂ *THE SACRED ROMANCE*, 93–95

*While Jesus was here on earth, he offered prayers and pleadings, with
a loud cry and tears, to the one who could deliver him.*
—Hebrews 5:7 nlt

H ebrews 5:7 doesn't sound like the way prayers are offered up
in most churches on a typical Sunday morning. "Dear Lord,
we thank you for this day, and we ask you to be with us in all we
say and do. Amen." No pleading here, no loud cries and tears.
Our prayers are cordial, modest, even reverent. Eugene Peterson
calls them "cut-flower prayers." They are not like Jesus' prayers or,
for that matter, like the psalms. The ranting and raving, the passion and ecstasy, the fury and desolation found in the psalms are
so far from our religious expression that it seems hard to believe
they were given to us as our *guide* to prayer. They seem so, well,
desperate. Yet E. M. Bounds reminds us,

> Desire gives fervor to prayer. The soul cannot be listless
> when some great desire fixes and inflames it . . . Strong
> desires make strong prayers . . . The neglect of prayer is the
> fearful token of dead spiritual desires . . . There can be no
> true praying without desire. (*Man of Prayer*)

❖   *The Journey of Desire*, 59–60

My soul yearns, even faints,
for the courts of the LORD;
my heart and my flesh cry out
for the living God.
—PSALM 84:2

I came to know a delightful woman with a poet's heart, whose soul was buried beneath years not so much of tragedy but of neglect. This one particular afternoon, we had spoken for more than an hour of how deeply she longed for love, how almost completely ignored and misunderstood she felt her entire life. It was a tender, honest, and deeply moving session. As our time drew to a close, I asked her if she would pray with me. I could hardly believe what came next. She assumed a rather bland, religious tone to her voice and said something to the effect of "God, thank you for being here. Show me what I ought to do." I found myself speechless. *You've got to be kidding me*, I thought. *That's not how you feel at all. I know your heart's true cry. You are far more desperate than that.*

Why are we so embarrassed by our desire? Why do we pretend that we're doing fine, thank you, that we don't need a thing? The persistent widow wasn't too proud to seek help. Neither was the psalmist. Their humility allowed them to express their desire. How little we come to God with what really matters to us. How rare it is that we even admit it to ourselves. Wouldn't it be better to bury the disappointment and the yearning and just get on with life? As Larry Crabb has pointed out, pretending seems a much more reliable road to Christian maturity. The only price we pay is a loss of soul, of communion with God, a loss of direction, and a loss of hope.

❖ *THE JOURNEY OF DESIRE, 60–61*

One thing God has spoken,
two things have I heard:
that you, O God, are strong,
and that you, O Lord, are loving.
—PSALM 62:11–12

The reason a woman wants a beauty to unveil, the reason she asks, *Do you delight in me?* is simply that God does as well. God is captivating beauty. As David prays, "One thing I ask of the LORD, this is what I seek: that I may . . . gaze upon the beauty of the LORD" (Ps. 27:4). Can there be any doubt that God wants to be *worshiped*? That he wants to be seen, and for us to be captivated by what we see? As C. S. Lewis wrote, "The beauty of the female is the root of joy to the female as well as to the male . . . to desire the enjoying of her own beauty is the obedience of Eve, and to both it is in the lover that the beloved tastes of her own delightfulness."

This is far too simple an outline, I admit. There is so much more to say, and these are not hard and rigid categories. A man needs to be tender at times, and a woman will sometimes need to be fierce. But if a man is only tender, we know something is deeply wrong, and if a woman is only fierce, we sense she is not what she was meant to be. If you'll look at the essence of little boys and little girls, I think you'll find I am not far from my mark. Strength and beauty.

❖   *WILD AT HEART*, 37–38

So it is written: "The first man Adam became a living being"; the last Adam, a life-giving spirit. The spiritual did not come first, but the natural, and after that the spiritual. The first man was of the dust of the earth, the second man from heaven.

—1 CORINTHIANS 15:45–47

Jesus of Nazareth is given many names in Scripture. He is called the Lion of Judah. The Wonderful Counselor. The Prince of Peace. The Lamb of God. There are many, many more—each one a window into all that he truly is, all that he has done, all that he will do. But one name seems to have escaped our attention, and that might help explain our misunderstanding of the gospel. Paul refers to Jesus as the Last Adam and the Second Man (1 Cor. 15:45–47). Why is this important? Because of what happened through the *First* Adam.

Our first father, Adam, and our first mother, Eve, were destined to be the root and trunk of humanity. What they were meant to be, we were meant to be: the kings and queens of the earth, the rulers over all creation, the glorious image bearers of a glorious God. Our natures and our destinies were bound up in theirs. Their choices would forever shape our lives, for good or for evil. It is deep mystery, but we see something of a hint of it in the way children so often follow in the steps of their parents. As the old saying goes, the fruit doesn't fall far from the tree.

Our first parents chose, and it was on the side of evil. They broke the one command, the only command, God gave to them, and what followed you can watch any night on the news. The long lament of human history. Something went wrong in their hearts, something *shifted*, and that shift was passed along to each of us.

❁ *WAKING THE DEAD, 59–60*

Sin entered the world through one man . . . through the disobedience of the one man the many were made sinners.

—ROMANS 5:12, 19

Parents will often wonder where their toddlers learned to lie or how they came into the world so self-centered. It doesn't need to be taught to them; it is inherent to human nature. Paul makes clear in Romans. Of course, I am simply restating the doctrine of original sin, a core tenet of Christianity essential in Scripture.

But that is not the end of the Story, thank God. The first Adam was only "a pattern of the one to come" (Rom. 5:14). He would foreshadow another man, the head of a new race, the firstborn of a new creation, whose life would mean transformation to those who would become joined to him: "For just as through the disobedience of the one man Adam the many were made sinners, so also through the obedience of the one man Christ, the Last Adam the many will be made righteous" (Rom. 5:19).

A man comes down from heaven, slips into our world unnoticed, as Neo does in *The Matrix*, as Maximus does in *Gladiator*, as Wallace does in *Braveheart*. Yet he is no ordinary man, and his mission no ordinary mission. He comes as a substitute, a representative, as the destroyer of one system and the seed of something new. His death and resurrection break the power of the Matrix, release the prisoners, set the captives free. It is a historic fact. It really happened. And it is more than history. It is mythic in the first degree. Lewis said, "By becoming fact, it does not cease to be myth; that is the miracle."

❧ WAKING THE DEAD, 60

"Although you wash yourself with soda
and use an abundance of soap,
the stain of your guilt is still before me,"
declares the Sovereign LORD.

—JEREMIAH 2:22

In our psychological age, we have come to call our affairs "addictions," but God calls them "adultery." Listen again to his words to the Israelites through Jeremiah:

You are a swift she-camel
    running here and there,
a wild donkey accustomed to the desert,
    sniffing the wind in your craving—
    in your heat how can I restrain you?
Any males that pursue you need not tire themselves;
    at mating time they will find you.
Do not run until your feet are bare
    and your throat is dry. (Jer. 2:23–25)

Perhaps we can empathize with the ache God experienced as Israel's "husband" (and ours when we are living indulgently). Having raised Israel from childhood to a woman of grace and beauty, he astonishingly cannot win her heart from her adulterous lovers. The living God of the universe cannot win the only one he loves, not due to any lack on his part but because her heart is captured by her addictions, which is to say, her adulterous lovers.

❖ THE SACRED ROMANCE, 134–35

221

We have this hope as an anchor for the soul, firm and secure.
—HEBREWS 6:19

Once we come to accept that we can never find or hang on to the life we have been seeking, what then? As Dallas Willard writes, it matters for all the world to know that life is ahead of us.

> I meet many faithful Christians who, in spite of their faith, are deeply disappointed in how their lives have turned out. Sometimes it is simply a matter of how they experience aging, which they take to mean they no longer have a future. But often, due to circumstances or wrongful decisions and actions by others, what they had hoped to accomplish in life they did not . . . Much of the distress of these good people comes from a failure to realize that their life lies before them . . . the life that lies endlessly before us in the kingdom of God. (*The Divine Conspiracy*)

Pascal also observed, "We are never living, but hoping to live; and whilst we are always preparing to be happy, it is certain, we never shall be so, if we aspire to no other happiness than what can be enjoyed in this life."

Desire cannot live without hope. Yet, we can only hope for what we desire. There simply must be something more, something out there on the road ahead of us, that offers the life we prize. To sustain the life of the heart, the life of deep desire, we desperately need to possess a clearer picture of the life that lies before us.

❧ *THE JOURNEY OF DESIRE, 104–5*

I have much more to say to you, more than you can now bear. But when he, the Spirit of truth, comes, he will guide you into all truth.
—JOHN 16:12–13

There's more that Jesus wants to say to you, much more, and now that his Spirit resides in your heart, the conversation can continue. "He who belongs to God hears what God says" (John 8:47). Many good people never hear God speak to them personally for the simple fact that they've never been told that he *does*. But he does—generously, intimately. Jesus explains:

The man who enters by the gate is the shepherd of his sheep. The watchman opens the gate for him, and the sheep listen to his voice. He calls his own sheep by name and leads them out. When he has brought out all his own, he goes on ahead of them, and his sheep follow him because they know his voice . . . I am the good shepherd. (John 10:2–4, 11)

You don't just leave sheep to find their way in the world. They are famous for getting lost, being attacked by wild animals, falling into some pit, and that is why they must stay close to the shepherd, follow his voice. And no shepherd could be called good unless he personally guided his flock through danger. But that is precisely what he promises to do. He *wants* to speak to you; he wants to lead you to good pasture. Now, it doesn't happen in an instant. Walking with God is a way of life. It's something to be learned; our ability to hear God's voice and discern his word to us grows over time. As Brother Lawrence had it, we "practice the presence of God."

❖ WAKING THE DEAD, 102–3

He who belongs to God hears what God says.
—JOHN 8:47

When we set out to hear God's voice, we do not listen as though it will come from somewhere above us or in the room around us. It comes to us from *within*, from the heart, the dwelling place of God. Now, most of us haven't been trained in this, and it's going to take a little practice "tuning in" to all that's going on in there. And there's a lot going on in there, by the way. Many things are trying to play upon the beautiful instrument of the heart. The devil is a master at manipulating the heart. So are many people—though they would never admit that is what they are doing. How will you know what is compelling you? "Who can map out the various forces at play in one soul?" asked Augustine, a man who was the first to write out the story of listening to his heart. "Man is a great depth, O Lord . . . but the hairs of his head are easier by far to count than . . . the movements of his heart."

This can be distressing at times. All sorts of awful things can seem to issue from your heart—anger, lust, fear, petty jealousies. If you think it's you, a reflection of what's really going on in your heart, it will disable you. What you've encountered is either the voice of your flesh or an attempt of the Enemy to distress you by throwing all sorts of thoughts your way and blaming you for it. You must proceed on this assumption: if you are a believer in Jesus Christ, your heart is good.

❈ *WAKING THE DEAD, 105–6*

Behold, you desire truth in the innermost being.
—PSALM 51:6 NASB

Wise counsel doesn't just flow to us directly from Christ, *only* from him; it flows through his people as well. We need others—and need them deeply. Yes, the Spirit was sent to be our Counselor. Yes, Jesus speaks to us personally. But often he works through another human being. The fact is, we are usually too close to our lives to see what's going on. Because it's *our* story we're trying to understand, we sometimes don't know what's true or false, what's real or imagined. We can't see the forest for the trees. It often takes the eyes of someone to whom we can tell our story, bare our soul. The more dire our straits, the more difficult it can be to hear directly from God.

In every great story the hero or heroine must turn to someone older or wiser for the answer to some riddle. Dorothy seeks the Wizard; Frodo turns to Gandalf; Neo has Morpheus; and Curdie is helped by the Lady of the Silver Moon.

Having a doctrine pass before the mind is not what the Bible means by knowing the truth. It's only when it reaches down deep into the heart that the truth begins to set us free, just as a key must penetrate a lock to turn it, or as rainfall must saturate the earth down to the roots in order for your garden to grow.

Getting it there is the work of the stream we'll call Counseling.

❖ *WAKING THE DEAD, 124–27*

The people remained at a distance, while Moses approached the thick darkness where God was.

—EXODUS 20:21

Several years ago I went through one of the most painful trials of my professional life. The story involves a colleague whom I will call Dave. We spent many hours on the road together, speaking to churches about the Christian life. A point came when I needed to confront Dave about some issues in his life that were hurting his own ministry and the larger purposes of our team. In all fairness, I think I handled it poorly, but I was totally unprepared for what happened next. Dave turned on me with the ferocity of a cornered animal. He fabricated lies and spread rumors in an attempt to destroy my career. His actions were so out of proportion it was hard to believe we were reacting to the same events. He went to the head pastor in an attempt to have me dismissed. The attempt failed, but our friendship was lost, and several others were hurt in the process.

In the midst of the crisis, I spoke with Brent one afternoon about the turn of events and the awful pain of betrayal. He said "I wonder what God is up to in all this?"

"God?" I said. "What's *he* got to do with it?" My practical agnosticism was revealed. I was caught up in the socio-drama, the smaller story, completely blind to the true story at that point in my life. Brent's question arrested my attention and brought it to a higher level. In fact, the process of our sanctification, our journey, rests entirely on our ability to see life from the basis of that question.

❧ THE SACRED ROMANCE, 146–47

It is written in the Prophets: "They will all be taught by God."
Everyone who listens to the Father and learns from him comes to me.
—JOHN 6:45

There is wisdom, and there is revelation. They go together, hand in hand. "I keep asking that the God of our Lord Jesus Christ, the glorious Father, may give you the Spirit of wisdom and revelation, so that you may know him better" (Ephesians 1:17). From the Spirit come both wisdom and revelation. We need them both to walk with God, need them in generous doses. If you're the sort of person who tends to lean toward revelation (just asking God for direct guidance), then you need to balance your approach with wisdom. If you lean toward a wisdom approach to life, you must deliberately and consciously include revelation. Ask God. And if you operate for the most part with neither, you are in real trouble.

Knowing that, we need to admit that risk is always involved when we encourage others to walk with God. People have done a lot of really stupid things in the name of following Jesus. For that reason there are folks in the church who don't want to encourage this sort of risk, this "walking with God." Over the centuries they have tried to eliminate the messiness of personal relationship with Jesus by instituting rules, programs, formulas, methods, and procedures. Those things may have eliminated some of the goofy things that happen when people are encouraged to follow God for themselves. But those things also eliminated the very intimacy God calls us to.

Don't surrender this treasure of intimacy with God just because it can get messy.

❖ WALKING WITH GOD, 203–5

He wakens me morning by morning,
wakens my ear to listen like one being taught.
—ISAIAH 50:4

The Bible teaches that we hear God's voice:

> He calls his own sheep by name and leads them out . . . and
> his sheep follow him because they know his voice. I know
> my sheep and my sheep know me—just as the Father
> knows me and I know the Father—and I lay down my life
> for the sheep. I have other sheep that are not of this sheep
> pen. I must bring them also. They too will listen to my
> voice." (John 10:2–4, 14–16)

We are his sheep. Jesus says that his sheep hear his voice. "Here
I am! I stand at the door and knock. If anyone hears my voice and
opens the door, I will come in and eat with him, and he with me"
(Revelation 3:20). Jesus is speaking. He makes an offer. Who is
the offer for? "Anyone." That would include you.

What does Jesus say will happen? "Hears my voice." As in, hear
his voice. And if we respond to his voice and his knocking, what
will Jesus do? "I will come in and eat with him, and he with me."
He offers intimacy with us. What could be clearer? We are made
for intimacy with God. He wants intimacy with us. That intimacy
requires communication. God speaks to his people.

❖ *WALKING WITH GOD, 14–15*

We are the people of his pasture,
the flock under his care.
Today, if you hear his voice,
do not harden your hearts.
—PSALM 95:7–8

If you've been taught that God doesn't speak to you, then you're probably not going to be listening for his voice. This all comes down to what kind of relationship you think God offers. "It takes time," I said. "It's something we learn. Name one thing in your life that you really enjoy doing that didn't require practice to get there."

If you want to make music, you have to learn how to play an instrument. And in the beginning, it doesn't sound too good— all the squawks and squeaks and bad timing. You really *are* on your way to making music. It just sounds like you're strangling a pig. If you stick with it, something beautiful begins to emerge. Or how about snowboarding—learning to do that is really awkward at first. You fall down a lot. You feel like an idiot. But if you hang in there, you come to enjoy it. You get better. It starts to feel natural. That's when it becomes fun. This holds true for anything in life. Including our walk with God. It takes time and practice. It's awkward at first, and sometimes we feel stupid. But if we hang in there, we do begin to get it, and as it becomes more and more natural, our lives are filled with his presence and all the joy and beauty and pleasure that come with it.

It is something to be learned. And it is worth learning.

❁ *WALKING WITH GOD, 16–17*

When the woman saw that the fruit of the tree was good for food and
pleasing to the eye, and also desirable for gaining wisdom, she took
some and ate it. She also gave some to her husband, who was with her,
and he ate it.

—GENESIS 3:6

God gives Adam some instructions on the care of creation, and his role in the unfolding story. It's pretty basic, and very generous (see Gen. 2:16–17).

Adam doesn't need play-by-play instructions because this is what Adam is *for*. It's already there, everything he needs, in his design, in his heart.

Needless to say, the story doesn't go well. Adam fails; he fails Eve, and the rest of humanity. Let me ask you a question: Where is Adam, while the serpent is tempting Eve? He's standing right there: "She also gave some to her husband, who was with her. Then he ate it, too" (Gen. 3:6 NLT). The Hebrew for "with her" means right there, elbow to elbow. Adam isn't away in another part of the forest; he has no alibi. He is standing right there, watching the whole thing unravel. What does he do? Nothing. Absolutely nothing. He says not a word, doesn't lift a finger. He won't risk, he won't fight, and he won't rescue Eve. Our first father—the first real man—gave in to paralysis. He denied his very nature and went passive. And every man after him, every son of Adam, carries in his heart now the same failure.

Every man repeats the sin of Adam, every day. We won't risk, we won't fight, and we won't rescue Eve. We truly are a chip off the old block.

❖ WILD AT HEART, 50–51

All my longings lie open before you, O Lord;
my sighing is not hidden from you.
—PSALM 38:9

Indeed, if we will listen, a Sacred Romance calls to us through our hearts every moment of our lives. It whispers to us on the wind, invites us through the laughter of good friends, reaches out to us through the touch of someone we love. We've heard it in our favorite music, sensed it at the birth of our first child, been drawn to it while watching the shimmer of a sunset on the ocean. The Romance is even present in times of great personal suffering: the illness of a child, the loss of a marriage, the death of a friend. Something calls to us through experiences like these and rouses an inconsolable longing deep within our heart, wakening in us a yearning for intimacy, beauty, and adventure.

This longing is the most powerful part of any human personality. It fuels our search for meaning, for wholeness, for a sense of being truly alive. However we may describe this deep desire, it is the most important thing about us, our heart of hearts, the passion of our life. And the voice that calls to us in this place is none other than the voice of God.

We cannot hear this voice if we have lost touch with our hearts.

❀ *THE SACRED ROMANCE, 6–7*

Whom have I in heaven but you?
And earth has nothing I desire besides you.
My flesh and my heart may fail,
but God is the strength of my heart
and my portion forever.
—PSALM 73:25–26

"God is good," the Romance tells us. "You can release the well-being of your heart to him." The Arrows of Satan strike back, "Don't ever let life out of your control," and they seem to impale with such authority, unlike the gentle urges of the Romance, that in the end we are driven to find some way to contain them. The only way seems to be to kill our longing for the Romance, much in the same way we harden our heart to someone who hurts us. *If I don't want so much*, we believe, *I won't be so vulnerable*. Instead of dealing with the Arrows, we silence the longing. That seems to be our only hope. And so we lose heart.

Which is the truer message? If we try to hang on to the Romance, what are we to do with our wounds and the awful tragedies of life? How can we keep our heart alive in the face of such deadly Arrows? How many losses can a heart take? If we deny the wounds or try to minimize them, we deny a part of our heart and end up living a shallow optimism that frequently becomes a demand that the world be better than it is. On the other hand, if we embrace the Arrows as the final word on life, we despair, which is another way to lose heart. To lose hope has the same effect on our heart as to stop breathing.

❖ *THE SACRED ROMANCE*, 33

I will not leave you as orphans; I will come to You.
—JOHN 14:18

What is it that he sees in us that causes him to act the jealous lover, to lay siege both on the kingdom of darkness and on our own idolatries as if on Troy—not to annihilate, but to win us once again for himself? This fierce intention, this reckless ambition that shoves all conventions aside, willing literally to move heaven and earth—what does he want from us?

We've been offered many explanations. From one religious camp we're told that what God wants is obedience, or sacrifice, or adherence to the right doctrines, or morality. Those are the answers offered by conservative churches. The more therapeutic churches suggest that no, God is after our contentment, or happiness, or self-actualization, or something else along those lines. He is concerned about all these things, of course, but they are not his primary concern. What he is after is *us*—our laughter, our tears, our dreams, our fears, our heart of hearts. How few of us truly believe this. We've never been wanted for our heart, our truest self, not really, not for long. The thought that God wants our heart seems too good to be true.

❖ *THE SACRED ROMANCE, 91*

There is a way that seems right to a man
but in the end it leads to death.
—PROVERBS 16:25

God thwarts our plan for salvation; he shatters the false self. Our plan for redemption is hard to let go of; it clings to our hearts like an octopus.

Why would God do something so terrible as to wound us in the place of our deepest wound? Jesus warned us that "whoever wants to save his life will lose it" (Luke 9:24). Christ is not using the word *bios* here; he's not talking about our physical life. The passage is not about trying to save your skin by ducking martyrdom or something like that. The word Christ uses for "life" is the word *psyche*—the word for our soul, our inner self, our heart. He says that the things we do to save our psyche, our self, those plans to save and protect our inner life—those are the things that will actually destroy us.

"There is a way that seems right to a man but in the end it leads to death," says Proverbs 16:25. The false self, our plan for redemption, seems so right to us. It shields us from pain and secures us a little love and admiration. But the false self is a lie; the whole plan is built on pretense. It's a deadly trap. God loves us too much to leave us there. So he thwarts us, in many, many different ways.

❧ WILD AT HEART, *107–8*

I will be a Father to you, and you will be my sons.
—2 CORINTHIANS 6:18

Life will test you, men. Like a ship at sea, you *will* be tested, and the storms will reveal the weak places in you as a person. They already have. How else do you account for the anger you feel, the fear, the vulnerability to certain temptations? Why can't you marry the girl? Having married, why can't you handle her emotions? Why haven't you found your life's mission? Why do financial crises send you into a rage or depression? You know what I speak of. And so our basic approach to life comes down to this: we stay in what we can handle, and steer clear of everything else. We engage where we feel we can or we must—as at work—and we hold back where we feel sure to fail, as in the deep waters of relating to our wife or our children, and in our spirituality.

You see, what we have now is a world of uninitiated men. Partial men. Boys, mostly, walking around in men's bodies, with men's jobs and families, finances, and responsibilities. The passing on of masculinity was never completed, if it was begun at all. The boy was never taken through the process of masculine initiation. That's why most of us are unfinished men. And therefore unable to truly live *as* men in whatever life throws at us. And unable to pass on to our sons and daughters what *they* need to become whole and holy men and women themselves.

❀ *FATHERED BY GOD, 6–7*

Your love, O LORD, reaches to the heavens,
your faithfulness to the skies.
Your righteousness is like the mighty mountains,
your justice like the great deep.
—PSALM 36:5–6

Down through its history, the church has held up the good, the true, and the beautiful as a sort of trinity of virtues. As we think over the stages of the masculine journey, we find that the boy begins to understand Good as he learns right from wrong, and the warrior fights for what is True, but when a man comes to see that the Beautiful is the best of the three, then is the lover awakened.

Awakening with his passion for a battle you will often find another longing emerging, a longing for . . . he knows not what. An ache, often expressed in music, or perhaps poetry, a film or a book that stirs him like never before. His soul is undergoing a sort of second birth. He begins to *notice*. Sees moonlight on water for the very first time. Is stopped by certain movements in a song he loves. Pauses to realize that a snowflake or a flower is really altogether amazing. Discovers authors that stir him with some special quality in their writings. Now yes, it is often aroused by a woman.

Woman is the personification of Beauty, and it often takes her to turn the young man's attention from adventure and battle, "turn his head," as the phrase has it, and his heart comes along for the turning too. But often the awakening comes in the world of Nature. You see this in the poetry of David, whose lines are filled with the sun and stars, the dew of the fields, the brooks from which he drank so deeply.

❀ *FATHERED BY GOD, 127–28*

Let love be your highest goal!
—1 CORINTHIANS 14:1

There are many reasons a man shies away from the world of the heart and from his own heart. It might be that he is shamed when he tries to go there by a father who thinks that art, creativity, and beauty "are girl's stuff." Thus, to him, the heart is a source of pain and embarrassment. He thinks a man cannot be a true man and live from the heart. It may be that he has simply never been invited to know his own heart.

But we must remember Adam's fall, and the fierce commitment fallen men all share: never be in a position where you don't know what to do. Reason and analysis are predictable, manageable. They make us feel that things are under our control. I believe that is why many men stay there. It's safe—even if it kills your soul.

The lover might come partially alive when a man meets a woman and falls in love, and for a time his heart seems alive and their romance blossoms. But things begin to fade, and neither he nor she knows why. The reason: he stopped the progression, never went on to know God as Lover. No woman can satisfy this longing in a man's heart, and no good woman wants to try. When he makes her the center of his universe, it feels romantic for a while, but then the planets start to collide. It's not a big enough romance. He will find his heart awakening again when he opens his heart to God, and though he might have to journey there for a season, he'll find he has something to offer his woman again.

❧ *FATHERED BY GOD, 143–44*

Choose for yourselves this day whom you will serve.
—JOSHUA 24:15

Watch how Moses leads Israel out of bondage and guides them to the Promised Land. Notice how every chapter telling the story of the Exodus begins, from chapter 6 to chapter 14: "Then the Lord said to Moses," and the rest of the chapter is Moses doing what God told him to do.

Is this how the men you know run their corporations, their churches, their families? I'm stunned by how little daily guidance Christian men seek from God. They have a good idea, and they just go do it. Not the great kings. Look at David. "In the course of time, David inquired of the Lord. 'Shall I go up to one of the towns of Judah?' he asked. The Lord said, 'Go up.' David asked, 'Where shall I go?' 'To Hebron,' the Lord answered. So David went up there" (2 Sam. 2:1–2). In his heart, and in his daily practice, David is a man yielded to God. He is called, may I remind you, a man after God's own heart.

Regardless of age, position, or natural abilities, a man is ready to become a king only when his heart is in the right place. Meaning, *yielded to God*.

❁ FATHERED BY GOD, *163*

The Lord God will give him the throne of his father David, and he will reign over the house of Jacob forever; his kingdom will never end.
—LUKE 1:32–33

This, my brother, is what has happened to you through the work of Christ. Let me repeat, for this understanding about the kingdom of God is not broadly explained in the church just now. Adam (and all his sons, including you) was given the earth to rule. Born a King. He abdicated that authority to Satan through his sin and fall. But Jesus came and won it back, the Father giving all authority on earth to him. Jesus in turn shares that authority with us, gives us his authority, to rule in his name. For as he said, the Father is delighted to give us the kingdom (Luke 12:32). The course of a man's life is coming to the place where he can be made a king in his experience, where all that Christ has bestowed can be *realized* in the man's life.

❀ *FATHERED BY GOD, 178–79*

*Pay attention and listen to the sayings of the wise;
apply your heart to what I teach.*
—PROVERBS 22:17

As the ministry we started in 2000 began to take off like a wild horse, I found myself in desperate need of counsel. I sought out a well-known pastor, whose humility I will respect by leaving him unnamed. We sat in a café while I riddled him with questions about the growth of his own ministry and how he handled it. He said, "Of course, it is my joy to do this. But God has asked me to do certain things I did not want to do, and yet I did them because the kingdom needed it."

That was the threshold I was about to step over—to accept the burden of becoming a king, a burden I did not want but felt God was asking me to bear. And while this old saint's counsel was immensely helpful to me, there was something more given during our two hours that even still I find hard to describe. To sit with a man who has walked with God some seventy-plus years, to be in the presence of a father, to have the eyes of a wise and gracious man fixed upon you, to have his heart willingly offer you affirmation and counsel—that is a sort of food the soul of a man craves. All my years of loneliness and fatherlessness came into stark contrast.

I could have wept.

❖ *FATHERED BY GOD, 198–99*

Though an army besiege me,
my heart will not fear;
though war break out against me,
even then will I be confident.
One thing I ask of the LORD,
this is what I seek:
that I may dwell in the house of the LORD
all the days of my life,
to gaze upon the beauty of the LORD
and to seek him in his temple.

—PSALM 27:3–4

Our life *is* a quest arranged by our Father, for our initiation. There are gifts along the way to remind us that we are his beloved sons. Adventures to call forth the cowboy, and battles to train the warrior. There is beauty to awaken the lover, and power on behalf of others to prepare the king. A lifetime of experience from which the sage will speak.

And now, the trail calls us on. Remember this: I will not leave you as orphans; I will come to you. . . . My Father will love him, and we will come to him and make our home with him (John 14:18, 23).

As George MacDonald so wisely stated, "Because we are the sons of God, we must become the sons of God."

❈ FATHERED BY GOD, *219*

Resist the devil, and he will flee from you.
—JAMES 4:7

Whenever I'm facing spiritual attack of any kind, the pull is nearly always to try and ignore it, push it off till later, or explain it away as bad digestion or my ongoing inadequacies or something else. Anything else. I see this in all my friends as well. We just don't want to deal with it.

God gave us a will. Learning to exercise it is a great part of maturing as a person. You don't want to get out of bed in the morning? You'll lose your job. You don't want to deny yourself anything? You'll go into debt. This is Growing Up 101. And there is nothing like spiritual warfare to teach you to exercise your will. For one thing, you won't want to deal with it. So the best thing you can do is turn, face the attack, and deal with it. Now. It strengthens your will. But most Christians end up not really praying directly against the attack. They'll pray something like *Jesus, I ask you to take this away.* If it's discouragement they're dealing with, they may pray, *I ask you to encourage me.* And it's a good thing to be encouraged. Or let's say it's lust they've been confronted with. Most folks will then pray, *Give me pure thoughts, Lord.* And it's a good thing to ask for pure thoughts. But they are still dodging the issue. As the Scripture urges, "Resist the devil, and he will flee from you" (James 4:7).

No resist, no flee.

❧ *WALKING WITH GOD, 53–54*

I have fought the good fight, I have finished the course, I have kept the faith.

—2 TIMOTHY 4:7

One day the young man Moses, prince of Egypt, went out to see for himself the oppression of his kinsmen. When he witnessed firsthand an Egyptian taskmaster beating a Hebrew slave, he couldn't bear it and killed the man. A rash act, for which he became a fugitive, but you see something of the warrior emerging in him. Years later, God sends him back to set all his people free, and, I might add, it is one intense fight to win that freedom. David also fights, battle after battle, to win the freedom of his people and unite the tribes of Israel. Something in the man compelled him, that same something that wouldn't allow Lincoln to simply sit by and watch the Union tear itself apart, wouldn't permit Churchill—despite the views of many of his own countrymen—to sit by and let the Nazis take over Europe unopposed. For he knew that in the end they would have England, too.

There are certain things worth fighting for. A marriage, for example, or the institution of marriage as a whole. Children, whether they are yours or not. Friendships will have to be fought for, as you've discovered by now, and churches, too, which seem bent on destroying themselves if they are not first destroyed by the enemy who hates them. Many people feel that earth itself is worth fighting for. Doctors fight for the lives of their patients, and teachers for the hearts and futures of their students. Take anything good, true, or beautiful upon this earth and ask yourself, "Can this be protected without a fight?"

❈ FATHERED BY GOD, 92–93

The LORD your God, who is going before you, will fight for you.
—DEUTERONOMY 1:29–30

O
ne of the saddest of all the sad stories in the history of God's people comes shortly after the dramatic exodus from Egypt, as they stood on the threshold of the Promised Land.

> But you were unwilling to go up; you rebelled against the command of the LORD your God. You grumbled in your tents and said, "The LORD hates us; so he brought us out of Egypt to deliver us into the hands of the Amorites to destroy us. Where can we go? . . . They say, 'The people are stronger and taller than we are; the cities are large, with walls up to the sky. We even saw the Anakites there.'" Then I said to you, "Do not be terrified; do not be afraid of them. The LORD your God, who is going before you, will fight for you. [Not "comfort you." Not "be with you in your distress, defeated by your enemies." *Fight for you*], as he did for you in Egypt, before your very eyes, and in the desert. There you saw how the LORD your God carried you, as a father carries his son, all the way you went until you reached this place." In spite of this, you did not trust in the LORD your God. . . . Then you replied, "We have sinned against the LORD. We will go up and fight, as the LORD our God commanded us." (Deut. 1:26–32, 41; my comment in brackets)

Their decision *not* to fight led to their desert wandering. They suffered the consequence of refusing to trust God, and fight.

❁ *FATHERED BY GOD*, 95–96

My dear child, don't shrug off God's discipline,
  but don't be crushed by it either.
It's the child he loves that he disciplines;
  the child he embraces, he also corrects.
—HEBREWS 12:5–6 *The Message*

Now, there is discipline and there is *discipline*. The church has largely presented discipline as "kill your heart and just do the right thing." That is terrible. It wearies the soul, and ends up destroying the heart. Good discipline *harnesses* the passions. When Jesus "set his face like flint" toward Jerusalem, he manifested an inner resolve that came from deep within, from his heart.

This inner resolve is what is so sorely tested in Jesus as Satan comes to him in the wilderness, probing his defenses, looking for some angle, some hook to get Christ to give in and yield to temptation. Christ does not. This is absolutely essential to the warrior, to develop an unyielding heart. This is where *we* will be most profoundly tested. Though Paul is stoned, whipped, thrown into prison for preaching the gospel, he is undaunted. He will not be turned, and for that we have the books of Ephesians, Philippians, Colossians, and Philemon. Bunyan wrote *Pilgrim's Progress* from prison, and Alexander Solzhenitsyn continued his resistance of Soviet Communism from the gulag. I will not yield, I will not be a quitter—that is the warrior coming out.

❉ *FATHERED BY GOD, 104–105*

But whenever anyone turns to the Lord, the veil is taken away. Now the Lord is the Spirit, and where the Spirit of the Lord is, there is freedom. And we, who with unveiled faces all reflect the Lord's glory, are being transformed into his likeness with ever-increasing glory, which comes from the Lord, who is the Spirit.

—2 CORINTHIANS 3:16–18

We have no idea who we really are. Whatever glory was bestowed, whatever glory is being restored, we thought this whole Christian thing was about . . . something else. Trying not to sin. Going to church. Being nice. Jesus says it is about healing your heart, setting it free, restoring your glory. A religious fog has tried to veil all that, put us under some sort of spell or amnesia, to keep us from coming alive. As Pascal said, "It is a monstrous thing . . . an incomprehensible enchantment, and a supernatural slumber." And, Paul said, it is time to take that veil away.

A veil removed, bringing freedom, transformation, glory. Do you see it? I am not making this up—though I have been accused of making the gospel better than it is. The charge is laughable. Could anyone be more generous than God? Could any of us come up with a story that beats the one God has come up with?

❈ WAKING THE DEAD, 80–81

Don't be deceived, my dear brothers. Every good and perfect gift is from above, coming down from the Father of the heavenly lights, who does not change like shifting shadows. He chose to give us birth through the word of truth, that we might be a kind of firstfruits of all he created.

—JAMES 1:16–18

Nelson Mandela wrote,

Our deepest fear is not that we are inadequate. Our deepest fear is that we are powerful beyond measure. It is our light, not our darkness, that most frightens us. We ask ourselves, "Who am I to be brilliant, gorgeous, talented and fabulous?" Actually, who are you not to be? You are a child of God. Your playing small doesn't serve the world. There's nothing enlightened about shrinking so that other people won't feel insecure around you. We were born to manifest the glory of God that is within us . . . And as we let our own light shine, we unconsciously give other people permission to do the same. As we are liberated from our own fear, our presence automatically liberates others.

We *do* fear our glory. We fear even heading this direction because, for one thing, it seems prideful. Now pride is a bad thing, to be sure, but it's not prideful to embrace the truth that you bear the image of God. We walk in humility because we know it is a glory *bestowed*. It reflects something of the Lord's glory.

❖ WAKING THE DEAD, 87

I have revealed you to those whom you gave me out of the world. They were yours; you gave them to me and they have obeyed your word.
—JOHN 17:6

What have we come to accept as "discipleship"? A friend of mine recently handed me a program from a large and successful church somewhere in the Midwest. It's a rather exemplary model of what the idea has fallen to. Their plan for discipleship involves, first, becoming a member of this particular church. Then they encourage you to take a course on doctrine. Be "faithful" in attending the Sunday morning service and a small group fellowship. Complete a special course on Christian growth. Live a life that demonstrates clear evidence of spiritual growth. Complete a class on evangelism. Consistently look for opportunities to evangelize. Complete a course on finances, one on marriage, and another on parenting (provided that you are married or a parent). Complete a leadership training course, a hermeneutics course, a course on spiritual gifts, and another on biblical counseling. Participate in missions. Carry a significant local church ministry "load."

You're probably surprised that I would question this sort of program; most churches are trying to get their folks to complete something like this, one way or another. No doubt a great deal of helpful information is passed on. My goodness, you could earn an MBA with less effort. But let me ask you: A program like this—does it teach a person how to apply principles, or how to walk with God?

They are not the same thing.

❖ *WAKING THE DEAD, 95–96*

Continue in what you have learned and have become convinced of,
because you know those from whom you learned it.

—2 TIMOTHY 3:14

We take folks through a discipleship program whereby they master any number of Christian precepts and miss the most important thing of all, the very thing for which we were created: intimacy with God. There are, after all, those troubling words Jesus spoke to those who were doing all the "right" things: "Then I will tell them plainly, 'I never knew you'" (Matt. 7:23). Knowing God. That's the point.

You might recall the old proverb: "Give a man a fish and you feed him for a day; teach a man to fish and you feed him for a lifetime." The same holds true here. Teach a man a rule and you help him solve a problem; teach a man to walk with God and you help him solve the rest of his life. Truth be told, you couldn't master enough principles to see yourself safely through this Story. There are too many surprises, ambiguities, exceptions to the rule. Things are hard at work—is it time to make a move? What *has* God called you to do with your life? Things are hard at home—is this just a phase your son is going through, or should you be more concerned? You can't seem to shake this depression—is it medical or something darker? What does the future hold for you—and how should you respond?

Only by walking with God can we hope to find the path that leads to life. *That* is what it means to be a disciple. After all—aren't we "followers of Christ"? Then by all means, let's actually follow him. Not ideas about him. Not just his principles. Him.

❖ *WAKING THE DEAD*, 96–97

Therefore, there is now no condemnation for those who are in
Christ Jesus.

—ROMANS 8:1

A ll sorts of awful things can seem to issue from your heart—
anger, lust, fear, petty jealousies. If you think it's you, a
reflection of what's really going on in your heart, it will disable
you. It could stop your journey dead in its tracks. What you've
encountered is either the voice of your flesh or an attempt of the
Enemy to distress you by throwing all sorts of thoughts your way
and blaming you for it. You must proceed on this assumption:
your heart is good. If it seems that some foul thing is at work there,
say to yourself, *Well then—this is not my heart. My heart is good.*
I reject this. Remember Paul in Romans 7? This is not me. *This is*
not me. And carry on in your journey.

We do the same with any counsel or word that presents itself
as being from God, but contradicts what he has said to us in his
written Word. We walk with wisdom and revelation. When I
hear something that seems really unwise, I test it again and again
before I launch out. The flesh will try to use your "freedom" to
get you to do things you shouldn't do. And now that the Enemy
knows you are trying to walk with God and tune in to your heart,
he'll play the ventriloquist and try to deceive you there. Any
"word" or suggestion that brings discouragement, condemnation,
accusation—that is not from God. Neither is confusion, nor any
counsel that would lead you to disobey what you do know. Reject
it all, and carry on in your journey.

❂ WAKING THE DEAD, 105–6

And I will ask the Father, and he will give you another Counselor
to be with you forever–the Spirit of truth.
—JOHN 14:16–17

Our life is a story. A rather long and complicated story that has unfolded over time. There are many scenes, large and small, and many "firsts." Your first step; your first word; your first day of school. There was your first best friend; your first recital; your first date; your first love; your first kiss; your first heartbreak. If you stop and think of it, your heart has lived through quite a story thus far. Over the course of that story your heart has learned many things. Some of what you learned is true; much of it is not. Not when it comes to the core questions about your heart and the heart of God. Is your heart good? Does your heart really matter? What has life taught you about that? Imagine for a moment that God is walking softly beside you. You sense his presence, feel his warm breath. He says, "Tell me your sorrows." What would you say in reply?

How would you feel if your spouse or a friend said to you, "I think you need some counseling, and so I've arranged for it. You start tomorrow; it'll probably take years"? I've got five bucks that says you'd get more than a little defensive. The combination of our pride—*I don't need any therapy, thank you very much*—and the fact that it's become a *profession*—Freud and Prozac and all that—has kept most of us from realizing that, in fact, we do need counseling. All of us. Jesus sends us his Spirit as Counselor; that ought to make it clear.

✤ WAKING THE DEAD, *112–13*

When the servant of the man of God got up and went out early the next morning, an army with horses and chariots had surrounded the city. "Oh, my lord, what shall we do?" the servant asked. "Don't be afraid," the prophet answered. "Those who are with us are more than those who are with them." And Elisha prayed, "O LORD, open his eyes so he may see." Then the LORD opened the servant's eyes, and he looked and saw the hills full of horses and chariots of fire all around Elisha.
—2 KINGS 6:15–17

Entering into the Sacred Romance begins with eyes to see and ears to hear. Where would we be today if Eve had looked at the serpent with different eyes, if she had seen at once that the beautiful creature with the charming voice and the reasonable proposition was in fact a fallen angel bent on the annihilation of the human race? Failure to see things as they truly are resulted in unspeakable tragedy. From that point on, the theme of blindness runs throughout Scripture. It's not merely a matter of failing to recognize temptation when we meet it; like Elisha's servant, we often fail to see the drama of redemption as well (2 Kings 6:15–17).

Needless to say, Elisha's servant suddenly saw from a whole different perspective. I think it's safe to assume he also experienced a bit of emotional relief—a recovery of heart. What for him had undoubtedly been a harrowing encounter became an exciting adventure.

❖ *THE SACRED ROMANCE, 145–46*

"Come, follow me," Jesus said, "and I will make you fishers of men."
— MATTHEW 4:19

So much of the journey forward involves letting go of all that once brought us life. We turn away from the familiar abiding places of the heart, the false selves we have lived out, and the strengths we have used to make a place for ourselves and all our false loves, and we venture forth in our hearts to trace the steps of the One who said, "Follow me." In a way, it means that we stop *pretending* that life is better than it is, that we are happier than we are, that the false selves we present to the world are really us. We respond to the haunting, the wooing, the longing for another life. A turning *away* from attachment and a turning *toward* desire. The freedom of heart needed to journey comes in the form of detachment. As Gerald May writes in *Addiction and Grace*,

> *Detachment* is the word used in spiritual traditions to describe freedom of desire. Not freedom *from* desire, but freedom *of* desire . . . An authentic spiritual understanding of detachment devalues neither desire nor the objects of desire. Instead, it "aims at correcting one's own anxious grasping in order to free oneself for committed relationship to God." According to Meister Eckhart, detachment "enkindles the heart, awakens the spirit, stimulates our longings, and shows us where God is."

With an awakened heart, we turn and face the road ahead, knowing that no one can take the trip for us, nor can anyone plan our way.

❖ *THE SACRED ROMANCE, 149*

See! The winter is past;
the rains are over and gone.
Flowers appear on the earth;
the season of singing has come.
—SONG OF SOLOMON 2:11–12

I was walking in the woods and fields behind our house one evening, four months after Brent's death. My heart was so aware of the loss—not only of Brent, but in some ways, of everything that mattered. I knew that one by one, I would lose everyone I cared about and the life I am still seeking.

In the east, a full moon was rising, bright and beautiful and enormous as it seems when it is just above the horizon. Toward the west, the clouds were turning peach and pink against a topaz sky. Telling myself to long for eternity feels like telling myself to let go of all I love—forever. It feels like accepting the teaching of Eastern religions, a *denial* of life and all God created. We lose it all too soon, before we can even begin to live and love.

But what if? What if nature is speaking to us? What if sunrise and sunset tell the tale every day, remembering Eden's glory, prophesying Eden's return? What if it shall all be restored?

❖ *THE JOURNEY OF DESIRE, 107–8*

Above all else, guard your heart,
for it is the wellspring of life.
—PROVERBS 4:23

Above all else, guard your heart." We usually hear this with a sense of "Keep an eye on that heart of yours," in the way you'd warn a deputy watching over some dangerous outlaw, or a bad dog the neighbors let run. "Don't let him out of your sight." Having so long believed our hearts are evil, we assume the warning is to keep us out of trouble. So we lock up our hearts and throw away the key, and then try to get on with our living.

But that isn't the spirit of the command at all. It doesn't say guard your heart because it's criminal; it says guard your heart because it is the wellspring of your life, because it is a *treasure*, because everything else depends on it. How kind of God to give us this warning, like someone's entrusting to a friend something precious to him, with the words: "Be careful with this—it means a lot to me."

What do you do on a daily basis to care for your heart? Okay, that wasn't fair. How about weekly? *Monthly?*

❂   WAKING THE DEAD, 207–8

In a flash, in the twinkling of an eye, at the last trumpet. For the trumpet will sound, the dead will be raised imperishable, and we will be changed.

—1 CORINTHIANS 15:52

Here in the Rocky Mountains, spring comes late and fitfully. We had snow during the second week in May. I've come to accept that spring here is really a wrestling match between winter and summer. It makes for a long time of waiting. You see, the flowers are pretty much gone in September. The first of October, the aspens start turning gold and drop their leaves in a week or two. Come November all is gray. Initially, I don't mind. The coming of winter has its joys, but after the new year, things begin to drag on. Through February and then March, the earth remains lifeless. The whole world lies shadowed in brown and gray tones, like an old photograph. Winter's novelty is long past, and by April we are longing for some sign of life—some color, some hope. It's too long.

And then, just this afternoon, I rounded the corner into our neighborhood, and suddenly, the world was green again. What had been rock and twig and dead mulch was a rich oriental carpet of green. I was shocked, stunned. How did it happen?

My surprise is telling. It seems natural to long for spring; it is another thing to be completely stunned by its return. I am truly and genuinely surprised, as if my reaction were, *Really? What are you doing here?* And then I realized, *I thought I'd never see you again.* I think in some deep place inside, I had accepted the fact that winter is what is really true . . . And so I am shocked by the return of spring. And I wonder, *Can the same thing happen for my soul?*

❖ THE JOURNEY OF DESIRE, 108–9

I tell you a mystery: We will not all sleep, but we will all be changed.
— 1 CORINTHIANS 15:51

Can it really happen? Can things in our lives be green again? No matter what our creeds may tell us, our hearts have settled into another belief. We have accepted the winter of this world as the final word and tried to get on without the hope of spring. *It will never come*, we have assumed, *and so I must find whatever life here that I can.* We have been so committed to arranging for our happiness that we have missed the signs of spring. We haven't given any serious thought to what might be around the corner. Were eternity to appear tomorrow, we would be as shocked as I have been with the return of spring this week, only more so. Our practical agnosticism would be revealed.

But of course we aspire to happiness we can enjoy now. Our hearts have no place else to go. We have made a nothing of eternity. If I told you that your income would triple next year, and that European vacation you've wanted is just around the corner, you'd be excited, hopeful. The future would look promising. It seems possible, *desirable*. But our ideas of heaven, while possible, aren't all that desirable. Whatever it is we think is coming in the next season of our existence, we don't think it is worth getting all that excited about. We make a nothing of eternity by enlarging the significance of this life and by diminishing the reality of what the next life is all about.

❂ *THE JOURNEY OF DESIRE, 110–11*

He has sent me to bind up the brokenhearted.
—ISAIAH 61:1

When the Bible tells us that Christ came to "redeem mankind" it offers a whole lot more than forgiveness. To simply forgive a broken man is like telling someone running a marathon, "It's okay that you've broken your leg. I won't hold that against you. Now finish the race." That is cruel, to leave him disabled that way. No, there is much more to our redemption. The core of Christ's mission is foretold in Isaiah 61:1.

The Spirit of the Sovereign LORD is on me,
because the LORD has anointed me
to preach good news to the poor.
He has sent me to bind up the brokenhearted,
to proclaim freedom for the captives
and release for the prisoners.

The Messiah will come, he says, to bind up and heal, to release and set free. *Your heart.* Christ comes to restore and release you, your soul, the true you. This is *the* central passage in the entire Bible about Jesus, the one he chooses to quote about himself when he steps into the spotlight in Luke 4 and announces his arrival. So take him at his word—ask him in to heal all the broken places within you and unite them into one whole and healed heart. Ask him to release you from all bondage and captivity, as he promised to do.

❖ *WILD AT HEART, 128–29*

Remain in me, and I will remain in you. No branch can bear fruit by itself; it must remain in the vine. Neither can you bear fruit unless you remain in me.

—JOHN 15:4

A biding in the love of God is our only hope, the only true home for our hearts. It's not that we mentally acknowledge that God loves us. It's that we let our hearts come home to him, and stay in his love. MacDonald says it this way:

> When our hearts turn to him, that is opening the door to him . . . then he comes in, not by our thought only, not in our idea only, but he comes himself, and of his own will. Thus the Lord, the Spirit, becomes the soul of our souls . . . Then indeed we *are*; then indeed we have life; the life of Jesus has . . . become life in us . . . we are one with God forever and ever. (*The Heart of George MacDonald*)

Or as St. John of the Cross echoes in *Living Flame of Love*, "O how gently and how lovingly dost thou lie awake in the depth and centre of my soul, where thou in secret and in silence alone, as its sole Lord, abidest, not only as in Thine own house or in Thine own chamber, but also as within my own bosom, in close and intimate union." This deep intimate union with Jesus and with his Father is the source of all our healing and all our strength. It is, as Leanne Payne says, "the central and unique truth of Christianity."

❖ *WILD AT HEART, 130–31*

I have forgiven in the sight of Christ for your sake, in order that
Satan might not outwit us. For we are not unaware of his schemes.
—2 CORINTHIANS 2:10–11

The devil no doubt has a place in our theology, but is he a category we even think about in the daily events of our lives? Has it ever crossed your mind that not every thought that crosses your mind comes from you? We are being lied to all the time. Yet we never stop to say, "Wait a minute . . . who else is speaking here? Where are those ideas coming from? Where are those *feelings* coming from?" If you read the saints from every age before the Modern Era—this pride-filled age of reason, science, and technology we all are thoroughly educated in—you'll find that they take the devil very seriously indeed. But we, the enlightened, have a much more commonsense approach to things. We look for a psychological or physical or even political explanation for every trouble we meet.

Who caused the Chaldeans to steal Job's herds and kill his servants? Satan, clearly (Job 1:12, 17). Yet do we even give him a passing thought when we hear of terrorism today? Who kept that poor woman bent over for eighteen years, the one Jesus healed on the Sabbath? Satan, clearly (Luke 13:16). But do we consider him when we are having a headache that keeps us from praying or reading Scripture? Who moved Ananias and Sapphira to lie to the apostles? Satan again (Acts 5:3). But do we really see his hand behind a fallout or schism in ministry?

Who was behind that brutal assault on your own strength, those wounds you've taken? There is a whole lot more going on behind the scenes of our lives than most of us have been led to believe.

❀ *WILD AT HEART, 152–53*

"All this I have spoken while still with you," Jesus said, as he was preparing his followers for life after his departure. "But the Counselor, the Holy Spirit, whom the Father will send in my name, will teach you all things and will remind you of everything I have said to you."

—JOHN 14:25–26

God speaks to us through the Bible. And what is said there has more authority than anything else in our lives. It is the bedrock of our faith, the test of all things, a living connection to the heart and mind of God—when we approach it with the help of the Spirit of God. I add that qualifier because we do well to remember that the Pharisees read and studied the Bible, "but their minds were made dull, for to this day the same veil remains when the old covenant is read. It has not been removed, because only in Christ is it taken away. Even to this day when Moses is read, a veil covers their hearts" (2 Corinthians 3:14–15). How very sad. They read it, but they didn't get it.

The Bible is not a magic book. It doesn't reveal its treasures simply because you read a passage. It doesn't make you holy simply because you hold it in high esteem. Many cults use the Bible. Even Satan quotes Scripture (see Luke 4:9–12). We need the Bible and all it has to say to us. Desperately. We also need the Spirit of God to guide us in our reading and study.

We need God to help us understand his Word. We can't separate a walk with God from our reading of Scripture. The two go hand in hand.

❖ WALKING WITH GOD, 40

If you love me, you will obey what I command. And I will ask
the Father, and he will give you another Counselor to be with you
forever—the Spirit of truth. The world cannot accept him, because it
neither sees him nor knows him. But you know him, for he lives with
you and will be in you.

—JOHN 14:15–17

We need God to help us understand his Word. We can't separate a walk with God from our reading of Scripture. The two go hand in hand. Like having a tour guide as you wander the halls of the Louvre. Unfortunately, too many people approach Scripture without an intimacy with God, and they either end up frustrated because they've gotten so little out of it or, far worse, amass an intellectual understanding quite apart from any real communion with God. It usually results in religious pride.

The Bible is meant to be read in fellowship with God. Things can get really weird if we don't. Let me say that the more we know the Scriptures and the more they become a part of us, the more we'll find that we *can* walk with God. Having spent a good deal of time in the Word of God, you'll give the Holy Spirit a library within you to draw upon.

❖ WALKING WITH GOD, *41–42*

Blessed are they who keep his statutes
and seek him with all their heart.
—PSALM 119:2

The more we know the Scriptures and, the more they become a part of us, the more we'll find that we *can* walk with God. For example, I'll be sitting in a meeting and getting mad, and the Spirit reminds me, "Man's anger does not bring about the righteous life that God desires" (James 1:20). I cool down. Or I'll see a gorgeous vista in the mountains, and because I know "the earth is the LORD's, and everything in it" (Ps. 24:1), I'll be reminded of what God is like through his creation.

There is no substitute for the written Word of God. No matter how precious a personal word may be to us, no matter how cool some insight may be, it doesn't compare to the written Word. I've seen too many immature Christians chase after "revelation" and go wacky because they are not rooted and grounded in the Scripture.

The ordinances of the LORD are sure
    and altogether righteous.
They are more precious than gold,
    than much pure gold;
they are sweeter than honey,
    than honey from the comb.
By them is your servant warned;
    in keeping them there is great reward. (Psalms 19:8–11)

❁ WALKING WITH GOD, 42–43

Who is this coming from Edom,
from Bozrah, with his garments stained crimson?
Who is this, robed in splendor,
striding forward in the greatness of his strength?
"It is I, speaking in righteousness,
mighty to save."
—ISAIAH 63:1

Picture in your mind's eye an image of a great warrior, a renowned champion, returning home from far-off lands. His fame has long preceded him, and now the reports of his feats are confirmed by the scars he bears, the remembrance of wounds more noble than any tokens of honor. With dignity he moves up the main causeway of the city, lined with the faces of his people, the very people for whom he has fought bravely, whose freedom he has secured. The warrior has returned after years on the field of battle, returning only when triumph has been achieved and not a moment before. This is his homecoming, and it is as a conquering hero he returns. Before him, at the head of the street, stands the king, who is his father. The scene is both a homecoming and a coronation. For the father-king will now hand the kingdom over to his son.

It could be a passage from David's life, for he came to the throne after proving himself as a warrior. But I am referring to Jesus, of course, and while this is all quite true—biblically, historically—I'm afraid the power of it eludes us. Few of us have ever lived in a kingdom, under a king. Even fewer have ever met one. Imagine what a great king is like.

❧ *FATHERED BY GOD, 156–57*

The highest heavens belong to the Lord,
but the earth he has given to man.
—PSALM 115:16

We come now to the goal, in some sense, of the masculine journey, the maturity for which God has been fathering the man since his first breath—to be a king. To wield power, influence, and property in his name. It is as great and noble an undertaking as it is difficult; history makes that very clear. The reason for many of our miseries upon the earth in these days is that we have lost our kings. Yes, we find men in power, but they are not true kings. It is not through initiation that they have come to the throne, nor do they have the heart of a king. And that is a dangerous situation indeed, when a man is made king who is unfit to be one, and it has brought the ruin of many kingdoms—homes, families, churches, ministries, businesses, nations.

Paul says the whole creation groans for the revealing of the sons of God (see Rom. 8:19–21). For we were meant to rule the earth, and this world is in anguish until we, the sons of God, are all that we were meant to be, and in being that can rule upon the earth in blessedness.

❀ *FATHERED BY GOD, 158–59*

Then God blessed them and said, "Be fruitful and multiply. Fill the earth and govern it. Reign . . ."
—GENESIS 1:28 NLT

We must recover the king in a man. This is the role for which man was created. The first man, Adam, was given the earth to rule (see Gen. 1:28), and he was intended to be the beginning of a race of kings. "The highest heavens belong to the Lord, but the earth he has given to man" (Ps. 115:16). But Adam failed, abdicated the throne through his sin, so another Man was sent to restore the line. Jesus was also born a King, and destined to rule, as the angel said to Mary, "The Lord God will give him the throne of his father David, and he will reign over the house of Jacob forever; his kingdom will never end" (Luke 1:32–33). And where Adam failed, Jesus triumphed.

Jesus is, of course, now the Ruler of heaven and earth. The Son of God, ruling on his Father's throne. You, my brother, are from that noble line. You are a redeemed son of Adam, now the son of God (1 John 3:1–2). You were born to rule, *and you were redeemed to rule*. Destined to become a king. "Do not be afraid, little flock, for your Father has been pleased to give you the kingdom. . . . And I confer on you a kingdom, just as my Father conferred one on me" (Luke 12:32; 22:29). Jesus redeems his brothers to share his throne, to rule in his name.

❖ FATHERED BY GOD, *158–59*

Do not let your hearts be troubled. Trust in God; trust also in me. In my Father's house are many rooms; if it were not so, I would have told you. I am going there to prepare a place for you.

—JOHN 14:1–2

There is the joy of having someone save a place for us. We walk into a crowded room at church or at a dinner party and someone across the way waves us over, pointing to a chair he's held on to especially for us. For a moment we feel a sense of relief, a taste of being on the inside. Christ promises that he is saving a place in heaven especially for each of us. When we walk into the crowded excitement of the wedding feast of the Lamb, with the sound of a thousand conversations, laughter and music, the clinking of glasses, and one more time our heart leaps with the hope that we might be let into the sacred circle, we will not be disappointed. We'll be welcomed to the table by our Lover himself. No one will have to scramble to find another chair, to make room for us at the end of the table, or rustle up a place setting. There will be a seat with our name on it, held open at Jesus' command for us and no other.

❖ *THE SACRED ROMANCE, 182–83*

Come, all you who are thirsty,
come to the waters;
and you who have no money,
come, buy and eat!
Come, buy wine and milk
without money and without cost.
—ISAIAH 55:1

The Sacred Romance calls to us every moment of our lives. It whispers to us on the wind, invites us through the laughter of good friends, reaches out to us through the touch of someone we love. We've heard it in our favorite music, sensed it at the birth of our first child, been drawn to it while watching the shimmer of a sunset on the ocean. It is even present in times of great personal suffering—the illness of a child, the loss of a marriage, the death of a friend. Something calls to us through experiences like these and rouses an inconsolable longing deep within our heart, wakening in us a yearning for intimacy, beauty, and adventure. This longing is the most powerful part of any human personality. It fuels our search for meaning, for wholeness, for a sense of being truly alive.

However we may describe this deep desire, it is the most important thing about us, our heart of hearts, the passion of our life. And the voice that calls to us in this place is none other than the voice of God.

❖ *THE SACRED ROMANCE, 195*

Why spend money on what is not bread,
and your labor on what does not satisfy?
Listen, listen to me, and eat what is good,
and your soul will delight in the richest of fare.
—ISAIAH 55:2

Where do we go from here? "This life," wrote Jonathan Edwards, "ought to be spent by us only as a journey towards heaven." That's the only story worth living in now. In the imagery of Hebrews, a race is set before us and we must run for all we're worth. Our prayers will have been answered if we've helped to lift some of the deadweight so that our hearts may rise to the call, hear it more clearly, respond with "eager feet." Our final thoughts echo the advice found in Hebrews:

Keep your eyes on *Jesus*, who both began and finished this race we're in. Study how he did it. Because he never lost sight of where he was headed . . . he could put up with anything along the way: cross, shame, whatever. And now he's *there*, in the place of honor, right alongside God. When you find yourselves flagging in your faith, go over that story again, item by item, that long litany of hostility he plowed through. (Hebrews 12:2–3 *The Message*)

Jesus remembered where he was headed, and he wanted to get there with all his heart. These two themes, memory and desire, will make all the difference in our journey ahead. Without them, we will not run well, if we run at all.

❖ *THE SACRED ROMANCE*, 196–97

What is man that you are mindful of him,
the son of man that you care for him?
You made him a little lower than the heavenly beings
and crowned him with glory and honor.
You made him ruler over the works of your hands;
you put everything under his feet.
—PSALM 8:4–6

During a long layover at O'Hare, I studied the man who sells popcorn from a little stand in one of the terminal hallways. He sat silently on a stool as thousands of people rushed by. Occasionally, someone would stop and buy a bag. He would scoop the popcorn from the bin, take the money, and make change—all without a word being spoken between them. When the brief encounter was over, he would resume his place on the stool, staring blankly, his shoulders hunched over. He seemed well past fifty. His face wore a weary expression of resignation tinged with shame. *Adam*, I thought, *what happened?* Did he know how far his situation was from his true design? Somehow he knew, even if he didn't know the Story. His sadness was testimony to it.

Some people love what they do, but most merely toil to survive. As a result, we've come to think of work as a result of the Fall. Many endure a life of futility and anonymity in the bowels of some large corporation. We yearn to be *fruitful*, to do something that flows naturally out of the gifts and capacities of our own soul. But of course—we were meant to be the kings and queens of the earth.

❖ THE JOURNEY OF DESIRE, 154–55

Then the King will say to those on his right, "Come, you who are
blessed by my Father; take your inheritance, the kingdom prepared for
you since the creation of the world."

—MATTHEW 25:34

In Romans 8, Paul says something outrageous. He says that all our sufferings are "not worth comparing" with the glory that will be revealed in us. It seems hard to believe, given the way life can break your heart. The human race has seen an unspeakable amount of suffering. What can possibly make that seem like nothing? "The glory that will be revealed in us" (Matt. 8:18). The Great Restoration. Paul then goes on to say, "The creation waits in eager expectation for the sons of God to be revealed" (Matt. 8:19). The release of a fully restored creation is being more or less held back, waiting upon *our* restoration. Why? Because only then can we handle it. Only when we ourselves have been restored can we take our place again as the kings and queens of creation. Or did you not know? The day is coming when Christ will appoint you as one of his regents over his great and beautiful universe. This has been his plan all along.

When the Son of Man comes in his glory, and all the angels with him, he will sit on his throne in heavenly glory. All the nations will be gathered before him, and he will separate the people one from another as a shepherd separates the sheep from the goats. He will put the sheep on his right and the goats on his left. Then the King will say to those on his right, "Come, you who are blessed by my Father; take your inheritance, *the kingdom pre-pared for you since the creation of the world*" (Matthew 25:31–34, emphasis added).

And they will *reign* forever and ever.

❖ THE JOURNEY OF DESIRE, 156–57

*Let us make man in our image, in our likeness, and let them rule over
the fish of the sea and the birds of the air, over the livestock,
over all the earth.*

—GENESIS 1:27

Let's come back for a moment to original glory, the glory of God given to us when we were created in his image. So much light could be shed on our lives if we would explore what we were *meant* to be before things started going wrong. What was it that we were created to *do*? What was our original job description?

> God said, "Let us make man in our image, in our likeness, and let them rule over the fish of the sea and the birds of the air, over the livestock, over all the earth, and over all the creatures that move along the ground." So God created man in his own image, in the image of God he created him; male and female he created them. God blessed them and said to them, "Be fruitful and increase in number; fill the earth and subdue it. Rule." (Gen. 1:26–28)

And let them *rule*. Like a foreman runs a ranch or like a skipper runs his ship. Better still, like a king rules a kingdom, God appoints us as the governors of his domain. We were created to be the kings and queens of the earth (small *k*, small *q*). Hebrew scholar Robert Alter has looked long and hard at this passage, mining it for its riches. He says the idea of *rule* means "a fierce exercise of mastery." It is active, engaged, passionate. It is *fierce*.

❧ WAKING THE DEAD, 165–66

As the Father has sent me, so I send you.

—JOHN 20:21 NRSV

After his resurrection, Jesus sent us *all* out to do what he did and he gives us his authority to do it: "All authority in heaven and on earth has been given to me. Therefore go" (Matt. 28:18–19). Why else would he have given us his authority if we weren't supposed to *use* it?

The attitude of so many Christians today is anything *but* fierce. We're passive, acquiescent. We're acting as if the battle were over, as if the wolf and the lamb were now fast friends. Good grief—we're beating swords into plowshares as the armies of the Evil One descend upon us. We've bought the lie of the Religious Spirit, which says, "You don't need to fight the Enemy. Let Jesus do that." It's nonsense. It's unbiblical. We are *commanded* to "resist the devil, and he will flee from you" (James 4:7). We are told, "Your enemy the devil prowls around like a roaring lion looking for someone to devour. Resist him" (1 Peter 5:8–9); "Fight the good fight" (1 Tim. 1:18); "Rescue those being led away to death" (Prov. 24:11).

Jesus has won the victory over Satan and his kingdom; *however*, the battle is not over. Look at 1 Corinthians 15:24–25: "Then the end will come, when he Jesus hands over the kingdom to God the Father after he has destroyed all dominion, authority and power. For he must reign until he has put all his enemies under his feet." *After* he has destroyed the rest of the Enemy's works. *Until* then, he must reign by bringing his enemies under his feet. Jesus is still at war, and he calls us to join him.

❖ WAKING THE DEAD, 167–68

Let us not give up meeting together, as some are in the habit of doing, but let us encourage one another–and all the more as you see the Day approaching.

—HEBREWS 10:25

You awake to find yourself in the midst of a great and terrible war. It is, in fact, your most desperate hour. Your King and dearest Friend calls you forth. Awake, come fully alive, your good heart set free and blazing for him and for those yet to be rescued. You have a glory that is needed. You are given a quest, a mission that will take you deep into the heart of the kingdom of darkness, to break down gates of bronze and cut through bars of iron so that your people might be set free from their bleak prisons. He asks that you heal them. Of course, you will face many dangers; you will be hunted.

Would you try and do this *alone*?

Something stronger than fate *has* chosen you. Evil *will* hunt you. And so a fellowship *must* protect you. Honestly, though he is a very brave and true hobbit, Frodo hasn't a chance without Sam, Merry, Pippin, Gandalf, Aragorn, Legolas, and Gimli. He has no real idea what dangers and trials lie ahead. The dark mines of Moria; the Balrog that awaits him there; the evil orcs called the Urak-hai that will hunt him; the wastes of the Emyn Muil. He will need his friends. And you will need yours. You must cling to those you have; you must search wide and far for those you do not yet have. *You must not go alone.* From the beginning, right there in Eden, the Enemy's strategy has relied upon a simple aim: divide and conquer. Get them isolated, and take them out.

❖ WAKING THE DEAD, 186–87

Fight the good fight.
—1 TIMOTHY 1:18

I am not letting men off the hook. God knows, we have a lot more repenting to do. I *am* saying that you won't begin to understand the long and sustained assault on femininity, on women, until you see it as part of something much larger. The most wicked force the world has ever known. The Enemy bears a special hatred for Eve. If you believe he has any role in the history of this world, you cannot help but see it.

The Evil One had a hand in all that has happened to you. If he didn't arrange for the assault directly—and certainly human sin has a large enough role to play—then he made sure he drove the message of the wounds home into your heart. He is the one who has dogged your heels with shame and self-doubt and accusation. He is the one who offers the false comforters to you in order to deepen your bondage. He is the one who has done these things in order to prevent your restoration. For that is what he fears. He fears who you are; what you are; what you might become. He fears your beauty and your life-giving heart.

You really won't understand the life of a woman until you understand this:

A woman is passionately loved by the God of the universe.

A woman is passionately hated by his Enemy.

And so, dear heart, it is time for restoration. For there is One greater than your Enemy, One who has sought you out from the beginning of time. He has come to heal the broken heart and restore the feminine soul.

❖ *CAPTIVATING, 89–91*

The Spirit of the Sovereign LORD is on me.
—ISAIAH 61:1

The purposes of Jesus Christ are not finished when one of his precious ones is forgiven. Not at all. Read this passage from Isaiah very slowly, carefully, out loud to yourself:

> *He has sent me to bind up the brokenhearted,*
>   *to proclaim freedom for the captives*
>   *and release from darkness for the prisoners,*
> *to proclaim the year of the LORD's favor*
>   *and the day of vengeance of our God,*
> *to comfort all who mourn,*
>   *and provide for those who grieve in Zion—*
> *to bestow on them a crown of beauty*
>   *instead of ashes,*
> *the oil of gladness*
>   *instead of mourning,*
> *and a garment of praise*
>   *instead of a spirit of despair.* (61:1–3)

This is the passage that Jesus pointed to when he began his ministry here on earth. Of all the Scriptures he could have chosen, this is the one he picked on the day he first publicly announced his mission. It must be important to him. It must be central.

Read it again, and ask him, *Jesus, is this true for me? Would you do this for me?*

He can, and he will . . . if you'll let him.

❖ CAPTIVATING, 94–95

> *Jesus entered the temple area and drove out all who were buying and*
> *selling there. He overturned the tables of the money changers and the*
> *benches of those selling doves.*
> — MATTHEW 21:12

Jesus ran because he wanted to, not simply because he had to or because the Father told him to. He ran "for the joy set before him," which means he ran out of *desire*. To use the familiar phrase, his heart was fully in it. We call the final week of our Savior's life his Passion Week. Look at the depth of his desire, the fire in his soul. Consumed with passion, he clears the temple of the charlatans who have turned his Father's house into a swap meet (Matt. 21:12). Later, he stands looking over the city that was to be his bride but now lies in the bondage of her adulteries and the oppression of her taskmasters. "O Jerusalem, Jerusalem," he cries, "how often I have *longed* to gather your children together, as a hen gathers her chicks under her wings, but you were not willing" (Matt. 23:37, emphasis added).

As the final hours of his greatest struggle approach, his passion intensifies. He gathers with his closest friends like a condemned criminal sitting down to his last meal. He alone knows what is about to unfold. "I have *eagerly desired* to eat this Passover with you," he says, "before I suffer" (Luke 22:15, emphasis added). Then on he presses, through the intensity of Gethsemane and the passion of the cross. Is it possible he went through any of it halfheartedly?

❂ *THE SACRED ROMANCE, 197–98*

But blessed are your eyes because they see, and your ears because they hear.
—MATTHEW 13:16

It's not what God is not giving, but what he is giving. In July, my family and I were canoeing the Snake River in Teton National Park. We absolutely love that place. It was evening, and I was guiding our family and some dear friends down a part of the river most folks don't get to see and rarely canoe at dusk. I knew we would be alone, at the prime time for wildlife to come down for a drink. Hopes were high of seeing bull moose, elk, and who knows what else. The evening could not have been more beautiful. As we glided along the banks, peering into the wild growth on either side, time slipped away. It could have been the 1800s. We were utterly alone on the silent river, at twilight, and I knew we were in for a treat.

We passed the den of some river otters we'd seen last year. Nobody home. We passed the island where moose are always hanging out. Nope. Just a beaver or two. Frustrated, I made the group paddle an extra mile through a back channel where I *knew* the moose had to be. But no. The sun passed behind Mount Moran, and everyone was enjoying a spectacular sunset in the clouds above. But I missed it entirely, because I was so disappointed we didn't see wildlife. I was focused on what God was *not* giving, and missed what he *was* giving. Only later, looking at the photos, did I see all that I missed. The sunset was truly stunning. Peaches and violets and reds above the black silhouette of the mountains, all reflected in the river.

I missed it.

❖ WALKING WITH GOD, 69–70

Elijah climbed to the top of Carmel, bent down to the ground and put his
*   face between his knees.*
"Go and look toward the sea," he told his servant. And he went up and looked.
"There is nothing there," he said.
Seven times Elijah said, "Go back."
The seventh time the servant reported, "A cloud as small as a man's hand
*   is rising from the sea."*
So Elijah said, "Go and tell Ahab, 'Hitch up your chariot and go down
*   before the rain stops you.'"*
Meanwhile, the sky grew black with clouds, the wind rose, a heavy rain
*   came on.*

—1 KINGS 18:42–45

I love it that Elijah kept sending his servant to have a look. Is it working? I love it that it took this mighty man seven rounds of prayer to get it going. James points to this story as the example: "Elijah was a man just like us. He prayed earnestly that it would not rain, and it did not rain on the land for three and a half years. Again he prayed, and the heavens gave rain, and the earth produced its crops" (James 5:16–18).

Now why did James make a point of saying that Elijah "was a man just like us"? Because of that thing in each of us that says, *I could never do that.* Because of that theology that says, "Those stories are exceptions." That sort of thinking cripples faith. It cuts your prayer life off at the knees. Why are we given stories about the power of godly people praying if our prayers really don't accomplish anything? James said that Elijah was just like you and me. This was no exception. Meaning, you can pray and do this too. You can pray and see things happen.

❧ WALKING WITH GOD, 71–72

> *We know that the whole creation has been groaning as in the pains of*
> *childbirth right up to the present time. Not only so, but we ourselves,*
> *who have the firstfruits of the Spirit, groan inwardly as we wait*
> *eagerly for our adoption as sons, the redemption of our bodies.*
> —ROMANS 8:22–23

The whole life of the good Christian," said Augustine, "is a holy longing." Sadly, many of us have been led to feel that somehow we ought to want less, not more. Shouldn't we be more content? Perhaps, but contentment is never wanting *less*; that's the easy way out. The real test is to have your heart burning within you and have the patience to enjoy what there is now to enjoy, while waiting with eager anticipation for the feast to come.

Contentment can only happen as we increase desire, let it run itself out toward its fulfillment, and carry us along with it. And so George Herbert prayed,

> *Immortal Heat, O let thy greater flame*
> *Attract the lesser to it: let those fires,*
> *Which shall consume the world, first make it tame;*
> *And kindle in our hearts such true desires,*
> *As may consume our lusts, and make thee way.*

There may be times when all we have to go on is a sense of duty. But in the end, if that is all we have, we will never make it. Our Hero is the example. He's run on before us and he's made it, he's there now. His life assures us it can be done, but only through passionate desire *for the joy set before us.*

❖ *THE SACRED ROMANCE, 199–200*

I run in the path of your commands,
for you have set my heart free.
— PSALMS 119:32

As your soul grows in the love of God and journeys forth toward him, your heart's capacities also grow and expand.

But the sword cuts both ways. While your heart grows in its capacity for pleasure, it grows in its capacity to know pain. What, then, shall we do with disappointment? To want is to suffer; the word *passion* means to suffer. This is why many Christians are reluctant to listen to their hearts: they know that their dullness is keeping them from feeling the pain of life. Many of us have chosen simply not to want so much; it's safer that way. It's also godless. That's stoicism, not Christianity. Sanctification is an awakening, the rousing of our souls from the dead sleep of sin into the fullness of their capacity for life.

Desire often feels like an enemy, because it awakens longings that cannot be fulfilled in the moment. In *The Wasteland* T. S. Eliot says,

April is the cruelest month, breeding
Lilacs out of the dead land, mixing
Memory and desire.

Spring awakens a desire for the summer that is not yet. Awakened souls are often disappointed, but our disappointment can lead us onward, actually increasing our desire and lifting it toward its true passion.

❖ *THE SACRED ROMANCE, 200–201*

My Father, if it is possible, may this cup be taken from me. Yet not as
I will, but as you will.
—MATTHEW 26:39

The time has come for us to quit playing chess with God over our lives. We cannot win, but we can delay the victory, dragging out the pain of grasping and the poison of possessing. You see, there are two kinds of losses in life. The first is shared by all mankind—the losses that come to us. Call them what you will—accidents, fate, acts of God. The point is that we have no control over them. We do not determine when, where, what, or even how. There is no predicting these losses; they happen *to* us. We choose only how we respond. The second kind is known only to the pilgrim. They are losses that we *choose*. A chosen loss is different from repentance, when we give up something that was never ours to have. With a chosen loss, we place on the altar something very dear to us, something innocent, whose only danger is in its goodness, that we might come to love it too much. It is the act of *consecration*, where little by little or all at once, we give over our lives to the only One who can truly keep them.

Spiritual surrender is not resignation. It is not choosing to care no longer. Nor is it Eastern mysticism, an attempt to get beyond the suffering of this life by going completely numb. As my dear friend Jan describes, "It is surrender *with* desire, or *in* desire." Desire is still present, felt, welcomed even. But the will to secure is made subject to the divine will in an act of abandoned trust. Think of Jesus in the Garden of Gethsemane.

❧ *THE JOURNEY OF DESIRE, 192–93*

*Only be careful, and watch yourselves closely so that you do not forget
the things your eyes have seen or let them slip from your heart as long
as you live.*
—DEUTERONOMY 4:9

Right above my bed I think I shall hang a sign that says, GOD
EXISTS. You see, I wake most mornings an unbeliever. It
seems that during the night, I slip into forgetfulness, and by the
time the new day comes, I am lost. The deep and precious truths
that God has brought to me over the years and even just yesterday seem a thousand miles away. It doesn't happen every morning,
but enough to make it an ongoing reality. And I know I am not
alone in this. As George MacDonald confessed in *Diary of an
Old Soul,*

*Sometimes I wake, and lo, I have forgot,
And drifted out upon an ebbing sea!
My soul that was at rest now resteth not,
For I am with myself and not with thee;
Truth seems a blind moon in a glaring morn,
　Where nothing is but sick-heart vanity.*

Forgetting is no small problem. Of all the enemies our
hearts must face, this may be the worst because it is insidious.
Forgetfulness does not come against us like an enemy in full
battle formation, banners waving. Nor does it come temptingly,
seductively, the lady in red. It works slowly, commonly, unno-
ticed. It cuts us off from our abundant life so slowly, we barely
notice, until one day the blooms of our faith are suddenly gone.

❖ *THE JOURNEY OF DESIRE, 199–200*

I have sent Timothy, my beloved and faithful child in the LORD. *He will remind you of how I follow Christ Jesus, just as I teach in all the churches wherever I go.*

—1 CORINTHIANS 4:17 NLT

We're certainly warned about forgetfulness in Scripture, both in word and by example. In the Old Testament, the pattern is so predictable, we come to expect it. God delivers his people from the cruel whips of Egypt by a stunning display of his power and his care—the plagues, the Passover, the Red Sea. The Israelites celebrate with singing and dancing. Three days later, they are complaining about the water supply. God provides sweet water from the bitter desert springs of Marah. They complain about the food. God drops breakfast out of the sky, every morning. Then it's the water again. God provides it from a rock. Enemies attack; God delivers. On and on it goes, for forty years. As they stand on the brink of the Promised Land, God issues a final warning: "Only be careful, and watch yourselves closely so that you do not forget the things your eyes have seen *or let them slip from your heart* as long as you live" (Deut. 4:9, emphasis added).

They do, of course, let it slip from their hearts. All of it. This becomes the pattern for the entire history of Israel. Things aren't changed much in the New Testament, but the contrast is greater, and the stakes are even higher. God shows up *in person*, and before he leaves, he gives us the sacraments along with this plea: *Do this to remember me*. But they don't remember him. Paul is "shocked" by the Galatians: they are "turning away so soon from God, who in his love and mercy called you to share the eternal life he gives through Christ" (Gal. 1:6 NLT).

❖ *THE JOURNEY OF DESIRE, 200–201*

Now that you have purified yourselves by obeying the truth so that you have sincere love for your brothers, love one another deeply, from the heart.

—1 PETER 1:22

Unveiling our beauty really just means unveiling our feminine hearts. It's scary, for sure. That is why it is our greatest expression of faith, because we are going to have to trust Jesus—really trust him. We'll have to trust him that we *have* a beauty, that what he has said of us is true. And we'll have to trust him with how it goes when we offer it, because that is out of our control. We'll have to trust him when it hurts, and we'll have to trust him when we are finally seen and enjoyed. That's why unveiling our beauty is *how* we live by faith.

Unveiling our beauty is our greatest expression of hope. We hope it will matter, that our beauty really does make a difference. We hope there is a greater and higher Beauty, hope we are reflecting that Beauty, and hope it will triumph. Our hope is that all is well because of Jesus, and that all will be well because of him. So we unveil beauty in hope.

And unveiling beauty is our greatest expression of love, because it is what the world most needs from us. When we choose not to hide, when we choose to offer our hearts, we are choosing to love. Jesus offers, he invites, he is present. That is how he loves. That is how we love—sincerely, as the Scripture says, "from the heart" (1 Peter 1:22). Our focus shifts from self-protection to the hearts of others. We offer Beauty so that their hearts might come alive, be healed, know God. That is love.

❈ CAPTIVATING, *147*

Therefore each of you must put off falsehood.
—EPHESIANS 4:25

For what shall we do when we wake one day to find we have lost touch with our heart and with it the very refuge where God's presence resides?

Starting very early, life has taught all of us to ignore and distrust the deepest yearnings of our hearts. Life, for the most part, teaches us to suppress our longings and live only in the external world where efficiency and performance are everything. We have learned from parents and peers, at school, at work, and even from our spiritual mentors that something else is wanted from us other than our hearts, which is to say, that which is most deeply *us*. Very seldom are we ever invited to live out of our hearts. If we are wanted, we are often wanted for what we can offer functionally: if rich, we are honored for our wealth; if beautiful, for our looks; if intelligent, for our brains. So we learn to offer only those parts of us that are approved, living out a carefully crafted performance to gain acceptance from those who represent life to us. We divorce ourselves from our hearts and begin to live a double life. Frederick Buechner expresses this phenomenon in his biographical work, *Telling Secrets*:

> Our original shimmering self gets buried so deep we hardly live out of it at all . . . rather, we learn to live out of all the other selves which we are constantly putting on and taking off like coats and hats against the world's weather.

❁ *THE SACRED ROMANCE, 5*

One thing I ask of the LORD, this is what I seek: that I may . . . gaze upon the beauty of the LORD.

—PSALM 27:4

Communion with God is replaced by activity for God. There is little time in this outer world for deep questions. Given the right plan, everything in life can be managed . . . except your heart.

The inner life, the story of our hearts, is the life of the deep places within us, our passions and dreams, our fears and our deepest wounds. It is the unseen life, the mystery within—what Buechner calls our "shimmering self." It cannot be managed like a corporation. The heart does not respond to principles and programs; it seeks not efficiency, but passion. Art, poetry, beauty, mystery, ecstasy: these are what rouse the heart. Indeed, they are the language that must be spoken if one wishes to communicate with the heart. It is why Jesus so often taught and related to people by telling stories and asking questions. His desire was not just to engage their intellects but to capture their hearts.

❖ *THE SACRED ROMANCE, 6–7*

*If anyone is thirsty, let him come to me and drink. Whoever believes
in me, as the Scripture has said, streams of living water will flow
from within him.*

—JOHN 7:37–38

The religious technocrats of Jesus' day confronted him with what they believed were the standards of a life pleasing to God. The external life, they argued, the life of ought and duty and service, was what mattered. "You're dead wrong," Jesus said. "In fact, you're just plain dead whitewashed tombs. What God cares about is the inner life, the life of the heart" (Matt. 23:25–28). Throughout the Old and New Testaments, the life of the heart is clearly God's central concern. When the people of Israel fell into a totally external life of ritual and observance, God lamented, "These people . . . honor me with their lips, but their hearts are far from me" (Isa. 29:13).

Our heart is the key to the Christian life.

The apostle Paul informs us that hardness of heart is behind all the addictions and evils of the human race (Rom. 1:21–25). To lose heart is to lose everything. Sadly, most of us watch the oil level in our car more carefully than we watch over the life of our heart.

In one of the greatest invitations ever offered to man, Christ stood up amid the crowds in Jerusalem and said, "If anyone is thirsty, let him come to me and drink. Whoever believes in me, as the Scripture has said, streams of living water will flow from within him" (John 7:37–38). If we aren't aware of our soul's deep thirst, his offer means nothing. But, if we will recall, it was from the longing of our hearts that most of us first responded to Jesus.

❖ THE SACRED ROMANCE, 9

Meanwhile we groan, longing to be clothed with our heavenly dwelling.

—2 CORINTHIANS 5:2

The heart," Blaise Pascal said, "has its reasons which reason knows nothing of." Something in us longs, hopes, maybe even at times believes that this is not the way things were supposed to be. Our desire fights the assault of death upon life. And so people with terminal illnesses get married. Prisoners in a concentration camp plant flowers. Lovers long divorced still reach out in the night to embrace one who is no longer there. It's like the phantom pain experienced by those who have lost a limb. Feelings still emanate from that region where once was a crucial part of them, and they will sometimes find themselves being careful not to bang the corner of a table or slam the car door on a leg or arm long since removed. Our hearts know a similar reality. At some deep level, we refuse to accept the fact that this is the way things are, or must be, or always will be.

Simone Weil was right: there are only two things that pierce the human heart—beauty and affliction. Moments we wish would last forever and moments we wish had never begun. What are we to make of these messengers?

❀ *THE JOURNEY OF DESIRE, 8–9*

Surely God is good to Israel,
to those who are pure in heart.
—PSALM 73:1

The Arrows strike at the most vital places in our hearts, at the things we care most about. The deepest questions we ever ask are directly related to our hearts' greatest needs and the answers life gives us shape our images of ourselves, of life, and of God.

Who am I? The Romance whispers that we are someone special, that our hearts are good because they are made for someone good; the arrows of Satan tell us we are a dime a dozen, worthless, even dark and twisted, dirty.

Where is life to be found? The Romance tells us life will flourish when we give it away in love and heroic sacrifice. The Arrows tell us that we must arrange for what little life there may be, manipulating our world and all the while watching our backs.

"God is good," the Romance tells us. "You can release the well-being of your heart to him." The Arrows strike back, "Don't ever let life out of your control," and they seem to impale with such authority, unlike the gentle urges of the Romance, that in the end we are driven to find some way to contain them.

The only way seems to be to kill our longing for the Romance, much in the same way we harden our heart to someone who hurts us. *If I don't want so much*, we believe, *I won't be so vulnerable.* Instead of dealing with the Arrows, we silence the longing. That seems to be our only hope.

And so we lose heart.

❖ *THE SACRED ROMANCE, 32–33*

I rejoice in following your statutes
as one rejoices in great riches.
I meditate on your precepts
and consider your ways.
—PSALM 119:14–15

We have lived for so long with a "propositional" approach to Christianity, we have nearly lost its true meaning. As Mary Stewart Van Leeuwen says,

> Much of it hinges on your view of scripture. Are you play-
> ing proof-text poker with Genesis plus the Gospels and
> Paul's epistles, with everything else just sort of a big mystery
> in between . . . ? Or do you see scripture as being a cosmic
> drama—creation, fall, redemption, future hope—dramatic
> narratives that you can apply to all areas of life? (Interview
> in *Prism*)

Our modern, rationalistic approach to life has stripped us of that, leaving a faith that is barely more than mere fact-telling. Modern evangelicalism reads like an IRS 1040 form. As British theologian Alister McGrath warns, "To reduce revelation to principles or concepts is to suppress the element of mystery, holiness and wonder to God's self-disclosure. 'First principles' may enlighten and inform; they do not force us to our knees in reverence and awe, as with Moses at the burning bush, or the disciples in the presence of the risen Christ."

❁ *THE SACRED ROMANCE, 45*

The secret things belong to the LORD our God, but the things revealed belong to us and to our children forever, that we may follow all the words of this law.

— DEUTERONOMY 29:29

Walter Brueggemann wisely stated, "We live our lives before the wild, dangerous, unfettered and free character of the living God."

The mysterious Romancing or the message of the Arrows — which captures the essence of life? Should we keep our hearts open to the Romance or concentrate on protecting ourselves from the Arrows? Should we live with hopeful abandon, trusting in a larger story whose ending is good, or should we live in our small stories and glean what we can from the Romance while trying to avoid the Arrows?

Perhaps God, as the Author of the story we're all living in, would tilt the scale in a favorable direction if we knew we could trust him. And therein lies our dilemma. There seems to be no direct correlation between the way we live our lives and the resulting fate God has in store for us, at least on this earth. Abraham's grandson, Jacob, lives the life of a manipulator and is blessed. Jesus lives for the sake of others and is crucified. And we never quite know when we're going to run into the uncertainty of the part God has written for us in his play, whether our character has significant lines yet to speak or will even survive the afternoon.

❖ *THE SACRED ROMANCE, 47*

O God, do not remain quiet;
Do not be silent and, O God, do not be still.
—PSALMS 83:1 NASB

The question lodged deep in our hearts, hidden from our conscious minds, is: "Do you care for me, God?"

What's under that question?

Blaise Pascal, in his *Pensées*, says, "The heart has its reasons which reason knows nothing of." Under that question are our personal stories, often punctuated by the message of the Arrows: parents who were emotionally absent, bedtimes without words or hugs, ears that were too big and noses that were too small, others chosen for playground games while we were not, and prayers about all these things seemingly met with silence. And embedded in our stories, deep down in our hearts, in a place so well guarded that they have rarely if ever been exposed to the light of day, are other grief-laden and often angry questions: "God, why did you allow this to happen to me? Why did you make me like this? What will you allow to happen next?"

In the secret places of our hearts, we believe God is the One who did not protect us from these things or even the One who perpetrated them upon us. Our questions about him make us begin to live with a deep apprehension that clings anxiously to the depths of our hearts. Do you really care for me, God?

This is the question that has shipwrecked many of our hearts, leaving them grounded on reefs of pain and doubt, no longer free to accompany us on spiritual pilgrimage. What are we to make of God's wildness in allowing these things to happen?

❖ *THE SACRED ROMANCE, 49–50*

What good will it be for a man if he gains the whole world, yet forfeits his soul?

—MATTHEW 16:26

Our troubles and our heartbreaks tell us something about our true destiny. Tragedies elicit the cry, "This isn't the way it was supposed to be!" are also telling the truth—it *isn't* the way it was supposed to be. Blaise Pascal writes,

> Man is so great that his greatness appears even in knowing himself to be miserable. A tree has no sense of its misery. It is true that to know we are miserable is to be miserable; but to know we are miserable is also to be great. Thus all the miseries of man prove his grandeur; they are the miseries of a dignified personage, the miseries of a dethroned monarch ... What can this incessant craving, and this impotence of attainment mean, unless there was once a happiness belonging to man, of which only the faintest traces remain, in that void which he attempts to fill with everything within his reach? (*Pensées*)

Should the king in exile pretend he is happy there? Should he not seek his own country? His miseries are his ally; they urge him on. And so let them grow, if need be. But do not forsake the secret of life; do not despise those kingly desires. We abandon the most important journey of our lives when we abandon desire.

❀ *THE JOURNEY OF DESIRE, 12–13*

The LORD is a warrior!
— EXODUS 15:3

I think even a quick read of the Old Testament would be enough to convince you that *war* is a central theme of God's activity. There is the Exodus, where God goes to war to set his captive people free. Blood. Hail. Locusts. Darkness. Death. Plague after plague descends on Egypt like a boxer's one-two punch, like the blows of some great ax. Pharaoh releases his grip, but only for a moment. The fleeing slaves are pinned against the Red Sea when Egypt makes a last charge, hurtling down on them in chariots. God drowns those soldiers in the sea, every last one of them. Standing in shock and joy on the opposite shore, the Hebrews proclaim, "The LORD is a warrior!" (Ex. 15:3). Yahweh is a warrior.

Then it's war to get *to* the Promised Land. Moses and company have to do battle against the Amalekites; again God comes through, and Moses shouts, "The LORD will be at war against the Amalekites from generation to generation" (Ex.17:16). Yahweh will be at war. Indeed. You ain't seen nothin' yet. Then it's war to get *into* the Promised Land—Joshua and the battle of Jericho, and all that. After the Jews gain the Promised Land, it's war after war to *keep* it. Israel battles the Canaanites, the Philistines, the Midianites, the Egyptians again, the Babylonians—and on and on it goes. Deborah goes to war; Gideon goes to war; King David goes to war. Elijah wars against the prophets of Baal; Jehoshaphat battles the Edomites. Are you getting the picture?

❁ WAKING THE DEAD, *14–15*

Gird your sword upon your side, O mighty one.
— PSALM 45:3

Many people think the theme of war ends with the Old Testament. Not at all. Jesus says, "I did not come to bring peace, but a sword" (Matt. 10:34). In fact, his birth involved another battle in heaven (Rev. 12:1–5, 7–8, 17).

The birth of Christ was an act of war, an *invasion*. The Enemy knew it and tried to kill him as a babe (Matt. 2:13). The whole life of Christ is marked by battle and confrontation. He kicks out demons with a stern command. He rebukes a fever and it leaves Peter's mother-in-law. He rebukes a storm and it subsides. He confronts the Pharisees time and again to set God's people free from legalism. In a loud voice he wakes Lazarus from the dead. He descends to hell, wrestles the keys of hell and death from Satan, and leads a train of captives free (Eph. 4:8–9; Rev. 1:18). And when he returns, I might point out, Jesus will come mounted on a steed of war, with his robe dipped in blood, armed for battle (Rev. 19:11–15).

War is not just one among many themes in the Bible. It is *the* backdrop for the whole Story, the context for everything else. God is at war. He is trampling out the vineyards where the grapes of wrath are stored. And what is he fighting for? Our freedom and restoration. The glory of God is man fully alive. In the meantime, Paul says, *arm yourselves,* and the first piece of equipment he urges us to don is the belt of truth (Eph. 6:10–18).

❖ WAKING THE DEAD, *15–16*

Hope deferred makes the heart sick.
—Proverbs 13:12 NLT

Despair," wrote James Houston, "is the fate of the desiring soul." How agonizing it can be to awaken desire! Over the past year, I have wrestled deeply with what it means to go on. God has come to me again and again, insisting that I not give up the dream. I have ranted and railed, fought him and dismissed him. It feels crazy to desire anymore. What does it mean to live the rest of my life without my closest friend?

But I am not alone in this. Most of you will by this time have lost a parent, a spouse, even a child. Your hopes for your career have not panned out. Your health has given way. Relationships have turned sour. We all know the dilemma of desire, how awful it feels to open our hearts to joy, only to have grief come in. They go together. We know that. What we don't know is what to do with it, how to live in this world with desire so deep in us and disappointment lurking behind every corner. After we've taken a few arrows, dare we even desire? Something in me knows that to kill desire is to kill my heart altogether. Langston Hughes wrote,

Hold fast to dreams
For if dreams die
Life is a broken-winged bird
That cannot fly.
  ("Dreams")

❀ The Journey of Desire, 22–23

Ask and it will be given to you; seek and you will find; knock and the door will be opened to you.

—MATTHEW 7:7

In the Gospel of John, Jesus extends the offer to anyone who realizes that his life just isn't touching his deep desire: "If you are thirsty, come to me! If you believe in me, come and drink! For the Scriptures declare that rivers of living water will flow out from within" (John 7:37–38 NLT). Surely, those scripturally learned Jews must have recalled God's long-standing invitation to them, spoken seven hundred years earlier through the prophet Isaiah,

Come, all you who are thirsty,
  come to the waters;
and you who have no money,
  come, buy and eat!
Come, buy wine and milk
  without money and without cost.
  (55:1)

Somehow, the message had gotten lost by the time Jesus showed up on the scene. The Jews of his day were practicing a very soul-killing spirituality, a lifeless religion of duty and obligation. They had abandoned desire and replaced it with knowledge and performance. Desire was out of the question; duty was the path that people must walk. No wonder they feared Jesus. He came along and started *appealing* to desire.

❖ *THE JOURNEY OF DESIRE, 37–38*

In him was life, and that life was the light of men.
—JOHN 1:4

Eternal life—we tend to think of it in terms of existence that never comes to an end. And the existence it seems to imply—a sort of religious experience in the sky—leaves us wondering if we *would* want it to go on forever. But Jesus is quite clear that when he speaks of eternal life, what he means is life that is absolutely wonderful and can never be diminished or stolen from you. He says, "I have come that they may have life, and have it to the full" (John 10:10). Not, "I have come to threaten you into line," or "I have come to exhaust you with a long list of demands." Not even, "I have come primarily to forgive you." But simply, *My purpose is to bring you life in all its fullness.* Dallas Willard writes in *The Divine Conspiracy,*

> Jesus offers himself as God's doorway into the life that is truly life. Confidence in him leads us today, as in other times, to become his apprentices in eternal living. "Those who come through me will be safe," he said. "They will go in and out and find all they need. I have come into their world that they may have life, and life to the limit."

In other words, eternal life is not primarily *duration* but *quality* of life, "life to the limit." It cannot be stolen from us, and so it does go on. But the focus is on the life itself.

❂ *The Journey of Desire*, 38–39

Do not store up for yourselves treasures on earth, where moth and
rust destroy, and where thieves break in and steal. But store up for
yourselves treasures in heaven, where moth and rust do not destroy,
and where thieves do not break in and steal. For where your treasure
is, there your heart will be also.

—MATTHEW 6:19–23

God must, from time to time, and sometimes very insistently, disrupt our lives *so that* we release our grasping of life here and now. Usually through pain. God is asking us to let go of the things we love and have given our hearts to, so that we can give our hearts even more fully to him. He thwarts us in our attempts to make life work so that our efforts fail, and we must face the fact that we don't really look to God for life. Our first reaction is usually to get angry with him, which only serves to make the point. Don't you hear people say, "Why did God let this happen?" far more than you hear them say, "Why aren't I more fully given over to God?"

We see God as a means to an end rather than the end itself. God as the assistant to our life versus God *as* our life. We don't see the process of our life as coming to the place where we are fully his and he is our all.

❖ WALKING WITH GOD, 86–87

The LORD your God is testing you to find out whether you love him with all your heart and with all your soul.

—DEUTERONOMY 13:3

Until God has become our all, and we are fully his, we will continue to make idols of the good things he gives us. Whatever else might be the reason for our current suffering, we can know this: "The LORD your God is testing you to find out whether you love him with all your heart and with all your soul" (Deut. 13:3). We are so committed to arranging for a happy little life that God has to thwart us to bring us back to himself. It's a kind of regular purging, I suppose. A sort of cleansing for the soul. I have to yield not only all my hopes for this fall, but my basic approach to life as well. Of all tests, I do not want to fail this one.

Now, I am *not* suggesting that God causes all the pain in our lives. I don't believe he pushed me off my horse to make a point. In fact, I believe he saved my life. But pain does come, and what will we do with it? What does it reveal? What might God be up to? How might he redeem our pain? Those are questions worth asking.

Don't waste your pain.

❖ *WALKING WITH GOD*, 87–88

I no longer call you servants, because a servant does not know his master's business. Instead, I have called you friends, for everything that I learned from my Father I have made known to you.
—JOHN 15:15

If I were to choose one quality above all others to guide a man, it would be friendship with God. For if he has this, it will compensate for whatever other deficiencies the man may have, and if he does *not* have this, he will not become the king he could have been.

The passage from John's epistle describing the different levels of relationship with God gives special attention to "fathers," which in this case means mature men:

> I write to you, fathers,
>> because you have known him who is from the beginning.
>> . . . I write to you, fathers,
>> because you have known him who is from the beginning. (1 John 2:13, 14)

The same refrain is used twice. Something stable is implied here, something established and unchanging. They are the ones who "have known him who is from the beginning."

"Have," meaning it's been going on for some time now.

"Known," meaning actual, personal, intimate knowledge, as a man knows his best friend.

"Him who is from the beginning," meaning God. The fathers are the friends of God.

❖ FATHERED BY GOD, *181–182*

Be strong, and let us show ourselves courageous for the sake of our people and for the cities of our God; and may the LORD do what is good in His sight.

—2 SAMUEL 10:12 NASB

That strength so essential to men is also what makes them heroes. If a neighborhood is safe, it's because of the strength of men. Slavery was stopped by the strength of men, at a terrible price to them and their families. The Nazis were stopped by men. Apartheid wasn't defeated by women. Who gave their seats up on the lifeboats leaving the *Titanic*, so that women and children would be saved? And have we forgotten—it was a Man who let himself be nailed to Calvary's cross. This isn't to say women can't be heroic. I know many heroic women. It's simply to remind us that God made men the way they are because we desperately *need* them to be the way they are. Yes, a man is a dangerous thing. So is a scalpel. It can wound or it can save your life. You don't make it safe by making it dull; you put it in the hands of someone who knows what he's doing.

If you've spent any time around horses, you know a stallion can be a major problem. They're strong, very strong, and they've got a mind of their own. Stallions typically don't like to be bridled, and they can get downright aggressive—especially if there are mares around. A stallion is hard to tame. If you want a safer, quieter animal, there's an easy solution: castrate him. A gelding is much more compliant. You can lead him around by the nose; he'll do what he's told without putting up a fuss.

There's only one problem: Geldings don't give life.

❖ *WILD AT HEART*, 83–84

*For if you live according to the flesh you will die; but if by the Spirit
you put to death the deeds of the sinful nature you will live.*
—ROMANS 8:13 NKJV

There sure isn't any good thing in me." It's so common this
mind-set, this idea that we are no-good wretches, ready to sin
at a moment's notice, incapable of goodness, and certainly far
from any glory.

It's also unbiblical.

The passage people think they are referring to is Romans 7:18,
where Paul says, "For I know that in me (that is, in my flesh,)
dwelleth no good thing" (KJV). Notice the distinction he makes.
He does *not* say, "there is nothing good in me. Period." What he
says is that *"in my flesh* dwelleth no good thing." The flesh is the
old nature, the old life, crucified with Christ. The flesh is the very
thing God removed from our hearts when he circumcised them
by his Spirit. In Galatians Paul goes on to explain, "Those who
belong to Christ Jesus have crucified the sinful nature of the flesh
with its passions and desires" (5:24). He does *not* say, "I am incapable of good." He says, *"In my flesh* dwelleth no good thing."

Yes, we still battle with sin. *Yes,* we still have to crucify our flesh
on a daily basis. We have to *choose* to live from the new heart,
and our old nature doesn't go down without a fight. The question
on the table is: Does the Bible teach that Christians are nothing
but sinners—that there is nothing good in us? The answer is *no!*
Christ lives in you. You have a new heart. Your heart is good. That
sinful nature you battle *is not who you are.*

❀ WAKING THE DEAD, 75–76

Surely you have heard about the . . . grace that was given to me for you, that is, the mystery made known to me by revelation, as I have already written briefly. In reading this, then, you will be able to understand my insight into the mystery of Christ, which was not made known to men in other generations as it has now been revealed to me.

—EPHESIANS 3:2–5

Twice, in the famous chapter of Romans 7, where Paul presents a first-person angst about our battle against sin:

> As it is, *it is no longer I myself* who do it, but sin living in me. I know that nothing good lives in me, that is, in my sinful nature . . . Now if I do what I do not want to do, *it is no longer I* who do it, but it is sin living in me that does it . . . For in my inner being I delight in God's law." (vv. 17–18, 20, emphasis added)

Paul is making a crucial distinction. *This is not me; this is not my true heart.* Listen to how he talks about himself in other places. He opens every letter by introducing himself as "Paul, an apostle." Not as a sinner, but as an apostle, writing to "the saints." Dump the religiosity; think about this *mythically.* Paul, appointed as a Great One in the kingdom, writing other Great Allies of the kingdom. How bold of him. There is no false humility, no groveling.

Paul is unashamed to say that he knows things no man before him knew. He even assumes they've heard about him, the mysteries revealed to him. That is part of his glory. His humility comes through clearly, in that he quickly admits that it's all been a gift, and in fact, a gift given to him *for others.*

❀ WAKING THE DEAD, 76–77

O LORD, our Lord,
how majestic is your name in all the earth!
You have set your glory
above the heavens.

—PSALM 8:1

I just let out a deep sigh. That we even need to explain how beauty is so *absolutely essential* to God only shows how dull we have grown to him, to the world in which we live, and to Eve. Far too many years of our own spiritual lives were lived with barely a nod to beauty, to the central role that beauty plays in the life of God, and in our own lives. How could we have missed this?

Beauty is essential to God. No—that's not putting it strongly enough. Beauty is the essence of God.

The first way we know this is through nature, the world God has given us. Scripture says that the created world is filled with the glory of God (Isa. 6:3). In what way? Primarily through its *beauty*. Nature is not primarily functional. It is primarily beautiful. Stop for a moment and let that sink in. We're so used to evaluating everything (and everyone) by their usefulness, this thought will take a minute or two to dawn on us. Nature is not primarily functional. It is primarily *beautiful*. Which is to say, beauty is in and of itself a great and glorious good, something we need in large and daily doses (for our God has seen fit to arrange for this). Nature at the height of its glory shouts *Beauty is essential!* revealing that Beauty is the essence of God. The whole world is full of his glory.

❀ CAPTIVATING, 23–24

*I will go before you
and will level the mountains;
I will break down gates of bronze
and cut through bars of iron.
I will give you the treasures of darkness,
riches stored in secret places,
so that you may know that I am the LORD,
the God of Israel, who summons you by name.*
—ISAIAH 45:2–3

God's imagery of going before us lets us know that he desires us to go on a journey. This is not so frightening. Most of us are aware that the Christian life requires a pilgrimage of some sort. We know we are sojourners. What we have sometimes not given much thought to is what kind of a journey we are to be taking.

As we stand at this intersection of God's calling, we look down two highways that travel in very different directions. The first highway quickly takes a turn and disappears from our view. We cannot see clearly where it leads, but there are ominous clouds in the near distance. Standing still long enough to look down this road makes us aware of an anxiety inside, an anxiety that threatens to crystallize into unhealed pain and forgotten disappointment. We check our valise and find no up-to-date road map but only the smudged parchment containing the scribbled anecdotes and warnings by a few who have traveled the way of the heart before us. They encourage us to follow, but their rambling gives no real answers to our queries on how to navigate the highway.

❖ THE SACRED ROMANCE, 127–28

All these I have kept since I was a boy," he said. When Jesus heard this, he said to him, "You still lack one thing. Sell everything you have and give to the poor, and you will have treasure in heaven. Then come, follow me." When he heard this, he became very sad, because he was a man of great wealth.

—LUKE 18:21–23

The Evil One has basically two ploys. If he cannot get us to kill our hearts and bury our desire, then he is delighted to seduce our desire into a trap. Once we give over our desire for life to any object other than God, we become ensnared. We become slaves to any number of things that we thought would serve us. Repression of desire is a much less dangerous stage in the process. Addiction is far worse, for as May explains,

> Our addictions are our own worst enemies. They enslave us with chains that are of our own making and yet that, paradoxically, are virtually beyond our control. Addiction also makes idolaters of us all . . . preventing us from truly, freely loving God and one another. (*Addiction and Grace*)

Like the rich young ruler, we find we cannot give up our treasured possessions, even though God himself is standing before us with a better offer. If you think this sad story is not also your own, you are out of touch with yourself. The father of lies turns our most precious treasure—our longing for God and for his kingdom— into our worst enemy. It is truly diabolical.

❖ THE JOURNEY OF DESIRE, *84*

What I feared has come upon me;
what I dreaded has happened to me.
—JOB 3:25

It seems at times that God will go to any length to thwart the very thing we most deeply want. We can't get a job. Our attempt to find a spouse never pans out. The doctors aren't able to help us with our infertility. Isn't this precisely the reason we fear to desire in the first place? Life is hard enough as it is, but to think that God himself is working against us is more than disheartening.

As Job cried out, "What do you gain by oppressing me? . . . You hunt me like a lion and display your awesome power against me" (10:3, 16 NLT).

I want to state very clearly that not every trial in our life is specially arranged for us by God. Much of the heartache we know comes from living in a broken world filled with broken people. But there are times when God seems to be set *against* us. Unless we understand our desperate hearts and our incredible tenacity to arrange for the life we want, these events will just seem cruel.

When we lived in Eden, there was virtually no restriction on the pleasure around us. We could eat *freely* from any tree in the Garden. Our desire was innocent and fully satisfied. We had it all, but we threw it away. By mistrusting God's heart, by reaching to take control of what we wanted, Adam and Eve set in motion a process in our hearts, a desperate grasping that can be described only as *addiction*. Desire goes mad within us.

❧ *THE JOURNEY OF DESIRE, 91–92*

Whoever wants to save his life will lose it.
—LUKE 9:24

From the place of our woundedness we construct a false self. We find a few gifts that work for us, and we try to live off them. Stuart found he was good at math and science. He shut down his heart and spent all his energies perfecting his "Spock" persona. There, in the academy, he was safe; he was also recognized and rewarded. "When I was eight," confesses Brennan Manning, "the impostor, or false self, was born as a defense against pain. The impostor within whispered, 'Brennan, don't ever be your real self anymore because nobody likes you as you are. Invent a new self that everybody will admire and nobody will know.'" Notice the key phrase: "as a defense against pain," as a way of saving himself. The impostor is our plan for salvation.

So God must take it all away. He thwarts our plan for salvation; he shatters the false self. Our plan for redemption is hard to let go of; it clings to our hearts like an octopus.

❖ *WILD AT HEART,* 107–8

Apart from me you can do nothing.
—JOHN 15:5

Guys are unanimously embarrassed by their emptiness and woundedness; it is for most of us a tremendous source of shame. But it need not be. From the very beginning, back before the Fall and the assault, ours was meant to be a desperately dependent existence.

It's like a tree and its branches, explains Christ. You are the branches, I am the trunk. From me you draw your life; that's how it was meant to be. He's not berating us or mocking us or even saying it with a sigh, all the while thinking, *I wish they'd pull it together and stop needing me so much.* Not at all. We are *made* to depend on God; we are made for union with him, and nothing about us works right without it. As C. S. Lewis wrote,

> A car is made to run on gasoline, and it would not run properly on anything else. Now God designed the human machine to run on himself. He himself is the fuel our spirits were designed to burn, or the food our spirits were designed to feed on. There is no other.

Our sin is that stubborn part inside that wants, above all else, to be independent. There's a part of us fiercely committed to living in a way where we do not have to depend on anyone—especially God. We come to believe deep in our hearts that needing anyone for anything is a sort of weakness, a handicap.

❧ *WILD AT HEART, 121–22*

Jesus put his hands on the man's eyes. Then his eyes were opened, his sight was restored, and he saw everything clearly.
—MARK 8:25

If you wanted to learn how to heal the blind and you thought that following Christ around and watching how he did it would make things clear, you'd wind up pretty frustrated. He never does it the same way twice. He spits on one guy; for another, he spits on the ground and makes mud and puts that on his eyes. To a third he simply speaks, a fourth he touches, and a fifth he kicks out a demon. There are no formulas with God. The way in which God heals our wound is a deeply personal process. He is a person and he insists on working personally. For some, it comes in a moment of divine touch. For others, it takes place over time and through the help of another, maybe several others. As Agnes Sanford says, "There are in many of us wounds so deep that only the mediation of someone else to whom we may 'bare our grief' can heal us."

Remember—masculinity is bestowed by masculinity. The point is this: healing never happens outside of intimacy with Christ. The healing of our wound flows out of our union with him.

❊ *WILD AT HEART, 127–28*

Guard my life and rescue me;
let me not be put to shame,
for I take refuge in you.
—PSALM 25:20

The deeper reason we fear our own glory is that once we let others see it, they will have seen the truest us, and that is nakedness indeed. We can repent of our sin. We can work on our "issues." But there is nothing to be "done" about our glory. It's so naked. It's just there—the truest us. It is an awkward thing to shimmer when everyone else around you is not, to walk in your glory with an unveiled face when everyone else is veiling his or hers. For a woman to be truly feminine and beautiful is to invite suspicion, jealousy, misunderstanding. A friend confided in me, "When you walk into a room, every woman looks at you to see—are you prettier than they are? Are you a threat?"

And that is why living from your glory is the only loving thing to do. You cannot love another person from a false self. You cannot love another while you are still hiding. You cannot love another unless you offer her your heart. It takes courage to live from your heart.

Our deepest fear of all: we will need to live from it. To admit we do have a new heart and a glory from God, to begin to let it be unveiled and embrace it as true—that means the next thing God will do is ask us to live from it. Come out of the boat. Take the throne. Be what he meant us to be. And that feels risky . . . really risky. But it is also exciting. It is coming fully alive.

❖ WAKING THE DEAD, 87–88

*The gate is small and the way is narrow that leads to life, and there
are few who find it.*

—MATTHEW 7:14

Either we wake to tackle our "to do" list, get things done, guided by our morals and whatever clarity we may at the moment have (both rather lacking to the need, I might add); or we wake in the midst of a dangerous story, as God's intimate ally, following him into the unknown.

If you're not pursuing a dangerous quest with your life, well, then, you don't need a Guide. If you haven't found yourself in the midst of a ferocious war, then you won't need a seasoned Captain. If you've settled in your mind to live as though this is a fairly neutral world and you are simply trying to live your life as best you can, then you can probably get by with the Christianity of tips and techniques. Maybe. I'll give you about a fifty-fifty chance. But if you intend to live in the Story that God is telling, and if you want the life he offers, then you are going to need more than a handful of principles, however noble they may be. There are too many twists and turns in the road ahead, too many ambushes waiting only God knows where, too much at stake. You cannot possibly prepare yourself for every situation. Narrow is the way, said Jesus. How shall we be sure to find it? We need God intimately, and we need him desperately.

"You have made known to me the path of life," David said (Ps. 16:11). Yes—that's it. In all the ins and outs of this thing we call living, there is one narrow path to life, and we need help finding it.

❧ WAKING THE DEAD, 95

"Lord," Ananias answered, "I have heard many reports about this man and all the harm he has done to your saints in Jerusalem. And he has come here with authority from the chief priests to arrest all who call on your name." But the Lord said to Ananias, "Go!"

—ACTS 9:13–15

Wisdom is crucial. But wisdom is not enough. Wisdom is essential . . . and insufficient.

Saul of Tarsus was headed to Damascus, "breathing out murderous threats against the Lord's disciples," with official documents granting him permission to arrest all Christians in the city and have them sent to prison (Acts 9:1–2). Now, you and I know that Jesus changed Saul's agenda rather radically before he ever reached the city—the blinding light, the voice from heaven, the total realignment of his worldview. But the believers in Damascus don't know all this. As they wait in fear for Saul's arrival, God speaks to one of them, a man named Ananias, and tells him to go to the house where Saul is staying, lay hands on him, and pray for him.

Understandably, Ananias suggests this is not such a good idea. "Lord . . . I have heard many reports about this man and all the harm he has done to your saints in Jerusalem. And he has come here with authority from the chief priests to arrest all who call on your name" (9:13–14). It's okay, God says, he's my man now. Against wisdom Ananias goes, and the greatest of all the apostles is launched.

The Bible is full of such counterintuitive direction from God.

❖ *WAKING THE DEAD, 100–101*

*My teaching is not my own. It comes from him who sent me. If anyone
chooses to do God's will, he will find out whether my teaching comes
from God or whether I speak on my own."*

—JOHN 7:16–17

E ven Jesus endured assault—not the open accusation that he
had a wicked heart, but the more subtle kind, the seemingly
"innocent" arrows that come through "misunderstanding."

When the Jewish Feast of Tabernacles was near, Jesus'
brothers said to him, "You ought to leave here and go to
Judea, so that your disciples may see the miracles you do.
No one who wants to become a public figure acts in secret.
Since you are doing these things, show yourself to the
world." For even his own brothers did not believe in him.
(John 7:2–5)

I think we can relate to that. Did your family believe in you? Did
they even notice your heart at all? Have they been thrilled by your
choices, or has their disappointment made it clear that you just
aren't what you're supposed to be? At another point in his ministry,
Jesus' family shows up to collect him. "Your mother and brothers
are standing outside, wanting to see you" (Luke 8:19). They thinks
he's lost it, and they've come to bring him home, poor man.

Misunderstanding is damaging, more insidious because we
don't identify it as an attack on the heart. How subtly it comes,
sowing doubt and discouragement where there should have been
validation and support. There must be something wrong with us.

❊ WAKING THE DEAD, *117*

> *Early in the morning, Jesus stood on the shore, but the disciples did*
> *not realize that it was Jesus.*
> *He called out to them, "Friends, haven't you any fish?"*
> *"No," they answered.*
> *He said, "Throw your net on the right side of the boat and you will*
> *find some." When they did, they were unable to haul the net in*
> *because of the large number of fish.*
> *Then the disciple whom Jesus loved said to Peter, "It is the Lord!" . . .*
> *When they landed, they saw a fire of burning coals there with fish*
> *on it, and some bread . . . Jesus said to them, "Come and have*
> *breakfast."*

—JOHN 21:4–7, 9, 12

Now think about this for a minute. You're the Son of God. You've just accomplished the greatest work of your life, the stunning rescue of mankind. You rose from the dead. What would you do next? Have a cookout with a few friends? It seems so unspiritual, so *ordinary*. Do you see that eternal life does not become something totally "other," but rather that life goes on— only as it should be?

Jesus did not vanish into a mystical spirituality, becoming one with the cosmic vibration. Jesus has a body, and it's *his* body. His wounds have been healed, but the scars remain—not gruesome, but lovely, a remembrance of all he did for us. His friends recognize him. They share a bite to eat. This is our future as well—our lives will be healed and we shall go on, never to taste death again.

❖ *THE JOURNEY OF DESIRE, 118*

*Get rid of all bitterness, rage and anger, brawling and slander, along
with every form of malice. Be kind and compassionate to one another,
forgiving each other, just as in Christ God forgave you.*
—Ephesians 4:31–32

Time has come for us to forgive our fathers. Paul warns us that
unforgiveness and bitterness can wreck our lives and the lives
of others (Eph. 4:31; Heb. 12:15). I am sorry to think of all the
years my wife endured the anger and bitterness that I redirected
at her from my father. As someone has said, forgiveness is setting
a prisoner free and then discovering the prisoner was you.

Now you must understand: forgiveness is a choice. It is not
a feeling, but an act of the will. As Neil Anderson has written,
"Don't wait to forgive until you feel like forgiving; you will never
get there. Feelings take time to heal after the choice to forgive
is made." We allow God to bring the hurt up from our past, for
"if your forgiveness doesn't visit the emotional core of your life,
it will be incomplete." We acknowledge that it hurt, that it mattered, and we choose to extend forgiveness to our fathers. This is
not saying, "It didn't really matter"; it is *not* saying, "I probably
deserved part of it anyway." Forgiveness says, "It was wrong, it
mattered, and I release you."

And then we ask God to father us, and to tell us our true name.

❖ *Wild at Heart, 131–32*

The glory of young men is their strength,
gray hair the splendor of the old.
—PROVERBS 20:29

I have had no formal mentor in writing, no earthly father to father me in this beautiful, awful, lonely calling, fraught with dangers. But the Father has fathered me, and he has sent a sage or two along at just the right moment. One sage has been Norman Maclean, author of *A River Runs Through It*. (An important reminder that mentors and fathers need not be physically present, nor even still living.)

Late in his life, Maclean began work on *Young Men and Fire*. It was, for him, essential to what he called his "anti-shuffleboard philosophy," his defense against simply fading away with age. Maclean recounted:

> I wanted this possible extension of life to be hard as always, but also new, something not done before, like writing stories. That would be sure to be hard, and to make stories fresh I would have to find a new way of looking at things I had known nearly all my life, such as scholarship and the woods.

Maclean wrote this in his eighties—the research for the book requiring years of inquiry—and yet he wants to make his life *harder*? *Fresher*? I am amazed.

Maclean undertakes a very difficult book, hoping in part that it "might save me from feeding geese." This is the heart of the sage— to make his greatest contribution with the last years of his life.

❧ *FATHERED BY GOD, 188*

Set up road signs;
put up guideposts.
Take note of the highway,
the road that you take.
—JEREMIAH 31:21

Can a younger man be a sage? Certainly, to some extent. Solomon was king when he wrote Proverbs. But then again, he was given an extraordinary gift of wisdom from God. Certainly Jesus was a Sage, for there is no teaching that even comes close to his insight and compassion. And he was just into his thirties. So yes, a younger man can offer wisdom, advice, experience, counsel—certainly that is what I've tried to do in my writing.

And yet . . . there are some things we just cannot know or understand until we have passed through the years that gray hair signifies. Say you are going to war in the Middle East. Would you rather spend an hour with a young officer from West Point, valedictorian of his class, who wrote his dissertation on Middle East conflicts, or, would you want to spend that time with Norman Schwarzkopf?

I rest my case. Just as you don't want a young man to become a king too soon, you don't want him to present himself as a sage too soon, either—whatever his credentials might be.

❖ FATHERED BY GOD, 195–96

*The news about him spread all the more, so that crowds of people
came to hear him and to be healed of their sicknesses. But Jesus often
withdrew to lonely places and prayed.*

—LUKE 5:15–16

One of the most profound surprises that has come about through walking with God has been with regard to people. People make up a very large part of our lives. We're surrounded by people. We deal with others every day, from the driver in front of us, to the waitress in the café, to the gal in the next office, to those who share our homes. And they are nearly always, one way or another, in some sort of need. Or crisis. Or self-inflicted drama. And one of the great dangers for the person who has begun to desire to please Christ is that we simply let our conscience be our guide in relating to others. We tend to jump in, as opposed to walking with God. Either we give too much or too little, or we offer what is needed, but at the wrong time.

It would be a revealing study to look at the way Jesus relates to people in the Gospel stories. Sometimes he stops mid-stride to offer a word or a kindness to what seems to me to be a pretty minor character, someone I think I would have ignored. Other times he ducks for cover, dodges an encounter completely (see Luke 5:12–16). He possesses a freedom toward others I find myself longing for. What would happen if we began to ask Jesus what *he* is saying when it comes to the people in our lives?

❀ *WALKING WITH GOD, 130–31*

Woe to you, teachers of the law and Pharisees, you hypocrites! You are like whitewashed tombs, which look beautiful on the outside but on the inside are full of dead men's bones and everything unclean.
— MATTHEW 23:7–8

Let's come back to something very basic to our pursuit of God and the transformation he is always after in our lives — everything we do has a reason behind it, a motive. Within the Christian community we tend to focus on behavior, and that is right and that is wrong. It matters how you treat people. It matters whether you lie or steal or commit adultery. Our actions have enormous consequences. However, according to Jesus, holiness is a matter of the heart. This is the gist of the Sermon on the Mount:

Why do you pray — to be seen as holy? Why do you give — to be seen as generous? Why do you fast — to impress others? Be careful not to do your 'acts of righteousness' before men, to be seen by them. If you do, you will have no reward from your Father in heaven. So when you give to the needy, do not announce it with trumpets, as the hypocrites do . . . And when you pray, do not be like the hypocrites, for they love to pray standing in the synagogues and on the street corners to be seen by men. (Matthew 6:1–2, 5)

Jesus is moving the whole question of genuine goodness to the internal, back to motive. If we will follow him in this, it will open up fields of goodness for us. If we'll be honest about what compels us.

❖ *WALKING WITH GOD, 155–56*

And you, my son Solomon, acknowledge the God of your father,
and serve him with wholehearted devotion and with a willing mind,
for the Lord searches every heart and understands every motive
behind the thoughts.

—1 CHRONICLES 28:9

Our motives are an essential category to consider when we are learning to walk with God.

I noticed that at the retreats we do, I am careful to be kind and attentive to people. Why is that? It could be love. But might it also be that I want to be *seen* as kind and attentive? I spent a lot of time working on this book. Why? Is it to bring the truth as best I can — or to impress you, to be thought well of, to avoid embarrassment?

You have something to say to a friend or coworker, and you choose e-mail. Why? Is it because it will help them understand you better or because it is easier to fire a shot from a distance? We're faithful to attend church. Why? Is it because we are really worshipping God or because we know people will talk if we don't? We hate confrontation, and we never speak up in a meeting. Why? Is it humility, or is it so that everyone will like us? We want our children to behave in public. Why? Might it have something to do with the fact that they are a reflection on us? How about what we choose to wear — is it because we like it? Or because it will cause others to think we're rugged or really cool or sexy, or because we desperately want to fit in and we're scared to death of what others will say?

Everything we do has a motive behind it.

❖ WALKING WITH GOD, *156–57*

*I have learned to be content whatever the circumstances. I know what
it is to be in need, and I know what it is to have plenty. I have learned
the secret of being content in any and every situation, whether well fed
or hungry, whether living in plenty or in want. I can do everything
through him who gives me strength.*

—PHILIPPIANS 4:11–13

There *are* things we are asked to live without. I have my list
and you have yours. What am I to do with the fact that despite
my walk with God, my willingness to follow, and my resolve to do
battle, there are things I have to live without?

As I was praying about my disappointments the other day, I
noticed something lingering beneath the surface. I realized that
somewhere along the way, I'd come to an agreement of sorts—I
need this. Not that I want it, and very much. But that I *need it*. It's
a very subtle and deadly shift. One that opens the door to despair
and a host of other enemies. I was coming to believe that God's
love and God's life are not enough. Isn't that what Adam and Eve
were seduced into believing—that God was not enough?

He had given them so much, but all they could see in their
fateful moment of temptation was the one thing they *didn't* have.
So they reached for it, even if it meant turning from God.

❖ *WALKING WITH GOD, 181–82*

The LORD God said, "It is not good for the man to be alone. I will make a helper suitable for him."
—GENESIS 2:18

Eve is God's relational specialist given to the world *to keep relationship a priority*.

Men have a way of letting these things slip. They'll go months without checking in on the health of their relationships. Years, even. And the world simply uses people, then spits them out when they are worn out and no longer "on top of their game." Our enemy despises relationship, hates love in any form, fears its redemptive power. This is why God sent Eve. Women are *needed* to protect relationships, bring them back to center stage where they belong.

Women frequently feel like the only ones who care. But as women, they must hang on to this—that because of the Trinity, relationship is *the* most important thing in the universe.

It is here, *starting* with our circles of intimacy, that women are first and foremost women. It is here that we must first turn our gaze to ask, "What does it look like to offer my Beauty, my fierce devotion, my love? How do they need me to be their *ezer*?" You have an irreplaceable role in your relationships. No one can be to the people in your life who you can be to them. No one can offer what you can offer. There are many things God calls us to do, but loving well always comes first. And don't your relationships feel *opposed*? Of course. They must be fought for.

You have been sent by the Trinity on behalf of love, of relationships. Fight for them.

❀ CAPTIVATING, *209–10*

What causes fights and quarrels among you? Don't they come from
your desires that battle within you? You want something but don't
get it. You kill and covet, but you cannot have what you want. You
quarrel and fight. You do not have, because you do not ask God.
—James 4:1–2

The life we have is so far from the life we truly want, and it doesn't take us long to find someone to blame. In order for our longings to be filled, we need the cooperation of others. I long for a loving embrace and a kind word when I get home. I long for my boys to listen attentively when I talk about important life lessons. I want my work to be appreciated. I want my friends to be there for me in hard times. "No man is an island," wrote John Donne, and he could have been speaking of desire. We need others—it's part of our design. Very few of our desires are self-fulfilling; *all* our deepest longings require others to come through for us. Inevitably, someone stands in the way.

At its best, the world is indifferent to my desires. The air traffic controllers aren't the least affected when I've been traveling for a week and the flight they've chosen to cancel is my last chance to get home to my family. So long as it doesn't affect them, they couldn't care less. We suffer the violation of indifference on a daily basis, from friends, from family, from complete strangers. We think we've grown to accept it as part of life, but the effect is building inside us. We weren't made to be ignored. And though we try to pretend it doesn't really matter, the collective effect of living in a world apathetic to our existence is doing damage to our souls.

❖ *The Journey of Desire, 25–26*

Come near to God and he will come near to you.
—JAMES 4:8

The reason we don't know what we want is that we're so *unacquainted* with our desire. We try to keep a safe distance between our daily lives and our heart's desire because it causes us so much trouble. We're surprised by our anger and threatened by what feels like a ravenous bear within us. Do we really want to open Pandora's box?

If you remember the Greek myth, Pandora was the wife of Epimetheus, given to him by Zeus. The gods provided many gifts to her, including a mysterious box, which she was warned never to open. Eventually, her curiosity got the better of her, and she lifted the lid. Immediately, a host of evils flew out, plagues against the mind and body of mankind. She tried to close the box, but to no avail; the troubles had been loosed.

Dare we awaken our hearts to their true desires? Dare we come alive? The dilemma is this: we can't seem to live with desire, and we can't live without it. In the face of this quandary most people decide to bury the whole question and put as much distance as they can between themselves and their desires. It is a logical and tragic act. The tragedy is increased tenfold when this suicide of soul is committed under the conviction that this is precisely what Christianity recommends. We have never been more mistaken.

❁ *THE JOURNEY OF DESIRE, 30*

All my longings lie open before you, O Lord;
my sighing is not hidden from you.
—Psalm 38:9

There are three desires that I have found essential to a woman's heart. Every woman yearns to be fought *for*. Listen to the longing of a woman's heart: she wants to be more than noticed—she wants to be *wanted*. She wants to be pursued.

Every woman also wants an adventure *to share*. To be cherished, pursued, fought for—yes. But also, I want to be strong and a *part* of the adventure. So many men make the mistake of thinking that the woman is the adventure. But that is where the relationship immediately goes downhill. A woman doesn't want to be the adventure; she wants to be caught up into something greater than herself.

And finally, every woman wants to have a beauty to unveil. Not to conjure, but to unveil. Most women feel the pressure to be beautiful from the time they are very young, but that is not what I speak of. There is also a deep desire to simply and truly *be* the beauty, and be delighted in.

The world kills a woman's heart when it tells her to be tough, efficient, and independent. Sadly, Christianity has missed her heart as well. Walk into most churches in America, look at what you find there. There is no doubt about it. You'd have to admit a Christian woman is . . . tired. All we've offered the feminine soul is pressure to "be a good servant." No one is fighting for her heart; there is no grand adventure to be swept up in; and every woman doubts very much that she has any beauty to unveil.

❀ *Wild at Heart*, 16–17

O God, you are my God,
earnestly I seek you;
my soul thirsts for you,
my body longs for you,
in a dry and weary land
where there is no water.
—PSALM 63:1

What if those deep desires in our hearts are telling us the truth, revealing to us the life we were *meant* to live? God gave us eyes so that we might see; he gave us ears that we might hear; he gave us wills that we might choose, and he gave us hearts that we might *live*. The way we handle the heart is everything. A man must *know* he is powerful; he must *know* he has what it takes. A woman must *know* she is beautiful; she must *know* she is worth fighting for.

"But you don't understand," said one woman to me. "I'm living with a hollow man." No, it's in there. His heart is there. "I don't know when I died," said another man. "But I feel like I'm just using up oxygen." I understand. Your heart may feel dead and gone, but it's there. Something wild and strong and valiant, just waiting to be released.

If you are going to know who you truly are *as a man*, if you are going to find a life worth living, if you are going to love a woman deeply and not pass on your confusion to your children, you simply must get your heart back. You must head up into the high country of the soul, into wild and uncharted regions and track down that elusive prey.

❀ *WILD AT HEART, 18*

*You have your heads in your Bibles constantly because you think you'll
find eternal life there. But you miss the forest for the trees. These
Scriptures are all about me! And here I am, standing right before you,
and you aren't willing to receive from me the life you say you want.*
—JOHN 5:39–40 *The Message*

The promise of life and the invitation to desire have again
been lost beneath a pile of religious teachings that put the
focus on knowledge and performance. Dallas Willard says,

> History has brought us to the point where the Christian
> message is thought to be essentially concerned only with
> how to deal with sin: with wrongdoing or wrong-being and
> its effects. Life, our actual existence, is not included in what
> is now presented as the heart of the Christian message, or it
> is included only marginally. (*The Divine Conspiracy*)

Thus Dallas describes the gospel we have today as "gospels of
sin management." Sin is the bottom line, and we have the cure.
Typically, it is a system of knowledge or performance, or a mixture
of both. Those in the knowledge camp put the emphasis on getting our doctrine in line. Right belief is seen as the means to life.
Desire is irrelevant; *content* is what matters. But notice this—the
Pharisees knew more about the Bible than most of us ever will,
and it *hardened* their hearts. Knowledge just isn't all it's cracked
up to be. If you are familiar with the biblical narrative, you will
remember that there were two special trees in Eden—the Tree
of Knowledge of Good and Evil and the Tree of Life. We got the
wrong tree. We got knowledge, and it hasn't done us much good.

I am coming to you now, but I say these things while I am still in the world, so that they may have the full measure of my joy within them.
—JOHN 17:13

Christianity is often presented as essentially the transfer of a body of knowledge. We learn about where the Philistines were from, and how much a drachma would be worth today, and all sorts of things about the original Greek. The information presented could not seem more irrelevant to our deepest desires.

Then there are the systems aimed at getting our behavior in line, one way or another. Regardless of where you go to church, there is nearly always an unspoken list of what you shouldn't do (tailored to your denomination and culture, but typically rather long) and a list of what you may do (usually much shorter—mostly religious activity that seems totally unrelated to our deepest desires and leaves us only exhausted). And this, we are told, is the good news. Know the right thing; do the right thing. This is life?

We don't need more facts, and we certainly don't need more things to do. We need *Life*, and we've been looking for it ever since we lost Paradise. Jesus appeals to our desire because he came to speak to it. When we abandon desire, we no longer hear or understand what he is saying. But we have returned to the message of the synagogue; we are preaching the law. And desire is the enemy. After all, desire is the single major hindrance to the goal—getting us in line. And so we are told to kill desire and call it sanctification. Or as Jesus put it to the Pharisees, "You load people down with rules and regulations, nearly breaking their backs, but never lift even a finger to help" (Luke 11:46 *The Message*).

❖ *THE JOURNEY OF DESIRE, 41–42*

As the deer pants for streams of water,
so my soul pants for you, O God.
My soul thirsts for God, for the living God.
When can I go and meet with God?
—PSALM 42:1–2

Compare the shriveled life held up as a model of Christian maturity with the life revealed in the book of Psalms:

You have made known to me the path of life;
*   you will fill me with joy in your presence,*
*   with eternal pleasures at your right hand. (16:11)*

O God, you are my God,
*   earnestly I seek you;*
My soul thirsts for you,
*   my body longs for you,*
in a dry and weary land,
*   where there is no water. (63:1)*

Ask yourself, could this person be promoted to a position of leadership in my church? Heavens, no. He is far too unstable, too passionate, too desirous. It's all about pleasure and desire and thirst. And David, who wrote most of the psalms, was called by God a "man after his own heart" (1 Sam. 13:14).

Christianity has nothing to say to the person who is completely happy with the way things are. Its message is for those who hunger and thirst—for those who desire life as it was meant to be.

❖ THE JOURNEY OF DESIRE, 42–43

But we have this treasure in jars of clay to show that this all-surpassing power is from God and not from us.

—2 CORINTHIANS 4:7

The reason we enjoy fairy tales—more than enjoy them—the reason we *identify with them* in some deep part of us is because they rest on two great truths: the hero really has a heart of gold and the beloved really possesses hidden beauty. I hope you got a glimpse of God's good heart. But what about the second great truth—could we possess hidden greatness? It seems too good to be true.

The theme of veiled identity runs through all great stories. As Buechner reminds us, "Not only does evil come disguised in the world of the fairy tale but often good does too." The heroines and heroes capture our hearts because we see long before they ever do their hidden beauty, courage, greatness. Cinderella, Sleeping Beauty, Snow White—they're not simple wenches after all. The beast and the frog—they're actually princes. Aladdin is "the diamond in the rough." If the narrative of the Scriptures teaches us anything, from the serpent in the Garden to the carpenter from Nazareth, it teaches us that things are rarely what they seem, that we shouldn't be fooled by appearances.

Your evaluation of your soul, which is drawn from a world filled with people still terribly confused about the nature of *their* souls, is probably wrong.

❖ *THE SACRED ROMANCE*, 92–93

"I am the Lord's servant," Mary answered. "May it be to me as you
have said." Then the angel left her. . . . And Mary said:
"My soul glorifies the Lord
and my spirit rejoices in God my Savior."
—LUKE 1:38, 46-47

When the history of the world is finally told rightly—one of the great joys when we reach the wedding feast of the Lamb—it will be as clear as day that women have been essential to the great moves of God upon this earth.

I wanted to say *"nearly* every great move," not wanting to overstate a crucial point and recognizing that there are moments when men have led the way. But Stasi chimed in and said, "Those men had mothers, didn't they?!" Okay. I concede. Women have been essential to every great movement of God.

In the Old Testament, there is the story of Rahab. It's clear that women supported the ministry of Jesus, financially and emotionally, and women were the ones who stayed with him when nearly all the men hightailed it and ran. In the New Testament, we encounter women such as Lydia, whose home became the staging point for the evangelism of Thyatira and Philippi. There is Priscilla, who risked her life to help Paul spread the gospel, and Junias, who was with Paul when he was in prison and whom he calls "outstanding among the apostles" (Rom. 16:7).

And of course, the salvation of mankind rested on the courage of a woman, a teenage girl. What if she had said, "No"? What if any of them had said, "No"?

❁   CAPTIVATING, 203–4

*Who is wise and understanding among you? Let him show it by his
good life, by deeds done in the humility that comes from wisdom.*
—JAMES 3:13

The fool may have seen many winters, but they do not seem to
have had any other effect on him beyond fatigue, or perhaps
cynicism. Scripture describes a fool as a man who will not submit
to wisdom, a man who refuses to be taught by all that life has to
teach him. "A fool spurns his father's discipline" (Prov. 15:5).
Sadly, there are many aged fools, as anyone who has spent time in
Congress, or a university, or in the bowels of religious bureaucra-
cies knows. Gray hair does not a sage make. No doubt you have
experienced that by now.

We need more men around who have lived through yesterday,
and even if they haven't conquered it, they have learned from it.
Young warriors will sometimes dismiss the older men in their lives
because those men no longer yearn for battle, or simply because
they don't come from "my generation." Thus the sixties adage,
"Never trust anyone over thirty." Insecure kings often dismiss the
older men around them, send them into early retirement, threatened because the older men know more than they do. And our
culture in the progressive West has dismissed the elderly for years
now, because we have worshipped adolescence. Our heroes are
the young and handsome.

The "winners." We've worshipped adolescence because we
don't want to grow up, don't want to pay the price of maturity.
That is why we have a world now of uninitiated men.

❖ *FATHERED BY GOD*, 202–3

I will not leave you as orphans; I will come to you. Before long, the
world will not see me anymore, but you will see me. Because I live, you
also will live. On that day you will realize that I am in my Father,
and you are in me, and I am in you.
—JOHN 14:18–20

Those of you older men who have been wounded or dismissed, I have seen something of how painful that can be. Seek the comfort and healing Christ offers. Let your heart be restored, for you *are* needed. This is also the story of George MacDonald, a prophet for the most part unwelcomed and unhonored in his time. His church ran him out because he unsettled them with his heart-centered theology and true holiness. One of his best books (in my opinion) is *Diary of an Old Soul*, which begins,

> *Lord, what I once had done with youthful might,*
> *Had I been from the first true to the truth,*
> *Grant me, now old, to do—with better sight,*
> *And humbler heart, if not the brain of youth;*
> *So wilt thou, in thy gentleness and truth,*
> *Lead back thy old soul, by the path of pain,*
> *Round to his best—young eyes and heart and brain.*

I am not alone in being profoundly grateful that he did. Much of what we have received from C. S. Lewis is a result of MacDonald's choice, for he became Lewis's mentor of sorts through his writings. In the spirit of MacDonald's prayer, what would you ask God for the strength now to do?

❧ *FATHERED BY GOD, 205*

I will give them an undivided heart and put a new spirit in them; I will remove from them their heart of stone and give them a heart of flesh.

—EZEKIEL 11:19

You have been ransomed by Christ. You are entirely pardoned for every wrong thought and desire and deed. This is what the vast majority of Christians understand as the central work of Christ for us. And make no mistake about it—it is a deep and stunning truth, one that will set you free and bring you joy. For a while. But the joy for most of us has proved fleeting, because we find that we need to be forgiven again and again.

Think of it: you are a shadow of the person you were meant to be. You have nothing close to the life you were meant to have. And you have no real chance of becoming that person or finding that life. However, you are forgiven. For the rest of your days, you will fail in your attempts to become what God wants you to be. You should seek forgiveness and try again. Eventually, shame and disappointment will cloud your understanding of yourself and your God. When this ongoing hell on earth is over, you will die, and you will be taken before your God for a full account of how you didn't measure up. But you will be forgiven. After that, you'll be asked to take your place in the choir of heaven. This is what we mean by "salvation."

The good news is . . . that is *not* Christianity. Oh, I know it is what most people now living *think* Christianity is all about, including the majority of Christians. Thank God, they are wrong. There is more. A *lot* more. And that "more" is what most of us have been longing for most of our lives.

❦ WAKING THE DEAD, *61–62*

*In Christ you were also circumcised, in the putting off of the sinful
nature, not with a circumcision done by the hands of men but with the
circumcision done by Christ.*

—COLOSSIANS 2:11

It's not just that the Cross did something *for* us. Something deep
and profound happened *to* us in the death of Christ.
Remember—the heart is the problem. God understands this better than anyone, and he goes for the root. God promised in the
new covenant to "take away your heart of stone." How? By joining
us to the death of Christ. Our nature was nailed to the cross with
Christ; we died there, with him, in him. Yes, it is a deep mystery—
"deep magic" as C. S. Lewis called it—but that does not make it
untrue. "The death he died, he died to sin once for all . . . In the
same way, count yourselves dead to sin" (Rom. 6:10–11). Jesus
was the Last Adam, the end of that terrible story.

You've been far more than forgiven. God has removed your
heart of stone. You've been delivered of what held you back from
what you were meant to be. You've been rescued from the part of
you that sabotages even your best intentions. Your heart has been
circumcised to God. Your heart has been set free.

❖ WAKING THE DEAD, 63

If Christ has not been raised, our preaching is useless and so is your faith . . . and if Christ has not been raised, your faith is futile; you are still in your sins.

—1 CORINTHIANS 15:14, 17

Most people assume that the Cross *is* the total work of Christ. The two go hand in hand in our minds—Jesus Christ and the Cross; the Cross and Jesus Christ. The Resurrection is impressive, but kind of . . . an afterthought. It was needed, of course, to get him out of the grave. Or the Resurrection is important because it proves Jesus was the Son of God. His death was the *real* work on our behalf. The Resurrection is like an epilogue to the real story, the extra point after the touchdown, the medal ceremony after the Olympic event. You can see which we think is more important. What image do we put on our churches, our Bibles, on jewelry? The cross is the symbol of Christianity worldwide. However . . .

The cross was never meant to be the only or even the central symbol of Christianity.

That you are shocked by what I've just said only proves how far we've strayed from the faith of the New Testament. The cross is not the sole focal point of Christianity. Paul says so himself: "If Christ has not been raised, our preaching is useless and so is your faith . . . and if Christ has not been raised, your faith is futile; you are still in your sins" (1 Cor. 15:14, 17).

❧ WAKING THE DEAD, 63–64

*The LORD God said, "It is not good for the man to be alone. I will
make a helper suitable for him."*
—GENESIS 2:18

E ve was created because things were not right without her.
Something was not good. "It is not good for the man to be
alone" (Gen. 2:18). This just staggers us. Think of it. The world
is young and completely unstained. Adam is yet in his innocence
and full of glory. He walks with God. Nothing stands between
them. They share something none of us have ever known, only
longed for: an unbroken friendship, untouched by sin. Yet something is not good. Something is missing. What could it possibly
be? Eve. Woman. Femininity. Wow. Talk about significance.

To be specific, what was "not good" was the fact that the man
was "alone." "It is not good for the human to be alone, I shall
make him a sustainer beside him" (Gen. 2:18 *Alter*). How true
this is. Whatever else we know about women, we know they are
relational creatures to their cores. While little boys are killing one
another in mock battles on the playground, little girls are negoti-
ating relationships.

This is so second nature, so assumed among women it goes
unnoticed by them. They care more about relationship than just
about anything else. Radio talk-show host Dennis Prager reports
that when the topic of the day on his show is a "macro issue" like
politics or finance, his callers will be Ed, Jack, Bill, and Dave. But
when the topic is a "micro issue" involving human relationships,
issues like dating or faithfulness or children, his callers will be
Jane, Joanne, Susan, and Karen.

   ❖ CAPTIVATING, 26–27

Remain in me, and I will remain in you. No branch can bear fruit by itself; it must remain in the vine. Neither can you bear fruit unless you remain in me.

—JOHN 15:4

Once we begin thinking of all the deceptions the Enemy is about with regard to our lives, we have a tendency to become obsessed with him, fearful of what he is going to do next. Once we take him seriously, he switches from his tactic of "I'm not here" to one of having us worry about him day and night, which is almost a form of worship.

God's intention, on the other hand, is to use spiritual warfare to draw us into deeper communion with himself. Satan's device is to isolate us and wear us out obsessing about what he has done and what he will do next. And he is very effective in using our particular Message of the Arrows to do it. God desires to use the Enemy's attacks to remove the obstacles between ourselves and him, to reestablish our dependency on him as his sons and daughters in a much deeper way. Once we understand that, the warfare we are in begins to feel totally different. It is not really even about Satan anymore, but about communion with God and abiding in Jesus as the source of life. The whole experience begins to feel more like a devotional.

❖ *THE SACRED ROMANCE, 119–20*

And the God of all grace, who called you to his eternal glory in Christ, after you have suffered a little while, will himself restore you and make you strong, firm and steadfast.

—1 PETER 5:10

Until the moment that the courier from the Palace arrives at her door, Cinderella's life seems set in stone. A cellar girl, her enemies will forever have the upper hand. No other life seems possible. This is her fate. Then, word from the Prince arrives— an invitation to a ball. All hell breaks loose. Her longings are awakened. Her enemies become enraged. And her life is never the same.

How gracious that it comes by invitation. A woman, doesn't need to strive or arrange; you don't need to make it happen. You only needs to respond. Granted—Cinderella's response took immense courage, courage that came only out of a deep desire to find the life her heart knew it was meant for. She *wanted* to go. But it took stead-fastness to press through her fears. It took courage not to abandon all hope. But she became the woman she was born to be, and the kingdom was never the same. It is a beautiful parable.

The invitations of our Prince come to us in all sorts of ways. Your heart itself, as a woman, is an invitation. An invitation delivered in the most intimate and personalized way. Your Lover has written something on your heart. It is a call to find a life of Romance and to protect that love affair as your most precious treasure. A call to cultivate the beauty you hold inside, and to unveil your beauty on behalf of others. And it is a call to adventure, to become the *ezer* the world desperately needs you to be.

I am always with you;
you hold me by my right hand.
—PSALM 73:23

When I consider all that is at stake in this journey I am on, how vulnerable are my heart and the hearts of those I love, how quickly I forget, I am moved to fall on my face and cry out to God for the grace to remember. George MacDonald says it better in poetry:

Remember thou, and prick me with love's goad.
When I can no more stir my soul to move,
And life is but the ashes of a fire;
When I can but remember that my heart
Once used to live and love, long and aspire—
Oh, be thou then the first, the one thou art;
Be thou the calling, before all answering love,
 And in me wake hope, fear, boundless desire. (Diary of an
 Old Soul)

The final burden of remembrance does not rest on us; if it did, we should all despair. The author of Hebrews called Jesus the "author and perfecter of our faith" (12:2). He is the One who put the Romance in our hearts and the One who first opened our eyes to see that our deepest desire is fulfilled in him. He started us on the journey, and he has bound himself to see us through. Even though we may for long seasons forget him, he does not forget us.

❖ *THE SACRED ROMANCE,* 208–9

*Even though I walk
through the valley of the shadow of death,
I will fear no evil,
for you are with me;
your rod and your staff,
they comfort me.*
—PSALM 23:4

We are now in the late stages of the long and vicious war against the human heart. I know—it sounds overly dramatic. But I am not hawking fear at all; I am speaking honestly about the nature of what is unfolding around us . . . *against us.* And until we call the situation what it is, we will not know what to do about it. In fact, this is where many people feel abandoned or betrayed by God. They thought that becoming a Christian would end their troubles, or at least reduce them. No one ever told them they were being moved to the front lines, and they seem shocked by the fact that they've been shot at.

The wound is too well aimed and far too consistent to be accidental. It was an attempt to take you out, to cripple or destroy your strength and get you out of the action. Do you know why there's been such an assault? The Enemy fears you. You are dangerous big-time. If you ever really got your heart back, lived from it with courage, you would be a huge problem to him. You would do a lot of damage . . . on the side of good. Remember how valiant and effective God has been in the history of the world? You are a stem of that victorious stalk.

❖ *WILD AT HEART,* 85–87

God saw all that he had made, and it was very good.
—GENESIS 1:31

Certainly, you will admit that God is glorious. Is there anyone more kind? Is there anyone more creative? Is there anyone more valiant? Is there anyone truer? Is there anyone more daring? Is there anyone more beautiful? Is there anyone wiser? Is there anyone more generous? You are his offspring. His child. His reflection. His likeness. You bear *his* image. Do remember that though he made the heavens and the earth in all their glory, the desert and the open sea, the meadow and the Milky Way, and said, "It is good," it was only *after* he made you that he said, "It is *very* good" (Gen. 1:31). Think of it: your original glory was greater than anything that's ever taken your breath away in nature. The psalmist says, "As for the saints who are in the land, / they are the glorious ones in whom is all my delight" (Ps. 16:3).

God endowed you with a glory when he created you, a glory so deep and mythic that all creation pales in comparison. A glory unique to you, just as your fingerprints are unique to you. Somewhere down deep inside, we've been looking for that glory ever since. A man wants to know that he is truly a man, that he could be brave; he longs to know that he is a warrior; and all his life he wonders, "Have I got what it takes?" A woman wants to know that she is truly a woman, that she is beautiful; she longs to know that she is captivating; and all her life she wonders, "Do I have a beauty to offer?"

❖ WAKING THE DEAD, 77–78

*As for the saints who are in the land,
they are the glorious ones in whom is all my delight.*
—Psalm 16:3

The poet Yeats wrote,

*If I make the lashes dark
And the eyes more bright
And the lips more scarlet,
Or ask if all be right
From mirror after mirror
No vanity's displayed:
I'm looking for the face I had
Before the world was made.*
("A Woman Young and Old")

Yes, that's it. When you take a second glance in the mirror, when you pause to look again at a photograph, you are looking for a glory you know you were meant to have. Your story didn't start with sin, and thank God, it does not end with sin. It ends with glory restored: "Those he justified, he also glorified" (Rom. 8:30). And "in the meantime," you have *been* transformed, and you are *being* transformed. God is restoring your glory. Because the glory of God is you fully alive.

"Well, then, if this is all true, why don't I see it?" Precisely. Exactly. Now we are reaching my point. The fact that you do not see your good heart and your glory is only proof of how effective the assault has been. We don't see ourselves clearly.

And the one who sat there had the appearance of jasper and carnelian.
A rainbow, resembling an emerald, encircled the throne. Also before
the throne there was what looked like a sea of glass, clear as crystal.

—Revelation 4:3, 6

Is there any doubt that the God John beheld was beautiful *beyond*
description? But of course. God must be even more glorious
than this glorious creation, for it "foretells" or "displays" the glory
that is God's. John said God was as radiant as gemstones, richly
adorned in golds and reds and greens and blues, shimmering as
crystal. Why, these are the very things that Cinderella is given—
the very things women still prefer to adorn themselves with when
they want to look their finest. Hmmm. And isn't that just what a
woman longs to hear? "You are radiant this evening. You are absolutely breathtaking."

The reason a woman wants a beauty to unveil, the reason she
asks, *Do you delight in me?* is simply that God does as well. God is
captivating beauty. As David prays, "One thing I ask of the Lord,
this is what I seek: that I may . . . gaze upon the beauty of the
Lord" (Ps. 27:4). That he wants to be seen, and for us to be captivated by what we see?

But in order to make the matter perfectly clear, God has given
us Eve. The crowning touch of creation. Beauty is the essence of a
woman. We want to be perfectly clear that we mean *both* a physical
beauty and a soulful (or spiritual) beauty. The one depends upon
and flows out of the other. Yes, the world cheapens and prostitutes
beauty, making it all about a perfect figure few women can attain.
But Christians minimize it too, or over-spiritualize it, making it all
about "character." We must recover the prize of Beauty.

❧ *Captivating*, 35–36

How beautiful you are, my darling!
Oh, how beautiful!
—SONG OF SOLOMON 1:15

God gave Eve a beautiful form *and* a beautiful spirit. She expresses beauty in both. Better, she expresses beauty simply in who she is. Like God, it is her *essence*.

Stasi and I just spent a weekend together in Santa Fe, New Mexico, where we wandered for hours through art galleries and gardens, looking for those works of art that particularly captured us. Toward the afternoon of our second day Stasi asked me, "Have you seen one painting of a naked man?" The point was startling. After days of looking at maybe a thousand pieces of art, we had not seen one painting devoted to the beauty of the naked masculine form. Not one. (Granted, there are a few examples down through history . . . but only a few.) However, the beauty of Woman was celebrated everywhere, hundreds of times over in paintings and sculptures. There is a reason for this.

For one thing, men look ridiculous lying on a bed buck naked, half covered with a sheet. It doesn't fit the essence of masculinity. Something in you wants to say, "Get up already and get a job. Cut the grass. Get to work." For Adam is captured best in motion, *doing* something. His essence is *strength in action*.

Eve speaks something different to the world than Adam does. Through her beauty.

❂ CAPTIVATING, 36–37

Oh! Ephraim is my dear, dear son,
my child in whom I take pleasure!
Every time I mention his name,
my heart bursts with longing for him!
Everything in me cries out for him.
Softly and tenderly I wait for him.
—JEREMIAH 31:20 *The Message*

Our lives are not a random series of events; they tell a Story that has meaning. We aren't in a movie we've arrived at twenty minutes late; we are in a Sacred Romance. Our Story is written by God, who is more than author; he is the romantic lead in our personal dramas. He created us for himself, and now he is moving heaven and earth to restore us to his side. His wooing seems wild because he seeks to free our hearts from the attachments and addictions we've chosen, thanks to the Arrows we've known.

And we—who are we, really? We are not pond scum, nor are we the lead in the story. We are the Beloved; our hearts are the most important thing about us, and our desire is wild because it is made for a wild God. We are the Beloved, and we are addicted. We've either given our heart to other lovers and can't get out of the relationships, or we've tried our best to kill desire (often with the help of others) and live lives of safe, orderly control. Either way, we play into the hands of the one who hates us. Satan is the mortal enemy of God and therefore ours as well, who comes with offers of less-wild lovers, hoping to deceive us in order to destroy our hearts and thus prevent our salvation or cripple our sanctification. These are the stage, the characters, and the plot in the broadest possible terms. Where do we go from here?

❧ *THE SACRED ROMANCE, 147–48*

The wolf will live with the lamb,
the leopard will lie down with the goat,
the calf and the lion and the yearling together.
—ISAIAH 11:6

Our search for the consummation of our deepest hope is not a search in vain; not at all. We've only had the timing wrong. We do not know exactly how God will do it, but we do know this: the kingdom of God brings restoration. The only things destroyed are the things that are outside God's realm—sin, disease, death. But we who are God's children, the heavens and the earth he has made, will go on. "The wolf will live with the lamb, the leopard will lie down with the goat, the calf and the lion and the yearling together" (Isa. 11:6). "And Jerusalem will be known as the Desirable Place," the place of the fulfillment of all our desires (Isa. 62:12 NLT). This is significant because it touches upon the question: What will we *do* in eternity? If all we've got are halos and harps, our options are pretty limited. But to have the whole cosmos before us—wow. Thus George MacDonald writes to his daughter, whom he was soon to lose to tuberculosis,

I do live expecting great things in the life that is ripening for me and all mine—when we shall have all the universe for our own, and be good merry helpful children in the great house of our father. Then, darling, you and I and all will have the grand liberty wherewith Christ makes free— opening his hand to send us out like white doves to range the universe. (*The Heart of George MacDonald*)

❖ THE JOURNEY OF DESIRE, 123

"For this reason a man will leave his father and mother and be united to his wife, and the two will become one flesh." This is a profound mystery—but I am talking about Christ and the church.

—EPHESIANS 5:31–32

After creating this stunning portrait of a total union, the man and woman becoming one, God turns the universe on its head when he tells us that this is what *he* is seeking with *us*. In fact, Paul says it is *why* God created gender and sexuality and marriage—to serve as a living metaphor.

A profound mystery indeed. All the breathtaking things in life are. The Cross is a great mystery, but we are helped in understanding it by looking back into the Old Testament and finding there the pattern of the sacrificial lamb. Those early believers did not understand the full meaning of what they were doing, but once Christ came, the whole period of ritual sacrifice was seen in a new light, and in turn gave a richer depth to our understanding of the Cross.

We must do the same with this stunning passage; we must look back and see the Bible for what it is—the greatest romance ever written. God creates mankind for intimacy with himself, as his beloved. We see it right at the start, when he gives us the highest freedom of all—the freedom to reject him. The reason is obvious: love is possible only when it is freely chosen. True love is never constrained; our hearts cannot be taken by force. So God sets out to woo his beloved and make her his queen.

❖ *THE JOURNEY OF DESIRE, 130*

I decide to do good, but I don't really do it; I decide not to do bad, but then I do it anyway. My decisions, such as they are, don't result in actions. Something has gone wrong deep within me and gets the better of me every time. It happens so regularly that it's predictable. The moment I decide to do good, sin is there to trip me up. I truly delight in God's commands, but it's pretty obvious that not all of me joins in that delight. Parts of me covertly rebel, and just when I least expect it, they take charge.

—ROMANS 7:19–21 *The Message*

Ever since that fateful day when Adam gave away the essence of his strength, men have struggled with a part of themselves that is ready at the drop of a hat to do the same. We don't want to speak up unless we know it will go well, and we don't want to move unless we're guaranteed success. What the Scriptures call the flesh, the old man, or the sinful nature, is that part of fallen Adam in every man that always wants the easiest way out. It's much easier to go down to the driving range and attack a bucket of balls than it is to face the people at work who are angry at you. It's much easier to clean the garage, organize your files, or cut the grass than it is to talk to your teenage daughter.

To put it bluntly, your flesh is a poser. And your flesh is *not you*. Did you know that? Your flesh is not the real you. When Paul gives us his famous passage on what it's like to struggle with sin (Rom. 7), he tells a story we are all too familiar with.

Paul says, "Hey, I know I struggle with sin. But I also know that *my sin is not me*—this is not my true heart."

❖ *WILD AT HEART, 143–44*

I will give you a new heart and put a new spirit in you; I will remove
from you your heart of stone and give you a heart of flesh.
—EZEKIEL 36:26

The Big Lie in the church today is that you are nothing more
than "a sinner saved by grace." You are a lot more than that.
You are a new creation in Christ. The New Testament calls you a
saint, a holy one, a son of God. In the core of your being you are
a good man. Yes, there is a war within us, but it is a *civil* war. The
battle is not between us and God; no, there is a traitor within us
who wars against our true heart fighting alongside the Spirit of
God in us.

> A new power is in operation. The Spirit of life in Christ, like
> a strong wind, has magnificently cleared the air, freeing you
> from a fated lifetime of brutal tyranny at the hands of sin and
> death . . . if the alive-and-present God who raised Jesus from
> the dead moves into your life, he'll do the same thing in you
> that he did in Jesus. (Rom. 8:2, 11 *The Message*)

The *real* you is on the side of God against the false self. Knowing
this makes all the difference in the world. The man who wants to
live valiantly will lose heart quickly if he believes that his heart is
nothing but sin. Why fight?

❧ WILD AT HEART, *144–45*

Teach me your way, O LORD,
and I will walk in your truth;
give me an undivided heart,
that I may fear your name.
I will praise you, O Lord my God, with all my heart;
I will glorify your name forever.
—PSALM 86:11–12

Walking with God leads to receiving his intimate counsel, and counseling leads to deep restoration. As we learn to walk with God and hear his voice, he is able to bring up issues in our hearts that need speaking to. Some of those wounds were enough to break our hearts, create a rift in the soul, and so we need his healing as well. This is something Jesus walks us into— sometimes through the help of another person who can listen and pray with us, sometimes with God alone. As David said in Psalm 23, He leads us away, to a quiet place, to restore the soul. Our first choice is to go with him there—to slow down, unplug, accept the invitation to come aside.

You won't find healing in the midst of the Matrix. We need time in the presence of God. This often comes on the heels of God's raising some issue in our hearts or after we've just relived an event that takes us straight to that broken place.

When we are in the presence of God, removed from distractions, we are able to hear him more clearly, and a secure environment has been established for the young and broken places in our hearts to surface.

❖ WAKING THE DEAD, 140–41

> *Now the serpent was more crafty than any of the wild animals the*
> *LORD God had made. He said to the woman, "Did God really say,*
> *'You must not eat from any tree in the garden'?"*
>
> —GENESIS 3:1

The assault on femininity—its long history, its utter vicious-ness—cannot be understood apart from the spiritual forces of evil we are warned against in the Scriptures. This is not to say that men (and women, for they, too, assault women) have no accountability in their treatment of women. Not at all. It is simply to say that no explanation for the assault upon Eve and her daughters is sufficient unless it opens our eyes to the Prince of Darkness and his special hatred of femininity.

Why does Satan make Eve the focus of his assault on humanity? Because she is captivating, uniquely glorious, and he cannot be. She is the incarnation of the Beauty of God. More than anything else in all creation, she embodies the glory of God. She allures the world to God. He hates it with a jealousy we can only imagine.

And there is more. The Evil One also hates Eve because she gives life. Women give birth, not men. Women nourish life. And they also bring life into the world soulfully, relationally, spiritually—in everything they touch. Satan is a murderer from the beginning (John 8:44). He brings death. His is a kingdom of death. And thus Eve is his greatest human threat, for she brings life. She is a lifesaver and a lifegiver. *Eve* means "life" or "life-producer." Put those two things together—that Eve incarnates the Beauty of God *and* she gives life to the world. His bitter heart cannot bear it. He assaults her with a special hatred.

Do you begin to see it?

❋ CAPTIVATING, 82–85

Who is this King of glory?
The Lord strong and mighty,
the Lord mighty in battle.
—PSALM 24:8

The story of your life is the story of the long and brutal assault on your heart by the one who knows what you could be.

I will go before you
  and will level the mountains;
I will break down gates of bronze
  and cut through bars of iron. . . .
so that you may know I am the LORD,
  the God of Israel, who summons you by name. (Isa. 45:2–3)

Doesn't the language of the Bible sometimes sound overblown? God is going to level mountains for us? We'd be happy if he just helped us get through the week. What's all that about breaking down gates of bronze and cutting through bars of iron? We'd settle for a parking place at the mall.

If we *are* in an epic battle, then the language of the Bible fits perfectly. We are at war. That war is against your heart, your glory. Once more, look at Isaiah 61:1.

He has sent me to bind up the brokenhearted,
to proclaim freedom for the captives
  and release from darkness for the prisoners.

❖ WAKING THE DEAD, 149–50

Do not let any unwholesome talk come out of your mouths, but only what is helpful for building others up according to their needs, that it may benefit those who listen.

—EPHESIANS 4:29

Over the years we've come to see that the only thing *more* tragic than the things that have happened to us is what we have done with them.

Words were said, painful words. Things were done, awful things. And they shaped us. Something inside us *shifted*. We embraced the messages of our wounds. And from that we chose a way of relating to our world. We made a vow never to be in that place again. We adopted strategies to protect ourselves from being hurt again. A woman who is living out of a broken, wounded heart is a woman who is living a self-protective life. She may not be aware of it, but it is true. It's our way of trying to "save ourselves."

We have also developed ways of trying to get something of the love our hearts cried out for. The problem is, our plan has nothing to do with God. The wounds we received and the messages they brought formed a sort of unholy alliance with our fallen nature. From Eve, we all received a deep mistrust in the heart of God toward us. Clearly, he's holding out on us. We'll just have to arrange for the life we want. We will control our world. But there is also an ache deep within, an ache for intimacy and for life. We'll have to find a way to fill it. A way that does not require us to trust anyone, especially God. A way that will not require vulnerability.

❖ CAPTIVATING, 74–75

He has risen!
—MARK 16:6

It's the great company at the party in *Titanic* that brings such happy tears. It's the boys making it safely home in *Apollo 13*. It's Maximus reunited with his family. So the fellowship finds Gandalf alive—no longer Gandalf the Grey, fallen beyond recovery in the mines of Moria, but Gandalf the White, whom death can never touch again. So Frodo and Sam are rescued from the slopes of Mount Doom, and when they wake, it is to a bright new morn with the sound of birds and the laughter of their friends.

This is our future.

After he laid down his life for us, Jesus of Nazareth was laid in a tomb. He was buried just like any other dead person. His family and friends mourned. His enemies rejoiced. And most of the world went on with business as usual, clueless to the Epic around them. Then, after three days, also at dawn, his story took a sudden and dramatic turn.

"Don't be alarmed," he said. "You are looking for Jesus the Nazarene, who was crucified. He has risen! He is not here. See the place where they laid him. But go, tell his disciples . . . 'He is going ahead of you into Galilee. There you will see him, just as he told you.'" (Mark 16:2–7)

Jesus came back. He showed up again. He was restored to them. He walked into the house where they had gathered to comfort one another in their grief and asked if they had anything to eat. It was the most stunning, unbelievable, happiest ending to a story you could possibly imagine.

And it is also ours.

❖ *Epic*, 85–87

How gladly would I treat you like sons.
—JEREMIAH 3:19

We aren't meant to figure life out on our own. This is an especially difficult truth for men to grasp. We struggle to accept that God wants to father us. The truth is, he *has* been fathering us for a long time—we just haven't had the eyes to see it. He wants to father us much more intimately, but we have to be in a posture to receive it. What that involves is a fundamental reorientation of how we look at life, and our situation in it.

First, we allow that we are unfinished men, partial men, mostly boy inside, and we need *initiation*. In many, many ways.

Second, we turn from our independence and all the ways we either charge at life or shrink from it; this may be one of the most basic and the most crucial ways a man repents. I say "repent" because our approach to life is based on the conviction that God, for the most part, doesn't show up much. I understand where the conviction came from, battle it constantly myself, but still—it's faithless, is it not? We must be willing to take an enormous risk, and open our hearts to the possibility that God *is* initiating us as men—maybe even in the very things in which we thought he'd abandoned us. We open ourselves up to being fathered.

I'll admit, it doesn't come easily. A sort of fundamental mistrust built on that core mistrust in God we inherited from Adam. Making the switch will feel awkward. As Gerald May says, the more we've become accustomed to seeking life apart from God, the more "abnormal and stressful" it seems "to look for God directly." *Especially* as a Father, fathering us.

❖ *FATHERED BY GOD, 11–12*

*I tell you the truth, unless you change and become like little children,
you will never enter the kingdom of heaven.*

—MATTHEW 18:3

Now, we don't know much about stages of development in our instant culture. We have someone else make our coffee for us. We no longer have to wait to have our photos developed—not even an hour—for now we have digital cameras that deliver the image to us instantly. We don't have to wait to get in touch with someone—we can e-mail them, page them, call them on a cell phone, instant-message them this moment. We don't need to wait for our leather jackets or our jeans or caps to age to get that rugged look—they come that way now, pre-faded, tattered. Character that can be bought and worn immediately.

But God is a God of *process*. If you want an oak tree, he has you start with an acorn. If you want a Bible, well, he delivers that over the course of more than a thousand years. If you want an adult, you must begin with the child. God ordained the stages of maturity. They are woven into the fabric of our being, just as the laws of nature are woven into the fabric of the earth. In fact, those who lived closer to the earth respected and embraced the stages for centuries upon centuries. We might think of them as the ancient paths. Only recently have we lost touch with them. At least one result of having abandoned masculine initiation is a world of unfinished, uninitiated men. But it doesn't have to be this way. We needn't wander in a fog. We don't have to live alone, striving, sulking, uncertain, angry. We don't have to figure life out for ourselves. There is another way.

❂ *FATHERED BY GOD*, 23–24

Greater love has no one than this, that he lay down his life for
his friends.
—JOHN 15:13

I urge that friendship with God is essential for a king for two reasons. First, because a man in power is positioned to do great good or great damage, and he will not have the wisdom to address every situation. Humility demands he turn to God, and often. Remember—the heart of the king is yielded to God. "For I did not speak of my own accord, but the Father who sent me commanded me what to say and how to say it. . . . So whatever I say is just what the Father has told me to say" (John 12:49–50).

But there is an even deeper reason than expedience. This is what a man was made for. To be a king and not know God intimately is like a son who runs part of the family business, but never talks to his father. Yes, we are here to serve as kings. But that service was never meant to take the place of our relationship with God. Your life as a man is a process of initiation into masculinity, offered to you by your true Father. Through the course of that journey, in all the many events of the beloved son, the cowboy, the warrior, the lover, whatever else you learn—you will learn to walk with God, for he is walking with you.

❀ *FATHERED BY GOD, 183–84*

Let us rejoice and be glad
and give him glory!
For the wedding of the Lamb has come,
and his bride has made herself ready.
—REVELATION 19:7

Have you no other daughters?" "No," said the man. "There is a little stunted kitchen wench which my late wife left behind her, but she cannot be the bride." The King's son said the man was to send her up to him, but the stepmother answered, "Oh no, she is much too dirty, she cannot show herself!" But he absolutely insisted on it, and Cinderella had to be called.

She first washed her hands and face clean, and then went and bowed down before the King's son, who gave her the golden slipper. Then she seated herself on a stool, drew her foot out of the heavy wooden shoe, and put it into the slipper, which fit like a glove. And when she rose up and the King's son looked at her face, he recognized the beautiful maiden who had danced with him and cried, "This is the true bride!"

The stepmother and two sisters were horrified and became pale with rage; he, however, took Cinderella on his horse and rode away with her.

I love this part of the story—to see the heroine unveiled in all her glory. To have her, *finally*, rise up to her full height. Mocked, hated, laughed at, spit upon—Cinderella is the one the slipper fits; she's the one the prince is in love with; *she's* the true bride. Just as we are.

❧ WAKING THE DEAD, 71–72

I have loved you with an everlasting love;
I have drawn you with loving-kindness.
I will build you up again
and you will be rebuilt. . . .
and go out to dance with the joyful.

—JEREMIAH 31:3–4

Everlasting love—that cuts right through the lie that love never stays. His love does. It is everlasting. Immoveable. True. We don't believe the Scriptures because they don't seem to align with what we are *feeling* right now. It has frustrated the livin' daylights out of me to see people clinging to their agreements and unbelief because that is what they are feeling in the moment. We are so stubborn in our unbelief because we aren't at that moment *experiencing* whatever it is God says is true.

He knows that we make agreements with all sorts of lies, distortions, and accusations. Now he invites us to agree with him in what is *true*. We cannot base our convictions on whether or not we are feeling or experiencing the truth of what God says. It is an arrogant posture, to let our immediate state of being be the judge of whether the Scripture is true for us. I know I have to start with the truth, embrace it, stake my all on it, and then later—sometimes right away, sometimes down the road—I will experience its truthfulness.

How great is the love the Father has lavished on us, that we should be called children of God! (1 John 3:1)

❖ *WALKING WITH GOD, 100–101*

No, a man is a Jew if he is one inwardly; and circumcision is
circumcision of the heart, by the Spirit.
—ROMANS 2:29

Your sin has been dealt with. Your Father has removed it from you "as far as the east is from the west" (Ps. 103:12). Your sins have been washed away (1 Cor. 6:11). When God looks at you he does not see your sin. He has not one condemning thought toward you (Rom. 8:1). But that's not all. You have a new heart. That's the promise of the new covenant: "I will give you a new heart and put a new spirit in you; I will remove from you your heart of stone and give you a heart of flesh. And I will put my Spirit in you and move you to follow my decrees and be careful to keep my laws" (Ezek. 36:26–27). There's a reason that it's called good news.

Too many Christians today are living back in the old covenant. They've had Jeremiah 17:9 drilled into them and they walk around believing *my heart is deceitfully wicked.* Not anymore it's not. Read the rest of the book. In Jeremiah 31:33, God announces the cure for all that: "I will put my law in their minds and write it on their hearts. I will be their God, and they will be my people." I will give you a new heart. Sin is not the deepest thing about you. You have a new heart. Did you hear me? Your heart is *good.*

❖ *WILD AT HEART, 133–34*

Behold, I stand at the door and knock.
—REVELATION 3:20 NKJV

This is what Jesus nearly always does when he comes to mend those rifts in our hearts. He brings his comfort and mercy to those times and places where we suffered the shattering blow, and the heart in that place often feels the same age as it was at the time of the event, even though it might have been decades ago.

It might be a surprise that Christ asks our permission to come in and heal, but he stands at the door and knocks. He doesn't force his way in, and the principle remains true after we have given Christ the initial access to our hearts that we call salvation. There are rooms we have kept locked up, places he has not had access to by our own will, and in order to experience his healing, we must also give him permission to come in there. *Will you let me heal you?*

The work of Christ in healing the soul is a deep mystery, more amazing than open-heart surgery. A friend described his experience as having Christ "holding the broken parts of my heart in his hands, and bringing them all together, holding them tenderly until his life brought a wholeness or a oneness to what was many pieces." That idea of "binding up" our brokenness involves bringing all the shattered pieces back together into one whole heart. Reintegrating those places broken off by tragedy or assault.

❦ *WAKING THE DEAD*, 138–40

ABOUT THE AUTHOR

John Eldredge is the founder and director of Ransomed Heart™ Ministries in Colorado Springs, Colorado, a fellowship devoted to helping people discover the heart of God. John is the author of numerous books, including *Epic*, *Waking the Dead*, *Wild at Heart*, and *Desire*, and coauthor of *Captivating* and *The Sacred Romance*. John lives in Colorado with his wife, Stasi, and their three sons, Samuel, Blaine, and Luke. He loves living in the Rocky Mountains so he can pursue his other passions, including fly-fishing, mountain climbing, and exploring the waters of the West in his canoe.

In *Fathered by God*, John Eldredge takes men down a paradigm-shifting path to a divinely ordained manhood. He unveils the six stages many men miss, stages they must complete in order to become the men God designed them to be. Inspiring, insightful, and challenging for men and the women in their lives, *Fathered by God* delivers the very thing every man needs, a way to forge companionship with God the Father while undergoing a transformation, releasing the fullness of life and the passion God designed him to live.

THOMAS NELSON
Since 1798

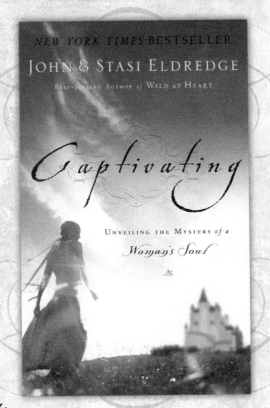

By revealing the core desires every woman shares—to be romanced, to play an irreplaceable role in a grand adventure, and to unveil beauty—John and Stasi Eldredge invite women to recover their feminine hearts, created in the image of an intimate and passionate God. Further, they encourage men to discover the secret of a woman's soul and to delight in the beauty and strength women were created to offer.

THOMAS NELSON
Since 1798